THE WINDS OF CHANGE

To Pat with healing & love x Stephanie x

Inner Sanctum

Published 2005
By
Inner Sanctum Publications

ISBN 978095424219X

'Just for today '
By
Stephanie J. King

Cover design by Damian Keenan

Inner Sanctum Publications
http://www.innersanctumpublications.com

Printed and bound by Antony Rowe Ltd, Eastbourne

The Winds of Change

By

Stephanie J. King
(Co-written with the aid of Spirit)

To my family…

Simon, Christopher

and Natasha

…with love

A special thank you is given to my spirit helpers, Mr Mie and Mr John Benjamin, for their patience and wisdom in pulling 'The Winds of Change' together. This book could not have been written without them.

Thank you too – to all my relations, for without their love and support, I would not be the person that I am, and in the place of life where I found this book.

I am

I can

I will

These words come to us from spirit

~ all we must do,
is decide how to use the time that is ours ~

the time that is given to us.

(I am I)

I have created man, so that I may experience first hand, the pleasure of life itself. It is only through this channel, that I may know all aspects of life on earth. Man is my own experience of experiencing.

(I am I)

Introduction

This book has been given to help man through his turmoil and fear. When read in the usual manner - front to back, it will unlock the truths that will then take you forward.

How can you know your potential, without first recognition of the walls that hold you back? The Winds of Change will help you.

When you need some extra advice, when alone, perturbed or confused, place the book quietly upon your lap. Close your eyes and listen to the rhythm of your heart. Take a moment to still your mind and then with your eyes shut, thumb through the pages. At a time when you feel compelled, open the book and read the section that your eyes are first drawn to.

The journey of your life is unique to you, therefore the assistance you require will be unique to you also.

You have the world at your feet and it needs you to find happiness in your life now. This is the reason you came.

Contents

Prologue

We all come from spirit. We are matter and energy beings. All we can see and touch is matter. Matter is energy at its slowest vibration frequency. The slower the vibration, the denser the object will be. The faster the more translucent. Science has explained this to us admirably over past years. It has also an explanation for many other things in the universe that we see, yet much more exists besides, that we can't. Only now is science even willing to acknowledge that there is indeed an underlying intelligence that governs and operates through the planet we live upon. Science has explained 'the how' of the universe, but cannot yet explain 'the why'. We are as much in the dark today as our ancestors and theirs before them, and we still don't understand our true connection to this planet that gives us life.

Chapter One

The Winds of the Past

<u>In the beginning</u>

Once upon a long time ago, this planet we live on was born. It existed only as pure, transparent energy. Then the conditions that surrounded it changed. Atoms and molecules began to move and rub against each other. Cells began to grow and split, just the same as cells in a mother's womb. In the universe conditions altered and the intelligence that made all things would begin to know itself. A drop of water will always be just that until it becomes part of a river, a lake, an ocean, or a cup of steaming hot tea. Things will always remain the same until the conditions that surround them change. And so it was at the start. The first energy was intelligent. It sensed the change coming within itself and all was good.

This energy in its true form vibrated at a frequency not yet known to man. As the changes began to occur, the frequency within its centre slowed further and further. The cells continued to grow and change and slow down at different levels just like a child grows in its mother's womb. The Earth we live upon grew and is still growing - just as it did in the beginning of time.

Man is part of that earth. He lives on its surface as bacteria lives on ours. We cannot see the germs that are upon all things until conditions ripen and they are allowed to grow. Man is the same. When conditions were ripe – we too began to grow, hence we were first created.

We are still in the belly of the energy that first existed, still growing as in its womb. It fills all space around us that the eye can see. It exists within and without us and in all

1

things. It can never be anywhere else and it is this that gives us life. We are botanical bodies that grow on the surface of this earth, just like the trees and flowers and animals do, but the difference is that we have consciousness. We have the ability to know ourselves and all things around us, just as the intelligent energy knows itself.

All things on this earth are interconnected and always have been. We have already stated that. All things are made of the same energy that grew from the one source, and we have even mentioned this too. Each living thing, large or small, has its own part to play in the existence of our planet, and this is no less true for man. Man in fact has the most important role of all and this is by no account big headed. Man has the role that was destined for him by earth itself, just as each limb we possess also plays an individual role that is unique only to itself and the body it belongs to. Man has the role of an energy converter. We are responsible for the smooth movement of energy between the earth and the sky around us. This role is uniquely suited to man.

All people everywhere play this part, regardless of who they are, where they live, what they know and what they possess. All people are the same, everywhere, and this cannot be stressed enough. Energy movement is the prime function of our body, but it appears that we often seem unable to do just that. Along the course of living life the energy channels we possess become blocked, just as guttering on the roof of a house can. When blockages arise the energy is unable to flow as it should, so we become ill. All illness is merely a form of blockage, regardless of the symptoms the ailment might produce.

Energy plays a vital role in all things. It existed before the earth was born and will do so after the earth is no more. It is eternal and it is this that is eternal within us, and all things. It is this that is unique to all things and can never

2

die. I, too, am made of Energy. That part of the whole that exists within us will always be imprinted with the essence of who we are and as we grow and change, so does the imprint we leave behind after our body has perished. It is this part of us that is eternal. It is this part of the earth that is responsible for all life and always shall be, and that is why it is so important. In the beginning, the all that was, began to grow and change. Each change took billions of years, because in the heart of the energy ball, matter began to grow, and we have said that matter vibrates at a slower rate than the pure energy of life does. Like steam is to water, water is to ice etc....

I, too, am energy. I, too, can never die. You can never die. Nothing ever dies; it can merely evolve back into its original form. The energy part of us has never separated from the rest of the energy ball and it is this part of us that is called our Soul. It is this part of us that experiences life and all that we know and do. It is this that is responsible for our joy and our pain, for our intelligence. Man has learnt how to recreate matter, how to grow trees and reproduce animal and human bodies, but the spark of life that exists within, man can never reproduce because it is not made of man. It is eternally a part of the whole of the planet that we live on. It is God.

Why 'God' many will ask. Why not? God is merely the name given to it for identification purposes. Just as we and every other thing on this earth have a name, a label, so does it. All things are part of this God and God is part of all things. Since time began.

I am a part of God. You are a part of God. We all are a little part of the whole thing that exists, much as a single strand of yarn is merely that, but put with others it completes a beautiful rug or anything else we attach it to. We are no different. Combined we form this planet we live upon. We have our own conscious intelligence but from space we are merely part of the earth that we inhabit.

3

It took millions of years for this earth to evolve. It will continue for many more, with or without our help, but our help is needed and urgently so. The role of man, apart from his own life, is to conduct energy between the sky and the dense matter of the planet. Together all this forms a living, breathing, growing, intelligent cell. The ground is its nucleus and the sky its food, its life force. Without man's function being properly carried out, this earth we love will die, just like the moon and other planets around it. We, man, are the keepers of the earth in a very real sense. We are vital to its continuation because we are part of it. We are what keeps it changing, for without us it would simply be as it was before. It is man that has consciousness. It is man that can grow and change and experience all there is to experience. It is man that can 'enjoy' what has been created like no other living species on the planet. It is man that helps the energy that is God – know itself. We are the vital link to the creative force that exists in all the world.

In the beginning the world was created. It grew as a consequence of the energy slowing itself enough when the conditions were right. All things became as they are today, the mountains, the trees, the animals and the seas. All things would still be just the same if man had not also grown. But man did grow. He was meant to, and because of that he is part of the mechanics of the world he lives upon. No 'part' of anything should not exist. It all matters, and so does man, that's why it is important for us to get our act together and sort our species out. We are not performing the function that nature gave us. We are not transferring the energy we are supposed to because too many of us are locked into the problems of our own daily life. We have become closed channels instead of open ones.

The bible was an early collection of books, written by early teachers who lived in those times. It was designed to help us understand ourselves and our connection to 'the all that is'. All bibles, regardless of their denomination, were designed for the same purpose, but man has become too tied up in their words. He is too tied up in the thought that only 'his' religion is correct, or the 'right' one to follow. Admittedly through the years that have passed many original words were changed to suit the power cravings of those who changed them, but the basic message within still remains. We are a product of the world around us. We live on a garden that was grown for our enjoyment. This is it. This is the Garden of Eden that was created long ago. We are here to enjoy it, to physically experience and grow ourselves and then to return back to our original energy form. We can come back here as often as we wish, or as often as we need, but the point is – that we do come back. We will experience the cause and effect of all we have ever done. We do not leave it behind. We come back to live here again by choice.

Now you can see the importance of this book you are reading. It is not a myth, or a fanciful fairy tale. We do come back and so it is important that we get this thing called life – right.

Chapter Two

The Winds of Growth

The way forward

The next step is acknowledging that changes need to occur. All of life exists as it was meant to be from the start. That is how things are. But now we have reached a plateau and it is time for personal growth and development. In order to proceed further, successfully along the course of life, man must know himself and his own connection to the world.

Many of us amble along our daily paths neither looking to the left or the right. We allow life, circumstance and other people to propel us, until all we can do is pick up their pieces along the way. We come to a standstill within ourselves. I, too, reached that point, but I was lucky enough to wake up in time to go forward to write this book.

All of man must reach and pass this point in his life. He must face the choices that are available to him, but the problem is – how does he know that he has reached a standstill? Life itself will show him. Life will offer him all that he needs - providing he can read the signs correctly.

All through life he has been following instructions. From infancy to adulthood, anything he needed to take the next step was provided. It was the next link in his life. Then he reached the point of saturation; too much of all things. Too much good living in any form you care to think of became the norm. Instead of wanting less, we became stuck in the programme of obtaining more; bigger houses, more money; better jobs, expensive clothes, more food than we could ever eat, more gold than we can comfortably wear etc, etc. Even holidays that extend into working time are gathered freely and without thought – or thanks to anyone.

The more we got the more we wanted, the more we felt we were owed or needed. Life has never been so good. We are living the dream we always wanted, the dream our ancestors gave their lives to achieve, but still we don't recognise what we have. We want more, we expect more and we want it faster, at any cost. We rarely even see the cost of this life we are living. It has to stop. It must stop or the world will burn itself out. A wheel will keep on turning as it was meant to do – for eternity if it is treated and handled properly, but if it is pushed too far, too hard, for too long, it will buckle, splinter and break. It will burn, or wear itself out and that is what we are doing to our planet. It cannot cope without a slowing down of life. All we could ever need is in front of us – for eternity, but right now we must take things easy. Not chill and sit still for days on end, but make a conscious decision to go slower and softer in our daily life.

Take a look at the world you live in. Not the world as a whole, but your own sector of it. Each man lives in his own universe and signs are present all around. Is there discomfort within your family, the lives of your work colleagues or friends? Is your own life as easy or free of worry as you would like it to be? Are you on an ever-moving treadmill of work, bills, arguments, illness etc? Is your life as good as you want it to be, even with all you have around you, even with your hard work and what you have achieved yourself? Can you even get a job at all, or do you feel at a dead end? Do you jump out of bed with a spring in your step and look forward to the day ahead, or is it a chore, a burden that must be faced before you are able to relax once more at the end of it? All these are clear indications as to the state of your life and your own happiness. Are you happy? Do you ever think to check?

We all strive for happiness every day of our lives, but many people rarely find or achieve it. Happiness is the most natural state in the world, but it can appear the hardest to come by. I, too, had to learn to achieve this state at the cost of much heartache along the way. Gurus and Holy Men take years to get there, so why should it be different for us? Happiness and peace are the greatest gifts we have and if we can pass it to others along the way then our lives are worth something. I, too, had to learn this. I, too, had to study. It was worth studying for.

We all are the same. We are made of the same substance. We feel the same emotions. We dream the same dreams. We are all the same as each other. I had to learn this after my own trials and tribulations came to a head. I had to learn to understand what I myself was doing to keep me exactly where I was in life. Again and again life appeared to let me down. I thought I had changed all I could, but still that was not enough to make the difference. Then I knew that it must be something I was doing. I began to search inside. I began to look at my own self in a way I had not done before. I began to see patterns of behaviour in me, in my family and in everyone else. I began to view the world about me from a different angle. The answers that were coming back were staggering. They were far, far too big for me alone. Yes, I could apply them to my own life, but my family would simply meet the same obstacles in their life when they went outside. I could choose to ignore them, but I would never feel right about doing so. I knew I had to share them and a book was the only answer.

We are born into life through our parents. From them we inherit family similarities and DNA, but that is all. Each soul born into a body is completely individual. It is a single part of the universal soul called God. It is a single part that is born to experience material life and all that comes with it. It comes to live and breathe and dance and cry. It comes to sing and laugh and eat and drink. It comes to feel the wind and the rain and the sun. It comes to be – exactly as we are right now. It also comes to be part of the planet we live upon and to make a difference some way, some how, to some body or some thing. It comes to create in the most basic form there is, the form of matter, because matter is everlasting – until it is not, by destruction or death. Every soul that is born into the world is individual in every sense of the word, yet it is not. It is also very much the same.

Life is life. Life can mean only that. All matter is not life; it is energy at its slowest vibration. It is energy that has converted itself into a form we can touch and hold and see. It is a solid, but it is not life. Life is a spark of conscious energy that exists in all things that live. This is the same from a flower, to a tree, to an animal, to man himself, but the difference is that only man can realise himself. Only man has the capacity to grow to be more than his original form. A flower can only grow to its limit and then it must die. It cannot grow beyond what it was destined to be. It cannot grow beyond its capabilities. The same applies to a tree or an animal. None can grow beyond its original form. An animal can only be just that. It can learn a few tricks, but it can never understand itself. It can never educate itself beyond the original limitations placed upon its form. But man can. Man is the only species on the planet's surface that can do all these things and more. Man has the capability to be anything he wants to be. He can experience anything and everything. He can know how it feels to fly like a bird, to swim like a fish, to hunt in the dark, to sing, to dance, to learn, to invent and investigate. None of these things are of necessity. They are of choice. They are not things he does because that is the nature of his species, but because he chooses to experience what those things are like. He chooses, while other species of life cannot. Each thing on earth has its proper place but man can exceed all his limitations – by choice, therefore, he has no limitations. He is free.

It is this freedom that we often take for granted. In fact, very often we even forget we have it. Never before has the

9

world had so much, yet we reach beyond these things again and again. Life for our ancestors was different than it is for us. Their time was neither better, nor worse, just different. Life for them was hard, but slower. The pace was slower, things could only be achieved slower, but today everything comes fast. This is not necessarily a bad thing, but it does mean that we have less scope for configuration or error. It is more important than ever that we get life right. The faster our pace the more compact our problems when they arise. It takes more effort to put things right than it does to do things properly in the first place and this is true for our own lives as well. We barge ahead, neither looking right nor left, to achieve what we think we desire or want, yet when we get there how often do those expectations fall short? How often do we wish we had waited a while, or searched a little longer? This seems to be a trend in the time that we live, yet it is not all doom and gloom. It is not too late to change our patterns or the course of life itself. The first step has been taken for you as you read this book. You are becoming more self-aware. You are also unable to argue with truths you already know. You are reaching a period of change, of clearing out old habits and behaviour patterns that no longer serve your needs.

Change of any kind takes time to manifest. But manifest it will, with or without your help. You can swim against a current and have a long and uncomfortable ride, or you can recognise the change in the tide and swim with it.

Change is inevitable. Just as the world must turn and the seasons rotate, change must occur, and so it is also with us. From the time of our birth we are destined to change, to grow, to alter. We push our limitations throughout the time we are given to walk the planet. Change is the nature of all life and all that we know. To remain stagnant is to be like stone and there would be no point to that at all, yet even stone must change as it crumbles and falls back to sand, then dust, then to nothing at all.

Chapter Three

The Winds that Stir

Our first inclination that something is amiss
We are born. We grow and change. We explore. We learn and understand. We store every shred of information we come across in our memory – even though we can't always recall it, but once we have seen or experienced something, it becomes a part of who and what we are. Life has deemed it so. Man is the product of every experience he has ever had since his time began, yet when does his time begin? If it were when he was born into this life, how can we explain brand new babies that already exhibit character at the time of their birth. How can we explain children that excel beyond their parental limits, within a family set up, or a child who always remains far behind his siblings even though the best of everything might have been the norm. Family differences are more than just that. They go deeper. Yes, the sameness can rub off between them as habits and opinions form, but deeper than that lays the difference. Each person is an individual soul. He/she is on her own individual journey that will take her through life. Members of a family might be born together and linked together chemically, but each one is a completely separate entity. He will go entirely where his life takes him, providing other limitations don't stop him. And sadly that has often been the case.

Looking Back
The life we live here is short. Old people can see that as they look back at all the years. Life whizzes by each and every day, but with each passing one we gain a sense of the rest that's still to come. We gain a purpose, a sense of

direction and a goal. We move in constant change that will lead us to something, somewhere. We choose where we aim to be and strive toward it.

But where do these urges come from? What is it inside that pushes us forward? And why is it so different within each and every one of us? The answer is old. It is that part of us that is our soul. It is the soul that yearns knowledge and experience. It is the soul that propels us forward – always. The soul we are given is an individual part of the whole that exists. Just like a leaf will never be the tree it came from, it will always remain a part of that tree. It could be nothing else, and so it is with us. We are part of the whole. I am part of the whole, you are part of the whole, your parents, siblings and friends are all individual, but equal parts of the whole. They are no more, or less important than each other, regardless of social position, or anything else. We are individual parts of the divine energy that has been given the chance to explore life as we see fit. Regardless of anything we may or may not do in that life, we still return back to our original state at the end – as part of the whole that exists.

We are primarily spirit beings (or energy ones – which ever you choose to be called). We have been on earth in a physical body many times since the world began; countless people have proved this over the years, but that is another subject for another book on another day. The point is simply that we do come back. We choose to come back to experience a new life in another form in another way, from another angle. Each time we come here, we learn and grow. We learn and grow some more to make a difference to ourselves and the world we live in. We also come here to reap what we have sown before, and this we call karma.

Each time we come back we choose what we need to experience in order to grow and perfect ourselves a little more. We choose the parents we shall have. We choose the situations and the lessons that will take us closest to the people we wish to become, and we often choose the people who will cross our path at specific times or points in our life. Right now most of us can recall a handful of people who have impacted our life at various stages – to take us in a new direction. There are no wasted meetings - ever. There is a reason behind everything, no matter how obscure it may seem at the time. Everything is part of the law of cause and effect. I, too, can see this at play when I look back over my own life. Not all was pleasant, but it took all of my experiences in all shapes and sizes to bring me to this point in time. Without any one of the things from my past I would be a different person than the one I am now. We are all the product of our complete life experiences and it is this that is taken back further than we even know. It is our past that influences us in the present.

I am also a product of my past. I, too, have quirky little ways that are unexplainable in the life I have now. For instance a fear of water, fire or heights, a fear of dogs, or horses, or anything else you could care to name, could stem from a past life experience, but so can the nice things. An immense love or interest of something could just as equally be bought forward by your psyche (or your soul). We are influenced as much by the far past as we are by the present. We are the product of every single experience encountered from the time we began to exist – however long ago that was, and this varies greatly from person to person, brother to sister etc. In fact, this is where the saying 'he's an old soul' comes from. I, too, am an old soul. I, too, have gained much experience, but I, too, have far yet to go and this is good. When you begin to realise that life is continuous, you appreciate the one you have now even more. It hammers home how precious every day, every moment, every instance it. Instead of wishing the weeks away, you want to hold on to them as long as possible, even the not so good ones can be seen as gems when you are able to look back with a balanced and open mind. It is not that we will enjoy the bad times more but that we can better understand what is occurring, and with greater understanding comes new lessons that carry us forward on a surer foot.

All lessons in life are necessary as part of a growth cycle. Nothing is ever for nothing and all things are necessary as part of who we are. Problems make us push past our limitations. They also help us to examine parts of our life that no longer work in our favour. They help us to take stock of what really matters and what does not. Problems are more help to us than we recognise, because they force the issue that needs addressing, or they make us change things that we have been putting off – either through laziness or fear. They even put our life in better order when we would prefer to be doing other things instead. Problems are a natural aspect of life that push us to greater heights. They are our friends, not our enemy's. Problems are no more to us than a flashing light is to a gadget or computer when things need attention or go wrong. They are warning signs that all is not as it really should be, and without them we would merely stagnate. We would just stay as we are – indefinitely.

Man is at a stage in life where problems exist all around. There seems to be trouble of one kind or another, everywhere. We have reached saturation point in many of the things we do, even to ourselves. We have passed the flashing light stage and the world at large is telling us to back off, to slow down and to take care. This is not all bad, but it is not good either, because we have to make changes to put things in order once again. The trouble is not what do we do, but where do we begin, and the obvious place is within ourselves.

We are each the centre of our own universe. We are each the central point in the life that we have. From our own vantage point – we experience and influence all that we do. Life begins to revolve about each and every one of us in a very influential manner. We alone are responsible for much that happens to us – day in and day out in our waking hours. We alone hold the keys to the sadness and the happiness we experience. Life has told us that the opposite is true, and we have in fact grown to believe it ourselves, but the truth is not this way. The truth lies in thoughts and feelings that flit through our head by the thousand each hour that passes, every day of our lives.

Man has earned the right to be happy. We have earned the right to begin again on a surer footing. It is time to put order to the chaos that surrounds and influences us on a daily basis. It is time to take stock of the life we are living, the dreams we are dreaming and the thoughts we are thinking, but before we can, we must realise the importance of such an undertaking.

Everyday hundreds of thoughts flit across the horizon of our mind. They are like lightening streaks that appear and disappear just as fast. Some are deep and meaningful, some connected to the time frame we are in, but most are absolute rubbish and mindless chatter. We take care of the food we put into our mouth, but do we consider the food we give our mind? Do we Ever? Likely, the answer is not. We allow our mind to wander freely wherever it wants. We hardly notice it at all. During the course of a normal day, millions of ideas come forward that have no resemblance to the things we are doing or saying. During the course of an average conversation, millions of possible answers are also available, but given the individuality of the people we are, how do we ever get the right one? Communication is an art unto itself, but to get it right we need a mind that is free from excess thought, clutter and emotion. How often are we ever like a blank page that allows the moment we experience to lead the way? Most often we rehearse our answers and responses before the situation we anticipate has even come into play. We imagine all the things our opponent will do and say – to our imaginary conversation

15

and actions, then, when the thing actually happens we put those rehearsals in to reality. We live a life of fantasy instead of reality and wonder why life rarely goes as we expected it to. We wonder achingly why we are never understood, or why no one understands what we are trying to achieve. Life is more like a game than the reality that it should be. We take the whole thing too much for granted and leave too much to haphazard imaginings. Life is not a game. It can be and should be fun, but it is a serious business all the same. I, too, had to learn this – in a not so easy a way, but it is possible and this book is proof. We all can be exactly what we want to be, but it will take a little more work than we often allow for. We have some growing 'in' to do.

We are spirit beings that live and operate through a biochemical, degradable body. This body is incapable of life on its own. It cannot do anything at all without the spirit part of itself being attached. A car is nothing more than a lump of components until the engine is switched on. A computer is nothing until electricity surges through its motherboard. A human or animal body is a lump of flesh, incapable of movement until it is united by its energy self – or spirit or soul, whatever you choose to call it. I, too, am unable to write this book without the use of a physical body. The two parts must unite to produce life as it is known on earth. A physical earth made of dense matter requires physical life of equally dense matter. That is how it was meant to be from the beginning.

Matter is incapable of intelligence. Intelligence is all the function of the soul. The soul completely enwraps the matter that exists within its space. The soul can be seen only because of its material body that gives it its physical shape in a physical world. The physical is necessary to anchor the soul – or energy to the ground, to the body of the earth itself. Now you can begin to see the importance of the soul connecting properly to the matter of the earth.

16

Now you can see the importance of man being an open channel for energy to pass through. Man is the true channel that must pass energy from the sky to the ground. Without this function operating at its best, the earth we live upon will die. It will be starved of the life force that exists all around it. It will die like the planets around its orbiting space. The earth needs man to sustain it and that is the importance of man being on earth. That is why we are here and that is why we must keep our species going, not in the materialistic, technological way we are now, but in a balanced healthy way that sustains both ourselves and the planet we live on. It is time for man to move to the next level of existence. It is time for man to fulfil his purpose; the purpose given to him by the planet that sustains his physical self.

Energy exists in abundance in the sky and in all the space that surrounds the physical earth. Everywhere man sees a space there is energy. The ozone layer is the outer skin of the spirit of the earth. It is the same as the outer membrane is to a single cell, the skin to frogspawn etc. The earth is a giant cell, nothing more. Beyond that man has no need to know – not yet and not in this book anyway. The earth is the matter that is growing in the heart of the cell it exists in. The cell is intelligent, just like any cell in any form of matter that exists. The cell knows what it is. It knows the shape it is to become. It knows all it needs to know, just like a sperm knows it must reach an egg, the earth knows it must continue to reach maturity. Once maturity is reached it can grow no more. It can only sustain what it has become. It can grow no more and that is that. The earth we live upon has reached that point. It can grow no more. It cannot change its shape or what it has become. It now needs nothing more than sustenance from the energy that surrounds it, but man is blocking the way. Man is stopping the life force from entering, as it should. Man is killing the earth in ways he does not understand. Not by mining and

17

using its resources, but by failing to perform his most basic function – that as a channel for the energy of the earth he lives upon.

Man does not realise the significance of his attachment to the earth. He is blind to it. All through the ages of history giant leaps have been made in the advancement of medicine, science, manufacturing and technology, but inside he still appears to be the same as he ever was. It is as though he has been asleep to his inner self, impervious to all except the outside world. Yes, history did not help his advancement, but in this age of freethinking it is time to wake up to reality. The truth is all around him clearly to be seen – if he could only allow his eyes to see it.

All of the life on this planet revolves around the balance and harmony set by nature itself. All of nature revolves around the balance and harmony set by the marriage of energies between the earth and the sky. All things must be in perfect union for life to continue as it should. The world lives in the state of balance caused by all things that exist on and above its surface. This is the way nature intended and the way it has been for millions upon millions of years, but now that balance is tilting and it is not in our favour.

Man holds the key to make or break the changes that are occurring. We have the choice to put things back as they should rightfully be – or to continue just as we are now. If we do continue we shall succeed in wiping ourselves out of the course of evolution. We shall relinquish the role we were given and that will be that. As things now stand – we have a chance, only a chance, to put things right, and this time has to be now or never.

Chapter Four

The Winds that can Change

The way we behave

Man has the power to change anything. He has the ability to think, act and foresee. He has also the ability to analyse and access. He knows what has been before and what might happen in the future, but the time that matters most is the time that is now. All of life exists strongest in this time frame. It is now and only now that change can commence to make its difference.

We can all see the evidence of mans progression as we look around and about us. I, too, helped in my little way to form the world as I see it. We each have lived as we saw fit and never really looked further than that. I am not saying that we stumbled aimlessly along, but we did live to achieve our individual aims. This is not so bad as long as we were happy, but the news each day is proving otherwise. Too many of us are sad and unhappy. We find ourselves wandering lost and alone in our thoughts and deeds. In fact many of us are unable to even glimpse the happiness that ought to be ours, no matter how much we try. And try we do – day in and day out, to get a balance and a straight run at life, but problems and people always get in the way. We catch glimpses of what we want in other peoples lives, but again when we get there ourselves, we see that that was not what we wanted either. We are lost in a sea of plenty. Times have never been so good. We can be anyone, do anything and have anything we could ever want. Our ancestors fought life and limb to get us to this point in life, yet we still don't recognise that we are living a real life dream. We have got where we wanted to go, but we still reach out for more. Man is locked into a pattern of striving

19

outwards as far as he can go, but inwardly we are no more than children. All day, everyday, we are little children in the games we play, the things we do and the things we say, but worse still is that we don't even recognise it. We are locked into a game of acquisition and power, and blow anyone else that gets in our way.

The world is our oyster. It is a balance of charm and destruction. It is fertile and it is barren. It is kind and it is ruthless, just like man himself. When the world was young there was no hostility. Yes there were savage animals, but they were just that, animals. They did purely what their instincts asked of them to survive. Now it is different. It is man who chooses to be hostile. Yes there is much good and kindness, but hostility and fear appears to be more widespread than the love that exists, and this is where our problems lie.

We are channels for the energy of the earth and sky to pass through. The earth needs this energy to survive. It needs it to keep the cycle of life in harmony and control. Nature needs this energy to function as well as it should. Life needs this energy to continue its cycle correctly. Man needs this energy for his own well-being and state of health. We all need this energy to survive.

Energy is supposed to flow freely between the earth and the sky. It is supposed to flow through us, day in and day out, for the whole of our lives. We were destined to live much longer upon this planet than we do, but we don't, neither now, nor in times past. I, too, was supposed to live much longer than I did, but I, too, let myself and the planet down. It is too late when we cease to live on earth, because our channels are then closed. We do not die, but we become part of the whole, part of the all that is, part of the energy once more. We become part of the life force that both man and the earth needs to keep itself going. We do not fulfil the same function after crossing over the bridge of seeming death. It is man that holds the key – when he is

20

physically alive, while he is still a part of the earth's matter. It is man who must love each other to keep the world alive; this is not a joke, or a fanciful story, it is for real. It is the Truth. It is all that matters now, all that will keep the earth turning as it should.

Earth is matter. Matter is energy. Energy vibrates at a high speed and matter at a slower one. The nearer we dig to the earth's core, the denser the matter, the slower the speed of its vibration. The core of the earth is all but dead to the eyes of man, while the surface seems more alive, because it vibrates faster and teams with life. The outer layer of most of the earth is still very much alive and will sustain itself for millions of years to come, yet the earth is dying - from the core. It has slowed its vibration too much. It has been starved and depleted of energy for too long by man himself.

History can clearly show us the destructive nature of man, not physically but mentally, emotionally. Throughout the ages there has never been a period where man was happy, either in his own self, or in the world about him. This is even more evident in the world we live in today. Man can only fulfil his purpose when he is relaxed and happy. Not the lay down and chill forever kind of happy, but deeply, mentally, emotionally happy, every working moment of each and every day. Man can only be a channel for the earth's life force when he is in a state of atunement with both himself and the world about him. He can only be 'open' when he is in a state of love – real love from deep within his being.

Man is a strange mixture of good and bad, happy and sad, love and hate. It is precisely this that makes him a good channel when he is operating properly. Life itself is good and bad, new and old, birth and death, destruction and eternal. It is a place of contradiction, of opposites. It is ending, yet unending. It is all, or nothing. This is the way it has always been and also the way it will always be. Man

21

is both the destroyer and the saviour of the world. He is capable of such love, such beautiful dreams and also of such devastation and hate. All these things are equal parts of the whole that make up the world. All these things must be in existence, or there can be no balance. Too much good is as tiresome as too much bad. Both things must be equal to keep the scale of balance at its most central point.

The world is born

In the beginning 'the all that was' or 'the intelligent energy' wanted to know itself, but there was nothing to measure against. If there was only hot – how could we know it was hot? Hot needs cold so that we can know the two, to experience and understand the one. The all that was began to grow and change as conditions that surrounded it changed also. Over millions of years the earth was formed, but the earth – or the all that was, did not know itself yet.

(I am I). I was not alive. I could not experience what had been created because there was no form of conscious thought on the planet. What was there was good and healthy and growing, but there was no way to be a part of it until man was born to experience, to feel, to think and to live the life that was offered. I had to live to know that all that was created would work as it should. I made man to be my eyes, my taste buds, my hearing, myself. I made man to complete this work of art, to finish what I had begun.

I made man as myself because I am the creator. I made man to think for himself because then he could create too. I made man to live myself – as I do now, upon the planet that sustains him. I made man so that I could experience the world I had made. I need man to help me now. I need man to help sustain all that has been made since time began. The world would continue if man was not here, sure enough, but it is presently in a state of imbalance and I need man to put it right on my

22

behalf. **Because man has total free choice, anything that I would do alone would countermand all that I stand for. The decision belongs to man alone. He must decide all by himself what he wants to do, but the key is this. He has been here before. He is here now and he will be again – not out of pressure or malice, but out of love, out of free will and choice. Man will be here again – to experience all he has created with his fellow men. (I am I).**

In order for the all that was to know itself and the world that had been created, opposites had to exist also. All things both good and bad are equal parts of the whole. Without one – the other could not be known, either by man, or by God itself. (Remember that the term 'God' is only a name. It is a reference point to be used like the names we ourselves are given). In order for man to experience life he had to be a conscious being. He had to have all the attributes of God. He had to think for himself alone. He had to have freedom of individual sight, touch, smell, hearing and taste. He had to be an explorer from the moment of his birth and that is why he had to be born completely helpless – like a blank page that was waiting for input; like a virgin computer programme. All his functions were there, he just needed to learn of their existence and then how to master and use them. Man is a born explorer of life. His life and what he shall make of it is totally his own affair, from its beginning – until its end. Yes, at the start he is at the mercy of his surroundings, but thereafter once he learns his free will, he can do as he pleases. This is the only way a true exploration can achieve results; unique, individual results. Just like a true explorer a child must have guidelines for safety, but thereafter, he will do what feels good for him.

Adult man is little different. He is the same. Each is the same as the other and yet the same as a child. Adults have also guidelines to follow, but each have the choice of free will to choose whether those guidelines are correct or not. He can push his boundaries at any time and redraw and refine them at others. Just as a child looks to his parents and peers for guidance, an adult should look within at the wealth of knowledge he has collected through his years. Each man has his own individual buttons and triggers. I, too, had those which served me and led me along my path of discovery. I, too, had freedom of choice, but unlike you, I did not realise where I was going until it was too late. Not too late to experience life - but too late to put it to good use. I had to cross the bridge to know my own self and my function.

Man is the master of his own life. He is slave to none. Our ancestors corrected this so we might enjoy the freedom we do. Man is here to enjoy and explore the life experience he is living. He is also here as a keeper of the earth. It is his job to pass the life force to the planet, but he can only do this when he is in a state of love and happiness. Only then is he a true open channel for energy.

Energy must pass freely between the sky and the planet body. As we have already learned, all things that we both see and don't see are energy based. It must and does radiate everywhere. We are living in an energy bubble. It is our life force. Man is the primary channel for the movement of this energy. When we are in a state of love and happiness we are open channels. When we are born we are completely open channels. I am a channel for energy. We all perform the same function, unless we don't, and that is the root of our problems. All of us get blocked at sometime in our life and unless we correct this we become ill or depressed. Life has become blocked within us. Imagine a long row of guttering that travels around the top of a house. It performs its function well, day in and day out. Then one day a twig is dropped in its path. Silt builds up; leaves get stuck, the blockage – bit by bit continues to grow until the water channel is completely blocked. It becomes ineffective for the purpose it was designed to do. Instead of water gently flowing along its surface to the down pipes, water spills over the sides or floods areas down below. At other times it will remain full to the brim of stale dirty water that has washed down from the roof, but whatever happens now, until it receives attention it looses its purpose. It becomes obsolete or destructive over a period of time, and the same thing happens to man. Only in a state of true love is he fully functional.

I, too, was once like this. Along the course of living my life I, too, became blocked. It took me much longer to free myself of this blockage, because as the years pass by it is far easier to compound the block. It is much easier to continue as we are than to stop and take stock of the person we have become and the life we are living. It is difficult to analyse your life's direction and focus, even with professional help. It is difficult – but it is possible. It is also necessary at some point. We need flushing out, just like the drainpipe or guttering did. We need to be living life as we should, not as we often do, to be fully functional as nature intended – or as nature desperately needs.

Chapter Five

The Winds that Blow

Our true being

I am a channel for life's energy to flow through. So are you. So are all the people – everywhere. I must remain open and unblocked, so must you and so must everyone else. This is our function. It is easy – yet so many of us fail to do it.

The earth needs energy to replenish itself. Energy keeps it moving in its regenerative state. It must flow freely between the earth and the sky. It is this that causes the weather to be as it should be. The earth needs the clear blue sky and the warmth of the sun, but it also needs the clouds and the rain and the storms that they bring. A good storm is nothing more than energy movement between the elements. The earth needs the power that is generated by the currents at work as much as it needs the heat from the sun and the moisture from the rain. Once again, in an ideal world all these things would be equally balanced, but once more it is not this way for us.

Energy must flow freely like water in a stream. Energy creates growth and harmony. It is the cause of all new life. It is the food that feeds all aspects of this world. It keeps nature on its course. It keeps the elements as they should be. It keeps the air fresh and healthy and it keeps all that we know as we know it to be. It keeps life on its course as it is.

Man is the main channel for energy and life that this planet has, but man is all too often blocked by the trials and tribulations of his life. The life force is not flowing through him as it should. Many areas of this earth we love are barren and dry. A good example would be the turmoil in

26

Afghanistan and the Middle East. There is trouble and unrest all over and this has been so for years. Their ground is dry and lifeless and the people are troubled and sad. Almost no growth exists either in the ground or above it. The energy that flows in this place is almost at a standstill. Similar examples of long term unrest, war and dis-ease can be seen throughout history, with similar life patterns too.

Man is in a state of flux. He is mostly discontented and disgruntled with his life, despite the many opportunities he has around him. He chooses those which suit him best, yet his life is still upside down. He finds it difficult to settle into a happy style of life. I, too, was the same. I, too, became upset with the content of my life because all that I was doing became a burden. Everything I had chosen out of choice and free will had become that burden. Everyday was an effort. I was tired and misunderstood. I had to work harder and harder for the recognition and love that I felt I needed.

I am now going to tell you a story about life...

Once upon a time there lived a man. He was a simple man both in his needs and his desires. Then one day he found a magic lamp. He rubbed the lamp and a genie appeared. "I can grant you your heart's desire," it said, "but only under the condition that it will bring you happiness." The man thought for a while. He considered all the options that were available to him – riches, travel, gems, women, friends and neighbours, fast cars, corporate business, holidays, jet planes, boats, fame etc. etc. He looked at the possibility of owning these things. He searched his mind for the outcome and the pleasure those things would offer him. He thought of the women... He thought of the popularity. He thought and thought about all it would bring and mean. At last he had made up his mind. "I wish for all man to be at peace with his life. I wish for heartache and sorrow, illness and fatigue to be a thing of the past. I wish for each person to attain their own personal goal and I wish for him to be

27

content with his choice. I wish for world hunger, illness and deprivation to be a thing of the past, as each person gets all that they need to survive, but most of all I wish for love. I wish for each and every man the deepest love he desires." The genie laughed. "But these things are yours already. All you ask is already in place." "How so?" said the man. "I look about me to see only famine and war. The people kill and others are sad. Most never reach their dream of success or their pot of gemstone or gold. They argue for love and the respect they deserve – along with their children and friends. Famine is ripe in half of the world, while the rest have more than their share. How can you say my wishes are here?" The genie smiled. He looked the man in his eye for a while and this is what he saw...

He looked to the right and destruction was there, desire and heartache too. Man's hopes and his dreams were catalogued well, his achievements and abilities too. He looked to the left and then once again, repeated that all was in place. All of mankind had still far to go in search of his true happiness. "I cannot do more to fulfil your request – all is in its proper place. It is up to mankind to fill in the blanks for a wonderful, love filled future." The man was put out, "but my wishes – where are they?" The genie just shook his head sadly. "I have given you the earth, the sky and free love. A life that is full to the brim. No more can I do – the rest is up to you, to love one another at once. If you cannot do that the rest will not matter, no riches and dreams will fulfil – the love in your heart that man searches for, is with you right now till the end." He was gone in a flash - no more than that, the old man just stood there a while. The genie was God, who had come to help man – the rest has still not been written.

Man holds the key to his own future. The past has been and gone. I am a product of today. My future will be fine, because the present that I live in is re-written day by day. It

28

is a product of love, of peace, of contentment and of hope. Hope that the future will be fine for us all. And it will be, as long as we each play our part. We do come back to live here again, so it matters very much what we make of the life we are in.

Over the strands of time man has done many things to make life comfortable for himself. He just keeps on going. I, too, enjoy the comfort of past inventions, but what do we do in the future? When life is as good as it can get, what will man want to put his efforts into? I, too, fell into that trap. I worked hard and enjoyed the fruits of that labour, but in the end did I really gain all that I thought I had? I did not, and neither does anyone else. All that money can bring is necessary to survive and be comfortable, but once this has been achieved, what more should we do?

We come into this world with nothing but the life we are given. When we leave we take that life force back with us, to the place where we all belong, but what of all the wealth and possessions we have accumulated during that life? What of all the good intentions we have about what we shall do with it? In most cases we leave our worldly goods to our relatives and friends, but does that serve a purpose other than for memories sake? The things that we hold near and dear do not have the same meaning to those who bequeath them. Possessions can never be anymore than that. I, too, have experienced this a few times in my life. I, too, wish I had done things a little differently in my time, but all too often we don't. It is easy with hindsight, but what matters most is none of that. What matters more than any possession is the way we have lived our life. The happiness and the love we have shared, the good things that have resulted from the fact that we have been here, the legacy of knowledge that we have left behind – even the smallest seed. That we take with us.

Only knowledge and truth and love hold any clout where we shall all end up. In that place we shall be seen as the sum total of our accumulation of these things. The rest will drop away – as meaningless.

Chapter Six

The Winds of Capability and Growth

<u>The way forward</u>

Only man is capable of growth. All other species of life remain within set limitations of their capacity to survive. A dog will always be a dog. His options are limited to what dogs always do. A bird will always be a bird for the same reasons, and so it goes on – with whatever we choose to look at, but man is different. He is born. He is actually far more helpless at birth than other species, but an in-built consciousness keeps him going forward. It is this that makes him different. It is this that makes him grow, and as he does he collects the data of his experiences just like a computer memory chip. Only man has this ability because only man will use the information accumulated at a later date.

We are like probes on an expedition of knowledge and experience. We are the sum total of all our experiences – not just those we choose to remember, but all of what we have ever said and done. We cannot lie a single thing aside, either good or bad, because then we are not who we have actually grown to be. There is in reality neither good nor bad. All things simply exist as they are at any given time in our lives. Each choice we made was right – or seemed right at the time, or we would not have chosen it, but then comes the consequence of those choices, and it is them that rule the next ones we make. I, too, am a product of consequence. I, too, am responsible for all of my past – whether I may like it or not, but I, too, have learned to step off that merry-go-round of chaos.

How we change our life is up to us, but do it we shall – each one of us, at some point in our life. How and when depends on how happy and content we are with the content and direction our life is experiencing now. We have total free will from the time of our birth. Yes we must operate within existing family boundaries and restrictions, but even from an early age, our likes, dislikes and preferences are our own. Very quickly we develop a character of our own and that uniqueness grows and develops stronger as the days, months and years go by. At some stage – at sometime, something inside will push us further forward or pull us farther back. We make the choices that keep us where we are or help us change direction. This is all part of the parcel of life. I, too, made choices many times that had great impact on the direction of my pathway, but more than once I came to realise that those choices were not all that I had anticipated them to be.

We are all the same. We are made of the same chemical components. We each feel happy, sad, lonely, angry and desirous. We all grow in an upward and outward direction that will conquer the obstacles placed in and along our path. Normal family restrictions are the first and keep us safe from harm, but later we push past those boundaries and explore. Only many can do this. We can analyse and assess all we encounter to measure and validate it for ourselves. We choose whether to remain on the plateau or level we are on or whether we might try a new one. All of our life is lived in this fashion. All of our life we aim and fire – to attain whatever our hearts desire at that time. A life without opportunity would be no life. We need to go forward to keep ourselves sane and happy. Growth is one of the most important of human characteristics. It keeps the world turning and the energy flowing as it should. Without the opportunity for growth, man would become stagnant, stale and fed up. He would appreciate little and individual choice would be a thing of the past. He would never reach up or out of his existing state and would never know the wonders that exist all around – for his interaction, entertainment, choice, enlightenment and delight.

Only man can be the eyes and ears of the creator. Only man has this capability. Only man is able to create and grow for himself, always on a journey of his own – forever more. That is the will of God – his creator, his consciousness and his soul.

The life we are given is a gift; a precious gift, but it is the nature of that life that we should change. First, we are who and what we are because of the choices and influences that were available to us at the time. We do all we can to be happy, to make others happy and to make something of ourselves, but too often now we are unhappy, dissatisfied and stuck in the life we are living. It seems that no matter what we do and how hard we try we still end up being misunderstood and unfulfilled. We search far and wide for the love we deserve but again people and life let us down. I, too, have been there, but the amazing thing is that so has everyone else. No matter what we are experiencing, even right now, so is everyone else. Everyone is the same. We are searching, looking for that niche in our life where we can undoubtedly fit and completely belong. Everyone is feeling the same thing – on one level or another in their life. Their packages might change, but underneath all things are the same.

The new millennium was a prime example. Every New Year – and the new millennium more than most, we look forward to the changes we hope they will bring, but as this time comes and goes we see that in reality nothing changes at all. All things remain very much the same. In reality how can one more day produce all we expect it too? The changes we desire are far deeper rooted and must come from within each of our own lives. The changes we require are on a more individual and personal level that when activated would alter not only ourselves, but others and how they relate to us too. I, too, had to learn and pass this point in my life, but I, too, do not look back in any way, shape or form with regret. To understand the changes on this personal level is like a breath of fresh air – or a wind that gains strength as it blows across the desert. It may be all consuming, but it blows with strength and conviction – and the promise of a brighter tomorrow.

Man cannot change the world alone but he can change his little part of it. He can make a conscious decision to alter the way he behaves and the way he reacts to others around him. Each man is the king of his own empire. That is the way of the world and of life itself. It does not matter if he is rich or poor, what matters is the kindness he gives to those who need his help. This is not to say that he should become a doormat. Some self-restraint will go a long way to earn both the respect of others and of himself. A man who does not even respect his own self is often full of sadness and despair. He has learnt to let others use him in anyway they like – just to feel that he is needed and that is not a good thing. Each man is totally responsible for his own life and all that it entails. Each man must gather his own strength, his own juicy bounty and his own rewards. There will be times in every life where one needs a helping hand, but when that hand is openly extended to another man – too often providing a life line - then the balance will quickly shift to burden, and no man should be a burden on another. The problem needs to be adjusted to give the first man back his independence. That is the will of the creator. Man must keep his own life in order – once the tools have been given him, and that is itself another story.

Only man can know the direction he must travel along the course of his life. Each one holds the key to his own failure or success, but this key is often hidden by fear or doubt. So many give up when the going gets a little tough while others still, soldier on for their whole life without seeming to get where they aim to be. This is life that has missed a beat. Somewhere along its pathway important

34

decisions or roads have been missed or misinterpreted. This, when apparent too often will place a man on a side road, completely cut off from those who could help him to establish the connection he needs. All that anyone could do at this point will be hard going, but the worst thing would be to give up or to throw in the towel. I, too, have been exactly here in many different ways during my lifetime, but I, just like many before me, managed to clamber back to the main stream of society and life. Only man has the ability to back track and change direction. Only man has the chance to change – anything that he may choose.

Only man has the need to change the rules of his life because only man can change his 'spots' so to speak. An animal of any description will always be just that – exactly the same as it has always been and exactly the same as all the others of its kind, but man changes at leisure into exactly what he desires to be. In years gone by, a life was the experience of one whole, complete experience but today we have the ability to taste many lives during the course of one lifetime. Because of the freedom of the world about us we can change direction many times, and each time we do we embark on another angle of that life. These little snippets of evolution all fruit the next experience we shall encounter along the course of our life pattern. Man can grow in any direction at any time in his life – but first must come the desire to do so. First must come the realisation that something more exists. Only man can find the key that fits into his own future destiny and that is why it is up to him alone to find and take the next step along the path of his journey.

The experience of any man is a completely individual affair. No two instances will ever be the same for any two people. Each situation that we encounter will lead us to the next piece in the puzzle of our life. When we rely too heavily on our friends and family to help us out, we can miss something that was vitally important as our next step, that only the individual concerned will ever see. Instead of dancing to our own tune we look to others for the answers we seek and in doing so – end up dancing to theirs. Very often that is what puts us and keeps us out of sync both with our own life and with reality. Only we can know what is right for us – and that might not be exactly what we want it to be. Only we can know at anyone time provided we can be honest with ourselves, and that too is a whole other story.

Only we know who and what we are. We know where we have come from (on an emotional as well as on a physical level) and we know exactly where we are going (or where we intend to be). Only we can also know the experiences we have encountered along the way, so it makes sense that only we can know the next step to take. Very often we do know – but choose to dither and dally instead, because we are fearful or unsure, and because of this, we look to others for confirmation of what we ourselves are thinking. We believe that others know better than we do and by their voicing an opinion about our next step, that all things will turn out much better. And they might for a while, but if anything was missed along the way, or if that solution was too quick or not right for us then we have to repeat the experience all over again, perhaps in a different form but the same none-the-less.

Life is a strange thing. We all begin at the same point and end in the same point also, but what goes on in the middle is a miracle itself. I, too, am a constant jumble of works in progress that can not be completed until the whole of my life has been lived, just like a priceless piece of art or a detailed Chinese rug cannot be what it is until the last bit of detail is accomplished. Only man can do that for himself.

Only man has the knowledge that is personally structured to fit his needs. He alone must learn what makes him tick, why he is happy, what makes him sad. Is he happy with his

36

life and if not, what areas need adjusting and why. Is there anymore he would like to accomplish with the time he has left? Are his friends and loved ones happy, or are there family feuds around him? Is his life full of stress and worry, pain and struggle – or is he carefree? I, too, had to delve down deep. I had to find out the reason that once more I was not as happy as I thought I should have been. Things were occurring, once again, that appeared out of my control – yet I somehow knew that I was also contributing to where I was. I had to find out what was bringing me down once more in my life, because like many others, I was not a bad person and I thought I was doing the best that I could with all that I had and was. I began to learn differently. I began to learn that we are all the same and in the same boat. We are all looking for happiness and a place to fit snugly in life. We are all constant works in progress that alter daily as time goes by. We add more to where we are in life than most of us realise. It is easy to blame others for our predicaments, indeed we are taught to do just that from a very early age, yet really it is down to us – but in more subtle ways that you can imagine at this time.

All of life is based on the laws of cause and effect. Nothing goes beyond this ruling. All of nature is based on the same thing – and we are part of nature itself. The world was born because of cause and effect, as conditions that surrounded the first energy, changed. Man thinks that this current span of life is his all, but it is not. He must work to grow and change his opinion of self, of whom and what he is. The Bible may be full of faults and changed texts that appear old and out of date, but it is also one of the earliest representations of our true selves. It clearly states that we are more than we think. It tells of our troubled past and the pressures of today, but it also holds the key to tomorrow. The words that are written (not only in the Bible, but other religious books too) tell a story of all that we are and all we are able to be. I, too, am the product that was written in its texts, but I, too, have realised my true connection to the divine. Only we can change the paths of distress, disease and destruction we find ourselves on, and only we can come back to do better than before. That is our given right in the scale of life and love itself. We have a chance to do better, to be more than we are and to claim our birthright here and now – in this lifetime.

Man is under the influence of his emotional self much more than he should be. Only we can make the necessary adjustments that are needed to correct this imbalance, but first we have to realise that a problem exists. From a very early age we learn to relate to the world about us by the way it feels. When some thing felt good we did it again and when something did not we shied away from it. Even our parents led us by our emotions and by their own ones too. We quickly learnt to read the emotional crosscurrents of all those who surrounded us. As we grew up, this experience extended to school and playmates and to anyone we encountered anywhere along the way. This is the nature of man, but what we did not know is that energy currents also flow from us – and it is those that trip our emotional switches just as much as the emotions and mood swings of other people. When we walk into a room that we have never been in before, we feel at ease or not, but we don't know why. What we are relating to is the energy that already exists in that space; the energy of what has gone on there before. Man is both physical and etheric. This means that we are equal parts of matter and energy. We are familiar with the 'matter or body' side of ourselves but often unfamiliar with the energy side. All energy flows around and about and through us, but like particles of dust settle down in a room, so do the residue of energy particles left there by other people. All objects that are used by man contain his residue and will affect the feel of the empty, yet furnished room.

38

Man is structured in a way that allows the free flow of energy to pass through him at all times. He is made to be happy and contented with his life, so when the opposite occurs he clams shut – just like a limpet on a rock face. Only peace and harmony allows him to perform the function he was made for and that is why it is written in the Bible 'that God does not recognise sorrow or fear, anger or war'. When man operates from within those behaviour traits, the energy that is his life force and also the planet's does not pass through. It cannot, because he has blocked its pathway or channel and this is how, as we said earlier, man is slowly killing the planet he loves. Its life force is not flowing as it should and therefore cannot reach as deep to the earth's core as is needed. Man is not doing this deliberately. He is not acting out of vindictiveness or vengeance. It is the cause and effect law in operation again. Man is unhappy, so both the planet and man himself get starved of the vital energy that they need. This is not God's will. It is not man's deliberate wish. It is simply the by-product of the life he lives at this time, and in past times, as history clearly shows.

Man lives to be happy. It was the way he was designed to be. He has around him all he could possibly want, need or desire. The possibilities for contentment have never been so great, so easy, yet it seems almost impossible for many. Somewhere deep down inside; love, laughter, happiness and contentment, are being lost or misplaced. Each and every day he treads the dreary, hard path of life and each day he fails to reach his goal posts. Something is wrong somewhere and that something lies embedded in each one of us. Only man can sort himself out because only man can find his own true happiness. That does not mean we should stamp on each other, point the finger of blame at those in its range or take drastic action to compensate, but it does mean that this will be a wake up call for many. Only time can put things right once more –

slowly, but we first need to understand there is a problem and why. We need to take stock, to understand that we ourselves play a greater part in our own unhappiness than we realise. It is easy to blame others around for their failings and for our own shortfalls, but these things are as much a product of their life as of ours. Nobody, anywhere deliberately sets forth to make those that they love or know unhappy, just as we don't set out to do the same to them. Miscommunication and misunderstanding play vital roles in this part of history, and we are all victims of it – not to mention our own overactive emotional behaviour traits.

Man is but a child, almost until his death. The life and time we spend here on earth is but a drop in an ocean of time and space, only at this moment, many of us don't realise or accept this to be true. That is the whole reason those we have loved and lost through seeming death are coming back to be with us once more. They are letting us know with every ounce of their being that death is not the end, it is only a transition. The life we live does go on – and so do the consequences. These are the laws of cause and effect. Those who take their life as a way out of sadness and turmoil simply continue where they left off as they cross over that bridge. The 'heaven' we all wait for is the continuation of the here and now. Here is the only place that we can make a difference. Here – on the face of the planet, on the physical body of the all that is, the body of God itself.

Many will throw out their hands in uproar of that statement, but only because they too are still asleep. They are deep in the path of their own life and beliefs, but that is not a problem. Many different ways lead up the mountain, but they all reach right to the top. There is nowhere else to go – unless they are on a round and round route. Each man will find his own truth. He will wake up at sometime – a time that is right for him, but it does not mean we should drag our feet and wait for them. We are on our own journey and if we speak words of truth and love, others too will see the light and follow. Truth needs no long lullaby to back it up. It stands straight and tall in its own merit, in its own strength, and once it is spoken something deep inside all of us makes its connection. We don't even have to realise. It will just happen because truth is like that. It is what man is unconsciously searching for – through the aeons of time he has been here.

Truth is an unchangeable force. Truth stands up in its own glory – regardless of what is thrown at it. Truth can be examined from any angle, and indeed it is, but each time the same conclusion is reached. Truth needs no coloration to make it palatable. It withstands time and space – eternally. Truth waits quietly by the side of man until he is ready to accept it, whether he believes in it or not. In fact believing or not believing does not alter a thing. Truth is truth and that is all there is to it.

I am truth. I am the light. I will lead you through the valley of death. These are words that hold great weight and meaning. These are words that are timeless. Yet these are words that are simple and true. Only now can we realise their full potential. Only now we can take them on board in our own life's situations. Knowledge of any kind is only useful if you put it to work in life; otherwise it is taken back and rendered useless by the mind. It is here and now that matters most and we have all that we need to help us make things work. Life is not a gamble. It is not a game. Only life that's lived moment by moment can be bought to successful fruition. Only this will make the difference that we all wait anxiously for. I am the light means that we have the light of truth and knowledge always – at all times within us. I am the truth means that we all, each and every moment know exactly what is best for us and what is the better option to take, but to recognise it fully we must still our emotions, because it is those that lead us astray. I will lead you through the valley of death, means exactly that

41

too. It is not concerned with physical death, because the transition we accomplish is automatic. We automatically return to whence we came. It is concerned though with the seeming death and fear of the spirit in life itself. It means that in our darkest, saddest, most fearful hours we will be taken by the hand and led back to peace and light. It means that we can always find that glimmer of hope that takes us forward to another day. A new day – and each new day is exactly that. It is a blank page that we can write upon – exactly as we would wish. It means that we do hold the key to our life firmly in our hand at all times and that we are not the victims of circumstance we like to think we are. There is always a better option available to everyone and we are led by the hand until we find it.

Man is boss of his own life and because of this only he can make the moves and the decision to change it. I, too, have had to pass this point and I still do on an ongoing basis. That is the nature of free will and individuality. We are not the product of our life and haphazard circumstances but of the choices that have taken us to this point in time. Each and everyday we have the option to change at least one little thing we don't like or something that no longer serves our purpose. That is all it will take to get the ball rolling; one little thing, or one issue at a time. Life does not call on us to make catastrophic alterations that will change its course overnight; indeed these are often the changes we should not make. But again these are more obvious with hindsight. I, too, have had my share of catastrophes, and have taken decisions that could have been better, but once again it is life that has shown me these things as I ponder and look back upon it. We all have a wealth of information and experience at our fingertips that we don't often access. We are too busy looking forward to where we would rather be than to notice exactly where we are right now. This seems to be the norm for today's fast lifestyle. We forget to stand and take stock of what is right under our nose.

Life comes at us – one step at a time. One day, one hour, one second. Every moment of everyday we have the opportunity to 'gently' say our truths, but do we? How often do we say exactly what we need to say to sort a problem out? If you are like I was, then the answer is not very often at all. It is easier to smile and keep the peace than to voice a truth that might bring conflict once it is aired. But that is not always the answer. Sometimes the signals we send out are not as clear or obvious as we would like to think, then we wonder why others don't seem to take any notice. But how can they when they are stuck in their own train of thought and behaviour. Signals are not clear enough. It is truth and kind words that are needed to put our point across. This is more necessary than we realise. Only man can help himself. There is no knight in shining armour that can come to whip our troubles, no magician and no genie. All of our future stems from us alone – and that will happen one single step at a time.

Chapter Seven

The Winds that will Wake Up

Each and every man is the same. We share the same hopes and the same dreams. We each look for love, hope and comfort. We would like world peace and world health. Each and every man deserves the most basic of human necessities as his birthright. We look to our parents to love and to guide us, to know us at least as well as we know ourselves and to be proud of who we are trying to be. We look to our friends to uplift us and to share our good times. We look to our siblings and children for a sense of belonging and understanding. We look to many people for many different reasons, but do we ever really look at ourselves? Do we know ourselves as well as we think we do? My guess is that we don't – not often anyway, yet we expect, completely expect others to know what we want and what we are thinking all the time. We look to others to mend the broken parts of us that we can't even fix ourselves, and then we wonder why life continually falls short of our expectations. But is it any wonder in reality?

Man is his own worst enemy. He travels through life dashing here and there without achieving anything. He travels miles along life's pathway that he need not travel at all. Much time is wasted in being busy that need not be spent – if he would only realise the pattern he is repeating. I, too, travel along this road. It's as if we need to be busy in order to prove our own worth, but in reality we do not. We could achieve more by consolidating our activity and focusing our attention on the task in hand. How often do we mindlessly perform menial tasks as our attention wanders all over the place? It takes us two or three times as long to perform something we could do in minutes – if we put our mind to it and focused properly. We rarely consider the connection between the task in hand and the thoughts we are thinking whilst doing it. Energy flows where attention goes and given that our attention wanders freely, no wonder we are tired and lethargic at the most inopportune times. I am also guilty of this. I waste my energy like water down a drain, and it's only with practice that we can stop. But how can we stop until someone tells us we are doing what we are doing in the first place? We are not taught things such as this ordinarily and we wonder why time flies so drastically fast. We rarely achieve what we set out to do in a day. Only we can know ourselves if we are guilty of this – and then only we can stop it from happening.

With our head in the future, the present that we experience passes by. It is easily done as we hold imaginary conversations with those we are intending to speak to. We enact dramas as if to practise what needs to be said and imagine what will happen in response, then when the event comes to be we wonder why those concerned do not react as we thought they would. Instead of relying completely on the moment we are in – we look to the future and rehearse it, either in our own mind or in conversation form with our friends or colleagues. And the same is said of the past. Not the distant past but this morning, yesterday, last week. We replay these scenarios as we would have liked them to be – so often that we invent the memory over and over again. How can we ever know the truth or let life take its course when we are not even present in the now. To be so we must experience every moment exactly as it occurs innocently, spontaneously – without coloration or rehearsal. How can we know how others will respond when we have not even reached that point? The answer is that we cannot possibly know. We think we do – based on past experience, but we don't really know at all. Each and every day, every event, every moment is individual. No two experiences are totally alike, so how can we anticipate them correctly?

Helping ourselves

We can help ourselves, but only in the moment we are in; in the 'now'. Yesterday has been and gone. Tomorrow is not yet here – and a hundred things could happen in the meantime, so it stands to reason that only 'now' can matter. This is where life is taking place. It is here that we can make a difference to our future - one step, one second, one minute at a time. It is here that all changes are possible and it is only here we can do the things that count for something.

Now is more important than we realise yet ironically it is the 'now' that we often leave to automatic pilot or chance. All decisions that need to be made are only of value in the now. All life exists at its highest state – in the now. Now is all that matters. Now is all that exists. This is not to say we should throw caution to the wind and totally ignore tomorrow and the future, on the contrary, this is not it at all. Our thoughts of the future show us the direction we want to travel in, the goals we need to head towards, but it is only in the 'now' that those changes can take shape – one step, one decision at a time. Only man has this capability of knowing. He holds all the keys in his own hand in every direction he looks and in all the decisions he makes. That is the law of consciousness.

Many hours are spent in longing. We long for different looks than we have, bigger and better jobs, houses, cars and lifestyles. Only a few are content with the lot they have and this is one of the saddest things that exist. We have more available to us – in every way we care to imagine, yet deep inside many are sad, discontented and even angry. I, too, have experienced my fair share of this kind of life. I, too, had to go within to understand what was going on. Each goal post that we reach should make us happy, but instead of enjoying the experience we look ahead to the next. How can we ever be pleased with our lot when we keep changing our mind? Yet there lies the paradox. We don't know our own mind. We don't even know what we want. Yes we have an idea. We really believe that we do; yet when we get there reality falls short of our high expectations and we often find that nothing has changed at all. We have all experienced this – in many forms and it is also why man today goes through many life changes. It used to take a lifetime to build up a home and raise a family, but today man can experience as many different lifestyles as he would like. The opportunity is there for all, and that is why it is time to get it right – but before we can we must know ourselves better than we do. Man is a complex machine. He is capable of so much, but achieves so little – too often. Apart from a few, many never reach their goals, their dreams or their desires and the saddest thing of all is that we don't even realise we could.

Only we can make the life we lead a happy one and only we can make it count. We travel this way to experience all that we can; to live, to love, to be happy and content, to make a difference – some way, some how, to someone, somewhere. We think that at death it is too late, that our time is up and we must face our maker as well as our flaws, but what we don't realise is that life carries on where we left off – just on another level, that's all. Life goes on. We do not die. There is no death – only change. We drop our bodies and they turn back to dust, but we ourselves live on in a more transparent way. What we do with our life, what we make of our choices and chances does matter. It matters very much, because when we get home it's too late. We shall see all the opportunities we missed – to do what we wanted to do. We shall regret plenty but then will try to put things right as best as we are able. We shall be the sum total of who we were before we came to earth plus the experiences and knowledge gained while in our physical form. It is here on earth that we matter the most. It is only here, in the now that makes any difference – either to the planet or to ourselves.

Man has the ability to do anything. He can go anywhere and be anybody that he would like himself to be. He is the keeper of his own life and master of his own destiny. No one anywhere can tell him otherwise. Yes he has responsibilities but even those are the outcome of past events or present necessity, and other than that he is free to come and go as he pleases. He alone makes up the rules he must live by. He again is responsible for the day to day running of his lifestyle. At some point in the past years of his life he himself has made every decision he now faces the consequence for, regardless of whether these have been in haste or not, or whether the outcome seems good or bad. He is responsible for exactly what he faces today. Again I hear people say "but what about this, what about that. If only they had done.... If only so and so had not put me in this situation, or that predicament..." There will always be a thousand if onlys, buts and maybes, but the truth will always remain the same. Each decision that was taken along the way has played a contributing factor and as each day passes man makes the best decisions he can at any given moment. How many of us can relate to this? How many of us have been to places, then done and said things that in hindsight we should have not? But at the end of the day we are only human and unless someone stands there and says "Hey – this is a better way", we carry on regardless. We are human and because of this we are our own worst enemies. We are all guilty of this trait – but then isn't that what being human is all about? We all like a quick fix, and if we see a short cut it would be unnatural not to take it, only it may not then be the best option in the long run. Only things won over time can last and pull through, the rest will fall by the wayside as quickly as they appeared.

Man must learn a better way to advent his options and to recognise the best route to take at any given moment.

We have already discussed how when we are young we look to our elders for direction and leadership, but what we don't realise is that those elders themselves are still searching for their own direction and answers in life. We come along, as innocent as the day is long and take on board every word that is said – until we learn otherwise. (That's if we ever do!). We are like sponges that soak up everything we find. We always think that others know better than us – but do they? In many cases they can only know what they themselves have been taught, and again this has not always been from the truest source. All that we see, hear and experience throughout our lifetime gets ingested into our head. We take on board all that interests us or we can relate to, and the rest gets discarded. That is our personal choice. But all that we keep is stored. It becomes a part of our belief system, and once we form a belief it remains with us through time – unless it gets challenged and we have cause to use or alter it. Most of the beliefs that we hold near and dear have been unaltered through time. We have very few reasons to check their validity or their content. They have been a part of us since childhood. But what if those beliefs are incorrect? We only know what we have been told by people older than us, and they too only know what they have been taught – and so it goes back through time.

Only man can know what his thoughts and beliefs are and these are as varied as the stars in the universe. We look to our beliefs to lead us through life but what happens when they are wrong or incomplete? Who knows? Who can tell? We are who we are, because of the life we have lived along the way. We are guided by our parents until we grow up – but when do we grow up? At what point in time do we know we have and who is around to tell us? It is assumed that once we leave school we can handle ourselves and our

49

life – but can we? All at once we seem to stop learning and get on with the job in hand – whether we are able to or not, but the truth is different. The truth is that many adults are more like children than the children are themselves. They are so busy surviving that everything else falls by the wayside. When do we grow up? Who says that we do?

What do we really know?

Life is full of ups and downs. Often we learn hard lessons along the way that appear cruel but are necessary. Problems we encounter are not meant to make us buckle and break, instead they are valuable lessons that we must learn and pass to take us to the next stage, the next place we are meant to be. As soon as we can recognise this – the quicker and easier we can overcome their existence. A problem is nothing more than a stepping-stone that will lead us to a smoother path. Yes, sometimes those stones feel more like boulders, but it is likely by then that we have missed a few red flags along the way. It is generally the case that we have buried our heads in the sand and ignored the signals, hoping they would go away, but if a problem gets bigger or keeps reoccurring it means that it needs our attention. Something needs addressing somewhere to instigate a change, and that is usually for the better in the long run – even if it hurts like mad at the time!

Man is working too hard. Everyday he gets up early and spends hours at his desk or in his office. Work is a natural part of life, but we have become 'stuck' in work mode. Only man spends his life cooped up in a room while the days of warmth and sunshine pass by. Days roll into one another and suddenly a month has past without his even realising. The time we have is precious. It is too important to waste. Man has become trapped by the rules and regulations of society, yet it is not society's fault. It is mans, because he uses and expects too much. We work hard to earn more money, to pay the bills and to buy more stuff. We are not content with waiting and saving, so we borrow money we don't yet have and this becomes a millstone around our neck. We work hard to pay it off, but in the meantime we need, or just buy more stuff. The money we borrowed gets higher or remains the same. We work harder to pay it off, but still keep living and buying and working and borrowing. We are stuck in a loop. In catch 22. The only way out is to stop; to get off that merry-go-round and stand still. Take a look at yourself. Do you really need all that you have around you? Is it worth working your life away? We all need a roof over our head because of the climate we live in. It's too cold to sleep outside forever as the Indians did! And we all need the basics, but we have enough clothes alone to cover a football pitch. We have enough stuff to keep a small village happy. Where does it all end? And who cares? We worked hard for it, we can do whatever we like, but are we happy? Because we buy and want so much society must create more and more to replenish its stocks and keep up. If we took stock and stopped for a while we might feel better for it. Just look about you and in the shops. Look at all the stock that is sitting there waiting to be bought. Imagine double; treble that amount, in the pipeline at all times waiting to come from manufacturers, in transit or on the drawing board as new lines for each new season. Do we need it? Should we really want it or should we take a look at ourselves and wake up? There is more to life than work and perhaps we should look to easing our load, to enjoy what is outside our window everyday. Alone we are small. We think we can't make a difference, but we are wrong. We so can make that difference. I, too, am one, but I am trying and that effort counts for more than I realise. **I can, I am and I will**.

Much of what we do today is totally unnecessary in the scale of life itself. If we pulled ourselves together and sorted our own life out we would be amazed, not pleasantly surprised, but amazed at how much we could accomplish. At this moment in time we are teaching our children to be exactly like us – to work and eat and sleep and work and spend and work and eat and sleep.... Is this what we actually want life to be like, or do we want more time to visit, to enjoy, to chill, to have fun, to savour the day? Only we can answer these questions. Only we can make that choice and instigate the changes that will make it happen, not overnight, not with rebellion or by skiving off work and our commitments but with one-step at a time, right here inside your self.

Man needs to reach a certain standard in his life to feel a sense of self worth and stability. He must reach the goal he sets for himself, but other than that this world is his oyster. He must work to survive and play but in reality that is all. However today this is often not the case. He is so used to working to achieve that now that is all he does. He works hard, too hard in a time in history where life has never been so good. There are more gadgets and gismos than ever before – and still he looks to produce bigger, smaller, faster, better ones that will cut his use of time even more. But what can he do with his time. Extra time is only of use if you appreciate having it, yet this is also not apparent today. We use that time instead to cook, eat, sleep and work some more. Man has ground to an emotional halt. He has lost his sense of enjoyment and zest for life. I, too, have been there, where every day is like the one before. I, too, had to leave the treadmill. It is easy to be bogged down by routine, and indeed we do need organisation, but when all is said and done, by the time we do get to sit down or relax, we are too tired for anything else. The hours slip by and off we go again. Is this the way of the western world – the so-called civilised high life? "It is a sign of the times" we say, but fail to recognise that we ourselves add to all that keeps us as we are, every single day. If we ate only when we were hungry and bought and wasted less, we would see that we need less. Because we need less we would buy less, therefore, we would be able to work less to produce less, and because we work less, we would have more free time to enjoy. It is another catch 22 loop hole that man has got himself caught up in. Notice the times you automatically do things you need not do and begin to curb your actions. It need not even be drastically, just one little thing at a time.

I was the same and still often am, but the more you can pull yourself back you will begin to break old habits. It is not comfortably possible to change overnight because then you feel deprived. When you feel deprived you want to spoil yourself to make yourself, feel better and so you begin the cycle again – until the next time... One step at a time is enough to dent the habit, and with practise it will slowly become a complete reversal. I, too, should know because I am still going through the motions myself. It is not easy and it sure takes time and patience, but keep on going and eventually you will get there!

Life is a joy to be lived. It is not always a bed of roses but then it's not supposed to be. If we never had anything bitter – how could we enjoy the sweet taste of honey? Life is equally good and bad and that is exactly the way it should be. It is a gift to wake up to each day. Each new day to live as we would like to live, to do whatever we desire to do. Work plays a vital role, but so do happiness, contentment and self-satisfaction. Yet given the fact it is necessary to work how many of us completely enjoy what we do? Too many hours are spent doing jobs that we really don't like. This is not to say we should not take a job that seems menial or below us, because in reality joy can be found in any vocation if you put your whole self into it, but why don't we find jobs that we would really enjoy instead of just working for a pay packet? The answer is that we sometimes forget what it was that we really wanted to be or become, then because we are so bogged down with necessity and the life we have formed for ourselves we have no possible means to backtrack. Life is too short to gamble and play at it. Before you know – time has run out. It is never too late to change your goal posts, but do it with love. Do it with consideration to yourself and to others, but do it. Look for that job that will fulfil you each day. It's too late when you go back across the bridge of death. What will you say? Yes, Thank you for my life, but I didn't enjoy it because... or Yes, I had the opportunity but I couldn't because... There will always be obstacles in your path but if you are sincere and move those boulders one stone at a time, you will gradually win through. Life is not a game. It is serious, and we seriously need to get happy – in all that we do. Make it count for you. Make it work like you would want it to and get happy in the process, not chilled out – drug type happy, but happily content with your lot. No one else can do it for you – so do it for yourself and all those around who love you. –

It is easy to put a smile on your face but even easier for someone else to remove it. Each and everyday, someone, somewhere can place a spoke in our works. Only we can stop them from doing this by making a choice. We can choose not to let them. Nine times out of ten those who spike us are only venting their own bad mood or anger anyway, so push it subconsciously back to them like a snow plough clearing snow (until you can learn how to recycle it). Make a decision that today no one can get to you and it's likely that they won't. We make that choice. Stand firm but happy in your own ground and the storm will pass you by. If you are worried make yourself subconsciously small, like a grain of sand and remain so until you know what to do. We are great at making our presence felt but if we did the opposite more often it would be better. Make yourself small everyday and life will flow much easier around you. If someone is causing a rumpus and you are quaking inside, send your thoughts up and ask for help.

Ask for them to be small as well. You can do this once or one hundred times in a day and it will always work. There is more that goes on in life than you realise – so have a little faith.

Life responds to us – we don't respond to it. This statement alone countermands much that many believe today. I, too, had to learn this in not so easy lessons. Life flows under its own rules and regulations. Peace and harmony follow. Man is given this life to live but he does not – or should not, control it. He is just a player, like a player to a team or an actor to a film. Man is the keeper of his own life but life also flows about him. I, too, learnt this when I was young. Life was not always as kind as it is today. Much has changed for the better yet we often barely notice. Only man can make his life work for him. Only he can help it flow in the direction of his choice – but that's exactly it, he must 'help' it. One day a man sat on a stone with his head in his hands. All day he had laboured to clear the leaves from a garden, but each time he did, the wind blew them back. All day this went on till at the end he gave up. The problem was not what he was trying to do but the way he was doing it. He was sweeping them into a pile to be picked up together at the end. If he had moved the pile out of the wind's reach or put them in a bag along the way, he would have been finished hours earlier. The moral is work with what is available to you in the most efficient way you can. Nature will lend a hand – but only if you stop working against it. Two streams that flow against each other will simply stand still and create a force, whereas two streams that meet as they follow the same direction will flow softly, softly until they reach the sea. Work with the currents that flow in your life – not always against them.

Signposts

Only we can determine the direction of our life, but if something is wrong we will always find out. These are the markers that keep us moving on. These are what keep life flowing and efficient. If we are on the wrong path for us – that door will close at some point and we are forced to reconsider or re-route entirely. This is one simple example of how life gently guides us to where we ought to be, to a smoother existence or plateau. Only we can make the alterations that will get us there but life gives us the signal first. We simply respond. It is us who decide the direction we wish to follow, because that is personal choice, but after we have, it is life that carries us there, that places the opportunity in our grasp. A baby with a rattle - at first cannot reach it. He does not know it is there and does not know it exists. Then he is shown it, but still he must reach out his hand for himself and that is what happens to us. One door closes and another takes its place. This is nature working with us. This is life at its best.

But who and what places these things in our pathway at exactly the right time? How do we know what we need before we have seen it? Someone does. How many times has a leaflet dropped onto your mat at just the right occasion? How often do we overhear a conversation and think 'that's funny'; I need or have experienced that too. We overhear the television, the radio or see a newspaper or magazine article that immediately connects to us at the exact time we need that information. I, too, have both experienced and read about this. It is called coincidence, but there is no such thing as a coincidence. Each time something of this nature occurs, it was meant to. You are being given a helping hand, or you are being shown an alternative direction that will help you out, or place you exactly where you need to be to receive another direction. All these happen so ordinarily that the average person thinks little of the incident, but begin to take notice from this time on. The more you notice and silently acknowledge that you have noticed, it will happen more often – with things that are more important to you. Usually we say 'if only I saw that last week' or 'I could have done with this yesterday'. If that is the case it is a sure sign that you are changing your mind too often. It can even signal that you live more in the future than the present. You are wishing your life away. Those that operate fully in the moment will be pleasantly surprised at how often coincidences occur, and they will continue to do so if you will let them.

Many of us believe that we must bombard ourselves through life to get what we can when we want it, but often this is wrong. How many times have we moved hell and high water to obtain something we thought we badly wanted – only to wish we had waited a little longer to get it? The answer is very often, if you are like the rest of society. We charge through life at a great rate of knots and miss much more than we see. It is time that we slowed down our pace - to allow the universe to catch up and help us once more. Man does not need to hurry through life quite as much as he presently does. Time passes the same whether we enjoy ourselves or not, so we may as well use it to our advantage. Only we can make life enjoyable for ourselves as well as for others, but that's not to say we take too much on board - because that is another problem.

Man as a race is good and kind (or the majority are). We look to make this life work as smoothly as possible. Life is hard sometimes for everyone, but usually at different times – for different reasons. As we pass through those difficulties we become wiser and stronger and happier. Life holds lessons for us all and we try to help those around us overcome theirs. We do this because we want to. We enjoy the end result when all goes well and often it does, but more often these difficulties only appear to be solved and if this is the case their problems will simply return and the person concerned will be back where he started once more. Every problem has a different lesson behind it – even if it appears to be the same on the surface. If that problem seems hard it is because it is meant to. Its lessons lie deeper than the surface will show. Usually a lot of things will need to be addressed and altered to make it disappear correctly, and never return. Only little things that get addressed at the time they arise will prevent a problem cascading. Only one step at a time and our lives would be different.

Life goes by in seconds, minutes, hours and days, but we don't notice the time at all. We are so wrapped up in the things that we do, that we hardly notice. We are forever on catch-up, rushing here and running there, without living the day at all. We are the only ones who can slow our time down. Only we can make it work for us and all we need do is ask. When time goes too slowly and the day appears to drag – send a signal up to your guides. Ask them to speed it up a little. When time seems to fly faster than you can work – ask again. Ask for it to be slowed right down, so you can achieve all that you want in the time that you have available for the project in hand. This can be done as often as you wish, but remember to put it back to normal when you are finished – or you may be on the opposite side of the problem. You have total charge over your perception of time. It can work for you – just as you need, but you must remember to ask for what you need. No one else can - because no one else knows. Only you do.

Only we can help ourselves but first we must realise that we can, and this is just one little trick of many that will work in your favour. We should be glad that we are not just skin and bones; that we are more and are capable of more than we understand right now, because all these things will work in our favour – forever, once they are mastered.

Life works for us depending on the rules by which we play. We set the scene and also the pace. We are able to choose pretty much everything. Yes, it often appears that we are at the mercy of outside events and people, but in truth, they are just living to their own beat, to their own rules and desires. If we are moved enough to become cross by them or their influence, it is because something somewhere has been overlooked. Wherever we are in life, it is because at that moment in time it is exactly where we are meant to be. When something needs to change we will know by the signals at work, or by our innermost feelings.

Only man can grow and change at will. He is the conductor of his own destiny. Just as a child reaches his upper ceiling of intelligence, so does man. He can only operate within the boundaries he sets for himself. When he is bored, or has had enough of the life about him, it is a sure sign that he needs to reach out and explore once again; new knowledge, new circles, new experiences and new energies to explore and digest. Sometimes this step may be small like joining a new club or doing a new activity, but at other times this may not be enough. Send out your thoughts once more that you need some help and watch closely to see what arises in response. Remain in a state of truth and love and openness and you will be surprised, but if you drop into depression, stress or fear you will only succeed in shutting out all that might be. You will clam yourself up once more and will feel the weight of the world upon your shoulders. Ask for help in an open, true and sincere way, and it really will come to you.

But again be watchful and remain open for new thoughts and experiences to filter through. Sometimes we are so bent on how we imagine the solution to be that we miss the subtle things that offer a change of direction. Don't be too rigid in your thinking – remain flexible. A solution may not appear in quite the same form as you anticipate. Don't rush headlong into counter activity and drastic measures. Be gentle with yourself. Imagine you can be as small as a grain of sand inside and sit tight for a while as things readjust or realign themselves around you. Be patient, be watchful to the signals and above all else be kind – not indulgent, but gentle on yourself. You are where you are now because that is where you were supposed to be at this time.

I have also travelled this not too considerate road and there are plenty of adjustments that need to be made. Notice others around you and you will see they too are often just as stuck or unhappy as you are. The wind that will blow your cobwebs away will also send gusts out to others who interact in your circles of movement. If you make the changes – no matter how small, that you need, you will also unblock the flow of life of others around. Sometimes these changes might feel a little painful but that is only because we are creatures of habit. We would rather remain unhappily as we are – in an uncomfortable situation, just because it is familiar to us. We can be too frightened to change because of the unknown factors it may bring, but life is like that. Life is like a pair of old slippers that we don't want to bin because of their comfort. They may be threadbare and inefficient, but we keep them just the same. We would rather remain unhappy and moan about it than alter the smallest thing, when really that is not the answer. We should instead obtain a happy and content frame of mind for many reasons. We must all love our life or it is not as it is supposed to be.

Only we can see the spokes in our works and the areas that cause us pain and discomfort, so only we can focus our attention on alterations that need to occur. Sometimes these changes will involve other people – but sometimes they might simply be down to a change in our own attitude. Don't do anything at all until you know exactly – without doubt, what to do. There are many books on the market that will open new windows of understanding for you. Only you can know how you feel, and if you are unhappy or stressed you need to understand the cause of it. We are each assigned at birth, a guardian angel. It does not matter whether you believe it - or not, because belief is not the key. They are there and will remain so until you die – or cross back over to home. The important part is that in your darkest moments, when you feel totally lost – you know you are not alone. You are being helped and guided. Go to a bookshop and browse in the self-help section. Notice the kind of book you are attracted to and read it. Remember to remain open and flexible. This will be the first of many stepping-stones that will lead you to a new understanding of yourself and of others around you. *'Families and how to survive them'* by John Cleese and Robin Skinner is a good starting point. If you are in relationship difficulties, try *'Men are From Mars and Women are from Venus'* by John Gray or *'The Relate Guide to Starting Again'* by Sarah Litvinoff (actually written by Relate). These are excellent starting points that will give you some food for thought and will also lead you to other books for other reasons. Remember all change starts within yourself. If you keep on doing what you have always been doing you will simply get what you've always been getting. A book is like a breath of fresh air. It is like discussing your problems with a friend or councillor and you will take on board only what you need. Your subconscious will do the work for you as it disregards all your rubbish. Change will come slowly, one step at a time, but just like a child, if you hold up your hand – someone, somewhere will answer your call. They were meant to.

Many of us are like children who need redirection and input from another source. When we are small we look to our parents and our teachers, but in adulthood we go forward as best as we can – often alone or by the guidance of others who are as stuck as we are. This is nobody's fault but everyone's problem. At this point in time you are luckier than most simply by your reading this book. You have already begun to wake up and look around you. You are sending out the ripples of alteration simply by recognising yourself in another way. The wheels of life are already beginning to alter. Be pleased and be happy.

Chapter Eight

The Winds of Youth

The child and the parent

We are born and we grow. We adapt to those around and to our surroundings. We simply fit into the surrounding influences that are in our path, but what proof do we have that those who surround us know as much as they think? We live by their rules, regulations and standards, but what if they themselves are out of sync with life as it should be? What if we ourselves have been swept along by the current of illusion, simply because we have followed an already illusional path? Should we not look to find out? Man is just the product of the life and influences that have surrounded him along the span of his time here. Whoever checks that the adults we follow, are on par with the world about them?

Anyone can be a parent. There are no restrictions of any kind. It takes all sorts to make a world and those all sorts operate on many different levels, thoughts and behaviour patterns. Many adults struggle daily to make their own lives work, then all of a sudden they become parents and it is assumed that they know what they are doing. Being a parent is the most important task in the world, yet most of the time we do it alone. We only know what to do from the examples we were being shown ourselves, but often those were way off the mark. Only man faces such a task as parenting alone and the stakes are too high to take risks with. We can never know how good we are doing, because there are no measures to measure ourselves by. Being a good parent is not easy. Being an adult or a child is not easy either. Perhaps we don't know as much as we think we do.

Anyone can have a child, but it is how we raise that child that is important. Out of love we make many mistakes, but how can we know? Who can tell us? There is no operator's manual. Each child, each family is completely different. It is a unique experience for us all, but should we experience it blindly and alone as we do? From birth until school age we are almost completely alone with our children. They are at our mercy, but should we carry this burden and should they? Is it right to leave such an important task to chance? People with learning difficulties have help with life, but they too are on their own in adulthood. We are trained for every job everywhere – yet we suddenly know how to be a good parent. We love our children and would lay down our own life for them if the need arises; yet we hurt them with our loving intentions all the time.

Children go through definite stages and behaviour patterns, but how often do we fully understand what they are and how to help them through their experiences? Many parents are too locked into their own trials and tribulations to notice. Small signals that would highlight a problem get taken on board as a child being naughty or needy, and then when a full blown problem comes to light we wonder where it came from. Children need our examples and guidance as well as our food and board. They tell us what they need at the time they need it, but then it's up to us to keep things balanced. Life is full of opportunity for a healthy happy child, but a child who is different in any way can come up against barriers that are hard to break. Teachers are trained for years to handle our children, but we expect to do it automatically, without help or guidance of any kind.

Only we can put this right, but first we need to know ourselves better than we do right now. We need to better understand what makes us tick. What pushes our buttons? Why do we laugh or cry? What makes us angry? Where are our boundaries and what are our beliefs? All these things and more, play a vital role in the person we see ourselves to be. It is the response behind the actions we take and the words we speak that is responsible for our drive, our hopes and our dreams. The way we see ourselves is the most important thing in the world, the world in which we live and grow and survive.

Only we can know the answers to these questions and more, but it is not as simple as taking a glance at yourself. Knowledge of this nature will only come to light as you pay attention to the things you do day by day, many of which are so ingrained and automatic that we don't even realise we do them at all. Only we can find the pieces of our mind and put them all together. Only we can rebuild ourselves, but in a much kinder yet mature way.

When we were small we learnt about the world from those around us, and by the time we reached school age we had a pretty big picture built up in our head. We learnt and continued to learn the way to behave, the way to respond and interact with others and also we knew better our likes and our dislikes. Our character was already well on the way to being formed. We learnt about family life, about our neighbours. We learnt about love and interaction and we had already decided whether the world was a good, kind place that made us feel safe and happy, or whether it was not. Many impressions such as these have stayed with us throughout our life into adulthood, but form just the tip of a tree of understanding that grows within us all.

We are who we are because we learnt to be that way. We learnt from our first understanding, how best to get along with life, how we should make others notice us, how to get attention, how best to get what we want or need, what to do or say to make others laugh and like us, or how to behave when there were bad vibrations around. We saw our parents work hard and we perhaps saw them argue or fight. We learnt how to make ourselves scarce and also how to stand up for ourselves against siblings. We liked what we liked and learnt what we didn't from the experience of others as well as our own. Only we had those experiences, no one else, and they all intermingled to become the base of who we are now. They were character forming years and we rarely have cause to examine them later. These were the times that had the greatest impact on us, because we were like blank pages that needed to be written upon, or like a blank computer that does not yet know what it is. We were 'open' for input in every way, shape or form we could get it, and that is how we formed who we are today.

Only we know ourselves whether we are comfortable within and how we feel the world relates to us. Try as we might it can be hard to be accepted and acknowledged for who and what we are. We are the ones that carry the weight of our thoughts on our shoulders and we are the only ones who can lighten that load once more, not by bullying and badgering our way through life, not by being a doormat, but with a new and deeper understanding of why we think and feel the things that we do. There is so much more to whom we are than we realise, not just in the way we look, act and talk, but more the thoughts we produce in our head, all day, and everyday. We are careful, almost to being extreme about the food we put in our bodies, but do we ever consider what we feed to our mind? We are susceptible to bombardment all day, everyday, from every direction. Thoughts we think roam free all over the place and we never consider them at all. In fact we grow up believing that we can think what we want to about anyone or anything, but that is so wrong; so very wrong.

We have already spoken about energy and the fact that it plays a larger part in our existence than we understand. Energy must flow freely both through us and around us at all times. Thought itself is energy, so wherever thoughts go - energy flows, always. When we are happy and relaxed

66

we are at one with the world and at peace with our surroundings. Even troubles seem to come and go without disturbing our equilibrium quite as much, but when we are stressed or sad we send out different thoughts. These are the difference between black and white. Kind thoughts are white, while others range from shades of grey to black, depending on our attitude at the time. When we are happy, pleased and balanced we send waves of love and contentment to all that we think of. These waves emanate from our bodies in a constant flow, and are felt by all around. A calm person will automatically calm all others they come into contact with, just by being themselves. Their presence will be felt in the whole room, while the opposite will be felt by stressed out, anxious or angry individuals. When we are uptight in any way, the vibes we expel fly out in all directions. They, too, will affect all they come into contact with, like sparks to dry kindling. All these come to pass from the thoughts we think, whether we believe they are in our control or not. Our thoughts do matter very much.

Only we can control the thoughts we think because they emanate from us. We blame other people all day long for putting us into a bad mood when the truth is that we allow them to do so. We let others control our every thought – without any recognition of the fact at all. We were taught to do just that by parents who were taught by their parents, for generations. We have allowed too much of ourselves to run on automatic pilot every second of every day, and it is this that needs addressing most urgently. Automatic pilot is a good thing when used properly, because it stops our systems from overloading. It takes the pressure out of the moment somewhat, but that is all it should be. It works to help us, because it temporarily removes our conscious attention from the repetitive and mundane tasks we are doing. Often these tasks are as natural as breathing, or blinking to us, so the automatic brain action can take over,

67

but the downside is that it leaves our mind and its chaotic thoughts free to wander at will. When we have better mastered our thought patterns, automatic pilot will be a good thing, but at the moment depending on our mood, our thoughts fire all over the place at random.

Mood swings hinder our lives and our productiveness, yet it was in childhood that we learnt how to react to them, when we took our cues from the standards and behaviour patterns of our elders. Adults who let their own emotions charge freely at one another give false information and signals to their young. We are told not to fight, not to get cross, not to be nasty etc., but is that enough to help us understand and harness these emotions? Mostly it is not, so we grow up feeling bad and frustrated when they surface. Many children learn to hide their emotions and push them deep inside themselves, while others are taught to spout themselves off at their leisure. Anger in its most basic form is as natural as laughter, and as necessary. It clears the air and puts your cards on the table, just like a good thunderstorm is sometimes necessary outside to clear hot, sticky conditions. When we are not taught to handle our anger in a more productive manner it bottles up and festers. Eventually, we explode like a pressure cooker and all sorts of things come tumbling out. Anger, properly vented should address only the moment you are experiencing – nothing more. What happened last week, last month or last year is irrelevant. That time has past and nothing can alter it now. Anger is a release of irritation and nothing more. It should be no more than that. Love is the strongest emotion we have – even though it seems the opposite is apparent. It is love that drives us all, quietly and directly. When we feel a flash of anger it should be recognised as a signal that not all is not as it should be. It is an indication of unbalance within, for either ourself, or our surroundings.

Anger is very recognisable. It always starts in the same way, as a feeling of being uptight in the stomach, or chest, or neck. This will differ depending on where you personally carry your stress and it would be helpful to help our children find and recognise theirs. An unusual, uncomfortable feeling inside is a good indication of what is building up. Once we recognise it we can address its source, much earlier and much better than by waiting for that anger to control us.

An angry child can become destructive, because he has no means of addressing and venting the strong emotions he experiences. He has not learnt how to handle his feelings, so it gathers strength within him, like a trickle of water becomes a raging torrent. He might live with parents who do not recognise their own emotions, or who themselves let their anger run wild. At other times he may live in such a restrictive family that showing emotion is out of the question. Being angry in its proper form (one that corresponds to the moment only) is as healthy as a smile and often truer to the circumstances.

Energy flows in every thought we think. It is a natural occurrence, because that is the way we were made to be. Energy flows with anger, energy flows with love, energy flows with every word we speak and every look we take. It is an unavoidable state of affairs. Man does not yet realise the immensity of everything he ever does during the course of a lifetime. Every minute of every day he is responsible for the vibrations that operate within his own self and those that he sends out to others. If he could see this energy transference he would be totally amazed. He would begin to understand not only what happens to his thoughts but also where he fits into the scale of life. He would begin to see his life in a completely new way. He would be awe inspired.

The fact that he is unaware and is unable to see all this with his eyes makes the whole thing no less real or important. It is part of the movement of nature. Just as the sea ebbs and flows with the tide and the moon, man does the same in the symphony of life. He is part of all things and all things are part of him. He is a vital part in the whole of life as he knows it to be.

Each long and lonely day we spend with ourselves, hooked into the thoughts we think, we omit energy waves to all that we think about. When we ponder part events – even of just this morning, we send energy to those occasions. We keep them alive and burning. I, too, play my part in this. We all do as we reminisce and wish things were still the same. At other times we replay conversations and interactions like a movie screen, reinventing all kinds of things we could have said and done differently at the time, but what is the use? That moment has been and gone. We can never get it back. Reinventing it only brings forward the emotions we felt – to tarnish the next time we meet up. Only we can put the past to bed properly by asking for help to do so. Imagine you could wrap up the events that cause pain and bad feeling. Close your eyes for a moment and bring a time such as this to mind. Place the whole thing – subconsciously, into a blue bin liner. Because you are doing this in your head the bin liner can be as big as you need it to be. Tie it up tight and let a huge hook come down to lift it up and take it away, like on a dry cleaners garment machine. Imagine as you watch it go that it gets smaller and smaller, until it disappears into the distance and moves out of sight. It is gone, but don't check because you are inviting it back to your consciousness. Just know and trust that it has. Know that it is being recycled for you and that all its pain and the hold that it had on your life has gone with it. You now are standing – relaxed, near the hole it came from. Imagine that hole being filled with warmth and light and love. A golden light that touches you and you feel good. Open your eyes and continue on with your day. This can be done as often as you wish. Once a day or twenty times in succession, but each time you do it will work. Some things might take more working on than

70

others to recycle, but eventually you will look back and the pain and emotional turmoil will be gone. It will not hurt you any more. The truth of the event – whatever it may be, will still remain the same, but you will not bring the emotional energy content forward to the present day to hurt you and keep you locked there. You will be relaxed, detached and in a more logical frame of mind. You will be able to meet with those concerned in a balanced manner – devoid of old anger, pain or regret. You will be able to operate completely in the moment you are in, without the invisible ties and strings that normally pull.

The past is past and how we choose to look at it is our own affair. It can have no strength or hold in the now. This is where you are and this is where life operates. It is here that all things matter and all things are possible. The future is no different to the past. It will be just the same unless we make the changes that matter – in the now. How often do we wish our lives away in a trance like state as we imagine how we want the future to be? And how often are we disappointed when the future gets here? We build it up to be any number of things, but when reality comes it lets us down. We build things up too high. We send all our energy, all our hopes and all our dreams forward to the day we hope they'll come true, to the events we think should make the difference, but when they come around – we deflate. How can things ever measure up to our high expectations when most of what could have happened has fallen by the wayside through our lack of attention in the now. We let time rush past us without changing anything at all in the meantime. Only we can know the reality of this statement, the times we said if only…. If only I had done this, if only I had done that… We bounce back once more to the past from the future, from the future to the past, over and over again. Life is here. It is now. It is in the here and now and nowhere else.

71

Only we can make life work. Only we can make it count. Only we can improve upon what we already have by relearning and readjusting ourselves to fit better into the world we live in. We hold the keys to all possibilities in life, so we make the choices that take us forward, or hold us back. There are no limits, no boundaries that we can't overcome and it all starts from within us. I, too, had to learn these lessons and this book is the result of that journey. We can each work wonders in the world in which we live, or our own little section of it. We each could make the difference between light and dark to somebody, somewhere, even just by being a better person, or a better parent. We presently do this job blindly and alone, but it need not be that way. It is the most important job in the world and our children, the children we love, deserve better. Our own parents did also the best that they could do. They, too, were just people like us, with their own hopes and their own dreams. Something needs altering somewhere, so let it begin right here – in our now.

Chapter Nine

The Winds of Love

Love. The most sought after word in the universe. Everybody wants it, everyone needs it, everyone searches for it, but few truly find it. Only a few even know what it really means.

Only man can understand the immensity of this word. Wars have been fought in its name; deaths have been arranged in its honour. Love. Only we can know what it really means – but that is the twist. What does it mean? It means something different to us all. Who can explain it? Who can put it accurately into words? Ballads have tried since the dawn of time; it makes the world go round. We love this word and hate it just as quick. Only we can make it work for us, but first we need to understand what it means to ourselves.

What is love and how do we know? At no point in our lives has someone explained it to us. We just know – or we think we do, from somewhere deep inside. We grow up with an expectation of love that reaches the moon. We expect it to warm us, to uplift us, to make us happy and to complete us. We love to love at all times, at all cost, all our lives.

We grew up feeling loved – or not as the case may be. Our impression of love and what we expected it to be grew with us. We unconsciously learnt to feel it from the first time we laid in our mother's arms – or not again as the case might be. Only those who experience it fully, innocently, can know and recognise it, while the rest can search all their life, but never really find it. They look past it without even knowing. Love is delicate. It is strong. It slams itself in your face, yet it creeps quietly along. Love has no definition; it just is what it is. We love with our hearts, our soul, and our mind. We love with every breath we take and every thought we think. We live for love all of our life.

We learn about love from our parents, from our brothers and sisters, from our friends and neighbours and grandparents. We unconsciously build up its picture all through our learning years. We recognise it by the way it makes us feel, depending on what we are doing and what we are thinking at the time. Slowly we build up a comprehensive picture that will lead us through life, and it is this that shapes all we are to do and become. All people everywhere just want to be accepted for the person they are. They just want to belong. Yet it is this sense of belonging that is so hard to come by, even when we are small, within our own family unit. Already, from a very early age we start ducking and diving the attentions and affections that are put upon us. We learn how to play each other to achieve favourable results and to score points. We learn that we like to be in our parent's good graces and also in those of other peers around. We gradually learn the difference between like and dislike, happiness and sadness, love and distress. It was these early influences that formed the basis of how we love and how we see love. They also taught us what we expect to feel when we experience love – of any kind.

Only we can know what love and being loved means to us, and that explanation will differ a hundred times by a hundred different people. Love is an individual experience, but one that we all hunger after. Love is the most important thing in our lives because without it – we feel like nothing. It is what gives us a sense of self respect and self esteem. It is what keeps us going through thick or through thin. In many cases it can seem like the be all and end all of life, but this is again another problem.

Love is important to us. It can fill our every waking thought, our whole being. It can lift us up as high as a cloud and we feel just as light – or it can dash us deep down into the ground. Love is the centre of all we feel; only it can rule our lives. It can be so strong that all other aspects of life seem to fade into nothingness. Only love can do so much with very little effort.

Only love. Only, only, only … but the cost of that only, can sometimes 'be' our life! Answer just with your heart as you read the next question. What do you need in order to feel loved?

Man is the only species to be driven blindly by this force. Only he will move mountains to get it. This is behind all he has ever done, all that he will ever do and all he will ever aspire to be. Love is the key to his life and also the kingdom of heaven and hell. Only we can know what it means to us and only we can harness its power. We can help it work within us, for us, or we can let it rule our world, but whatever we choose – it will always be with us as part of the person we are.

I, too, have had my share of this emotion. I have lived every day under its control until I knew nothing else. I, too, had to harness it and help it become a kinder, gentler but stronger love. I, too, have had my heart broken and have unmeaningly broken others – all in the name of love.

Only we can help ourselves. Only we can help each other, and only we can turn this thing around until it can be what it was made to be – the life force within us all.

Early lessons

From the time we are born we are subjected to its force. It fills our whole being at a time we have nothing more in our head. It gushes from our parents and all who come to see and welcome us. We don't know what it is – but we feel it. It feels good and it makes us feel good. We are happy and secure in our new form – our new home. We are

75

born into this world that is now our home. We reach out for this love for security every time we cry and unless we physically required something else – we got it. As we grew we learnt many things, but in the end the majority of what we received was love once more, gushing forth from our parents and others that we knew. We reached school and had to learn new rules that were sometimes less than kind and when things went well we learned to receive a different love, a different feeling – but a kind of love all the same. All love comes from the same source and it hits the same response points or buttons in us. Regardless of how old we are we need this interaction from all around. It is how we measure ourselves in the world. It is how we know if we are up to scratch or if we are way off the mark. It is how we fit into the life we carve out for ourselves, and that of our family too. A family that is too way out will not fit into society at large. They will feel uncomfortable and that the world and all its people are against them. When we fit, we have friends and happy neighbours. Life feels good. (Fitting in this instance is not the same as conforming to the same standard as everyone else – it just means that you are balanced and totally at peace with your life and yourself). To fit is to be happily content with your lot, and when you are content you are automatically in the love mode. The currents of life flow happily and easily along.

As we grow older from childhood to teens to adolescence we learn to express the feelings we have. We slowly learn to manipulate them, to let them work to our advantage. We learn to read others. We learn what helps us to feel good about ourselves and also what feels uncomfortable. Feeling either comfortable or uncomfortable about the choices we make and the actions we take is an important part of growing up. Feelings such as these keep us on track with our life and become signposts and guidelines to help us both now and in later years. We learn once more how to stay in the love mode – the happy, comfortable and good

76

side of life. We inch forward bit by bit into the person we will learn to become. We grow into our character and love is the force that urges us on.

Again, this is where good parenting comes in. Within a well-adjusted and balanced family all aspects of life are equally balanced. No one person has too much power over another. They are not pushing and pulling and shoving each other on a roller coaster ride of emotions and conditions. They are generally happy and able to speak their mind and their thoughts to interact successfully together. It will not be this way at all times – but then neither is it meant to be so. We have already discussed that anger is as healthy as laughter – but in a balanced way and in correct proportion to an event. All members in this family will see and respect each other as individual beings, who have a life and mind of their own. They live together, love each other and help each other along the course of their time together. They do not own each other – nor try to over control or protect each other. They just fit and interact, as friends would do. Being a blood relative is a privilege – not a hindrance - and in a happy family this is how it is seen.

Only we can relate to experiences that were individual to us. Only we can know if they were adequate or lacking in any way and if we were happily content for the most part – or not. Only we know if those about us understood and knew us or if they did totally not, but whatever we experienced, it was what it was at the time and now it's gone. All that remains is the product left behind and this is the total sum of us. We are what we have known and have experienced up to date and that's all there is to it. If we were lucky we would have had all that we needed, when we needed it – in an emotionally secure sense rather than a material one, but if we were not then the base bricks of our life will be scattered all over the place, like foundations that were not correctly set in a house. We will be fine of course because we learnt to be, but every now and again a little blip will arise, and the most obvious ones are in love, finance and parenthood. We have learnt to live so far from life's experienced examples, and if those themselves were also incomplete, then it is likely that we will have gaps in our subconscious instruction manual of life. We, too, will make the same mistakes that our parents made – as theirs did before them. Life is like that. It takes us all along the same route – until we choose it to be different. Yet that's just it - we 'can' choose.

Only we can make the choice and only we can learn to do it. Making a change is not as simple as changing your look, your partner, and your job. These things never really help at all because fundamentally we remain the same. We are still the same person, with the same base personality and life structure. We have still been subjected to the same things until now. We cannot run away from ourselves no matter how we might like to, so the only thing left is to look inside at the workings of your inner self. With time and effort you will discover how once more you are in exactly the same situations you always are – even though you thought you had changed the rules that you played by. I, too, have been in this place and it hurt. It hurt like mad, but it did get better. I, too, had to learn the things that put me there, and what was needed to get me out, but I did it – one step at a time, just like everyone does. It will get better and so will love. All that you have experienced so far, all that has bought you to this point, in some crazy way was meant to be. It has brought you to this point, to who and where you are now because without any single thing you would not be you. You would not be here but in some other place, probably facing a new and different set of problems and setbacks. Only being here – in the 'now' can take you forward to the next step, to the place you need to be - wherever that is.

Only man can love in the way that he does. Only he has the ability to love. Only he can know the ups and the downs, the ecstasy and the pain that this emotion can fetch. It is an emotion so strong that it can devour him at the drop of a hat, yet only we can know what it means for us; but do we know how we got there? Do we know what the word love means individually for us – in all the contexts that it affects? Do we understand the part that we play ourselves – to ourselves? We automatically look to others to give us what we need, but do we ever consider what we give to the self – to ourself? We play the greatest part in our own executions and it's all in our search for love.

Only we can sort this out and it won't be easy, but putting one step in front of another is a good beginning, and it all starts here, with you.

We have already discussed that the majority of us know little about the way we derived our opinions and expectations of love. At some point in our life they became automatic, a part of us that we think little about, but expect others to know exactly. Only we can know the answer to this riddle. Only we can know the love that we crave for and then help ourselves to find it. Only we can search within to reach the answers that fill the missing gaps in our life.

Man is driven by love. It is the force that lies behind all he ever has done. It is what helps us feel at home in our family surroundings. It is what attracts and attaches us to friends – new and old. It is what directs our work to be the person we are in all that we do and say. The job we choose, we do because we love it (or should) and the places we go, we do so because we thought we would love them too. The hobbies, the clothes, the food we eat, the music we enjoy, the colours we wear, the perfume, the car we drive, the name we call our child, the people we mix with, the person we date and perhaps eventually marry – we do so all because of love. It hides behind every decision we ever make in our lives. We are love – in its purest physical form.

During adolescence we play and explore the realms in which we find ourselves. We explore at leisure all avenues of adult life. We form opinions that will help us during that adult life and these stay with us until we either outgrow the need for them or until we find cause to update their content. I, too, had to re-examine many things that I strongly believed and found cause to empty my 'mind-set' closets. We carry so much outdated clutter in our head that we feel suffocated by our own thoughts. Just as a home needs periodical attention, so do our minds, our thoughts and our beliefs. By always remaining the same we become bored, boring and stale. A clean sweep of ourself goes a long way to inner peace and harmony. Adolescence plays a large part in clearing the mind of childish thoughts and notions that would otherwise cloud our judgement in later years. It helps us grow out of childhood – gently, but distinctly, into adult thoughts and beliefs. After early toddler years adolescence is the next vital step into becoming the individual character we shall be. It is the blueprint of the adult that is emerging from innocence.

We all need to pass through this stage under the safety of a secure family umbrella. All manners of things might happen and should happen during this period, but what remains the most important aspect is the emotional security that enables this function to take place. Any child that needs to hide aspects of him or herself is not being true to the character that is forming, and this in itself is a problem in the making. We all are the same, with the same hopes, dreams and desires, so in the end it's only natural we explore the same avenues and make the same mistakes. We are the sum total of all facets of ourselves, comprising the good and the bad, so having the freedom to make mistakes while still at home in the safety of our own family unit is priceless. We learn by the things we do in much greater depths than from words that are spoken or aimed in our direction, and these lessons will stay with us for life. That is why it's so important to live life in the now, without colour or illusion from the past or future. Only in the 'now' can we find balance to live life as it is.

During adolescence there is opportunity to play out beliefs and opinions we have formed and if we are lucky most of them will serve us well. We are also extremely sensitive to the opinion of others around, not just in a negative way, but we are liable to pick up all manner of things that are both good and bad, from every direction. This is the time that we need the most help, but ironically it is the time we are most likely to spurn that guidance. We are learning to survive on our own two feet, not only in all that we do, but in our emotions, thoughts and beliefs as well. We are cutting the apron strings that until now have been our lifeline.

We go to school, we grow up and leave home, we go to work, we stand alone on our own two feet, we fall in love and so it goes on and on... But how do we know that we are right? We only know what we know because somewhere along the line we were told what we were told. We saw what we saw and did what we did, but what happens when that information was flawed? Who will ever know? How will we know? And what happens to the next steps that we take? A building is only as straight as its foundations allow it to be and if in our earlier years the influences we had were incomplete, so will the next steps be too, unless we have cause to update those parts. But again, who knows – so who can help us or even notice and tell us? No one. No one can unless we go off the track we are following. All of us are in the same boat. We can't help it because humanity has been that way for generations. Not only have we passed advice, information and knowledge to one another, but we have passed on our flaws as well. I, too, had to understand what I was doing wrong.

In all of my life I was doing the best that I could. I was being the best person and giving the best effort in every way I believed. My life led me all over the place, yet fundamentally it was all the same. Nothing ever changed or got better, and again I found myself back in the past, repeating things I rather would not. I, too, had to step back and take stock; only it was not what I thought it would be.

Only we can know the thoughts we carry and the things we do. We know what we have seen, the people we have met and the experiences and influences we have had along the way. We know the hopes and dreams we have adhered to and we know those that were dashed. We know all that we did to feel accepted, happy and loved and we know exactly where that took us and where we are now. We know all the changes we made and the times we tried, and only we can say if these have worked or not – however the case may be.

Only a few appear to be lucky. They seem to have all they need to live life to the full and everything's great in their wake, but this is not always so easy for the rest of us. We try, we work, we try some more, but then it appears with each step we achieve – we only slip back even more. Sometimes years can go past and life seems fine. We turn a corner and wham. Everything stops. Not necessarily from our own doing, but more that life and other people let us down. We try to get up, to get going once again – and so it goes on and on and on.

Work, life, friendship, love; all these change; all these grow; all these fizzle out; but why? We do the best we can with all that we know, with all that is in our being. What determines what will work and what will not? We do all that we do with the best of intentions and effort, so what makes us fall down as fast as we try to get up? The answer – you will not believe. We cause our own destruction and our own heartache without even being aware. We do it all by ourselves - because we don't know any better.

We follow the path that many have trod because it appears to work at the time. We do all we do to the best of our knowledge because again it's right at the time. All we have been and all that we are, we did to the standard we could. Without any single page of our life, each and every event, we would not be in this place, yet here is where we are – and that is where we should be, even though it may not feel very right. We need to be here to take the next step because we are at a junction in time. Only we can move through this process. We can take stock, take a rest and take some time out. Even if your world is falling down - don't do anything more until you know what to do – and you will.

Man only loves with half of his heart, the rest of the time he waits for it to come to him. He waits in vain for the love of this life to appear to him. I, too, was guilty of this. For the whole of my life I felt alone – unloved, yet I was not.

From where do we derive our opinions of love? Who told us what it should be like? And how many of us even know what it is we are looking for? How do we know what we need to have - before we feel the love that is sitting on our laps? We love because we love and we wait for others to return it in the same fashion that we have given, but life is not like that. Love is an individual thing and no two people are ever the same (or at least hardly ever). Only we can know what we do for love and only we can know what we are looking for. We hope the people we care about will hit upon the buttons in our heart, but how can they do so when they don't know what they are, and even worse, neither do we.

Definitions of love

Love is a feeling. It is within each and every one of us as part of who we are. It is that part that determines how we feel about life, about others and about ourselves. It is the look of the world about us; it is the well-being in our heart.

83

It is the peace in our mind and the way we seem to swell when we are happy. It is the way we interact with each other and why we place their needs above our own. It is every ounce of our being that reaches out to touch the world we live in. Love is the way we care, the way we hope and the way we dream. It is the way we pick ourselves up, and others around, after they've fallen down. It is the first cry we make and the last breath we take. It emanates from our very beings everyday of our lives. It is the essence of all we are and all we can strive to be. Love is our life force. It is the energy that flows through the earth and it is this that the world is short of. It is this that can save our bacon. Love is the key to the rest of our life. It is the key to our own happiness and the key to the gates of paradise, whether you believe it or not.

Love will never fade away. It can never disappear. Love waits quietly in the wings of our life, waiting for us to notice. It is always there. Only we are stuck. We think we are lonely and alone when we are not. We close the doors to our own hearts and wait for others to turn the key, but how can they when we hold that key for ourselves. The doors are locked from within – not without. We have barred our own way through the unhappiness and pain we have felt. Every time we are sad and alone we place another obstacle in our way. We put another chink in our armour and bury ourselves deeper everyday without even realising. Only we can set our hearts free, because it was us that locked them up. No one can rescue us. No one can get even close until we allow them to do so. We make the decision within our own mind and it is us that must do this for ourselves. When the doors are flung open – of course it will hurt at times – like a breath of cold air produces a sharp intake of breath, but we can learn to take it. Life is full of ups and downs, but if we don't let them in, how will we ever weather ourselves to take them? If we lock out the pain, we also lock out the love. We trap our own feelings inside and wait for the love of another to reach in and knock on the door. Only we can help ourselves. Only we can love ourselves because when we learn to do this, the rest is automatic. It will come from God – and the angels who serve him, whether you believe in them or not. A parent loves his child no less for following his own path, his own dreams and his own opinions. A parent just loves. No frills, no flounces, no conditions. He just loves, and that is how it is for us. We are just loved – everyday of our lives – by the one who made it possible. We are love – so how can we ever be without it? Love is within – so let it out and it will attach itself to the love that is there, waiting for you.

First we must love ourselves because without that we can never love each other. Self-love is the most misunderstood form of love that exists in man. It is responsible for much of the heartache we experience, both by our own hand and by those of others. We are able to give of ourselves to everyone and every event that asks it of us, but to be kind to our own self seems almost impossible. How can we love ourselves when we alone know all the things we have been up to and are responsible for? How can we love ourselves when the largest part of who we are is buried deep where even we don't care to look? As soon as someone comes close we clam shut even tighter – just in case they might glimpse some scary sight. We learn to disown parts of ourselves from a very early age and because we have done it, so very well for so long, we don't even know we are doing it. We are the worst enemies to ourselves – much more in fact than we would ever allow others to be to us. We do all that we do as automatically as breathing.

Only we can lighten up on ourselves, but before we can we must learn how to do so. We must first recognise we have the problem before we can fix it. Life is full of love if we could only open up enough to receive it, and it must all begin again within each of us.

85

Only we can mend our broken spirit – and that is exactly what the problem is. We have allowed the whole of the world to trample us down until we lie battered, bruised and bleeding – emotionally. No one person is more responsible than another, no one person has done these things deliberately. It has just happened along the course of our life, slowly and surely, and the worse thing is that we helped them to do so, because somewhere deep inside we accepted it. We thought we deserved it. We know we will be hurt because we expect it from life. I, too, have lived this saga and in many ways still do; only now I am more aware of the process when it occurs. I can make the choice to let it be that way – or not. Life will not stop being the way it has always been, because that is the nature of life, but now I can choose how I will react to it. I can choose.

Only we can feel the emotions that are ours. We carry them all through our lives. Only we can fix those emotions with time and extra effort, but first we must recognise them and someone needs to show us how. Only we can love ourselves enough to make that difference in the thoughts that we have, the words that we speak and the things that we do and say. You decide what you are feeling at any one moment whether it be love and truth – or continued illusion, because without that choice all things remain as they always have been, and therefore just the same as they are. We can change the rules we live by – but not with force and battle, just love.

Man can change his mind. He alone makes the rules and regulations he moves within. He alone can make his life work, but before he is able he must understand the part he plays in his own turmoil. Life will support and help us if we let it, not in the lazy "I'll let life take care of me fashion", but with strength and courage and a clear head. If we stay out of illusion and deep in the truth we shall see much clearer the direction best to follow. Markers and signposts are all over the place, but first we must learn to read them. We must learn to see what we do see differently than we do right now.

The whole of life is like a symphony in motion. Each choice or decision leads up to the next. Cause and effect have more power over us than many care to know. We blame any number of things on the predicaments we are in, but very rarely look truthfully at our own input, and then when we do, we do it with anger and regret, very rarely with gentleness or love. It is the way we have learned to be. We have learnt very well indeed.

Chapter Ten

The Winds that Mend

Only man can mend his own heart. Time will help as well, but man must do the work. All through life he gets battered and bruised until at some stage he can barely take more. From a very early age we learn to blame ourselves for the misfortunes that befall us, and when this becomes too painful we make the switch to blaming others. We blame anyone for anything, from our being angry or cross to our worst nightmares in action. We blame all and sundry for the predicaments we are in, but most of all we blame them for the fact that we don't feel loved – or at least not in the way that we think we should.

Man has lost the key to his heart. He sits and waits for that feeling that's lost and when he can't find it he searches once more, but not in the direction that will serve him best. He searches outwardly, far and wide, for the emotions he seeks, when all the while it sits quietly within himself and has always done so since the beginning of time.

Man has lost his sense of wholeness and contentment. He is for the most part unsettled in his life. He constantly searches for the answers and the fulfilment that he feels he needs for his own self worth. This is not a problem - it is good. It means that he keeps on going forward in his restlessness. All through his life he has been used to others leading him on to the next faculty, the next chapter. The majority of men follow others who seem to know what they are doing. It is easy to look at someone else and see them as they are now. It is easy to mimic their lifestyle, their possessions and their manner, but are they really any happier than we are? We see the person today but do we consider the things they have been through to get them here in the first place? And do we know where it is they think they are going? Very few are happily content with their life; very few indeed. Only some are lucky enough to be happy and in love with their lot, yet this state is available to all, it is here for the taking. Everything we need is all about us, so what is the problem? Each new day is a brand new page; a brand new chance for another stab at life. Let's learn to use it to our advantage – not with force, but with a commitment to love, to self-love; to get on with the life we are capable of living.

When we were small we followed our parents. We followed their example and lived by the rules that they set. This was good, because it gave us a basic structure, a base grid to follow. As years went by we allowed others to add to that grid in the form of influence, experience and teaching. We have already discussed that we know what we know, because we have been taught or told, or have seen it somewhere in our life, and many of our opinions were formed by our own childish mind along the way, but what happens when those things are incomplete or rocky? Who can tell us? Who will really know? No one. We trundle along everyday thinking the thoughts that we think, just like others did before. We have also said that we are very careful what we feed to our bodies, but do we do the same to our minds? We allow anything and everything to pass through it – unfiltered, unprotected and uncensored. That is the nature of life, but we can only digest what we allow ourselves to digest and most of that depends on the opinions and boundaries we set up in early childhood. How can we determine at such an early age what is good and right for us? We rely heavily on our piers, but they, too, are in the same boat as us. They, too, have simply trundled along the path of life in the same fashion as we have until now. They, too, are looking to fit comfortably with life and be happy. They, too, are searching for their own life's completion. We are all following a blind path that seems to lead us nowhere. So who can help us? Who can tell us where to go and what we've been doing wrong?

Children today see the life that their parents have had. They witness first hand their dreams, trials and tribulations. They see their kind hearts and their good intentions. They live with their anger and emotional turmoil. They see the lovelessness that exists almost everywhere. They see the mistakes and the heartache that is all around. At different times they learn about the world, about love, about friendship, about sunshine and music and art. They are told that the world is their oyster and that love is all around – everywhere, but the majority live through the opposite – each and everyday.

I am. I can. I will. These words have been given to us from spirit. They mean simply that we are what we are, that we can change whatever and whenever we choose and that we will. They are simple words that can alter the way you see your life and also the place you are heading. Only we can know where we want to be in life and only we can instigate the steps that will take us there. All of our lives we try to be the best person we can be. We do all that we can for anyone yet still we feel unloved, misunderstood and alone. We change our jobs, our style, our partner, our outlook, each time in hope that that will do the trick, that that might be the missing link we are searching for. But all too often once again we find ourselves back almost exactly where we started. Years go past in this way and we are the only ones who can choose to not let this happen – ever again. We must make the changes from within our own selves – not without. We can change all we wish without – over and over again, but if we don't change ourselves – even just a bit, we shall always end up in exactly the same place. The missing denominator is within. It's not in anybody else anywhere.

A good example is love. How do we decide what love is? Do we ever stop to consider what it is that we think we are looking for – or what we need to feel that we are loved? Hardly ever! We just go right on looking for that something that will make us feel complete – but even in that statement is a problem itself. We wait for others to make us complete when we should be complete already. We should not look to another for this reason – yet we do. We use each other's strengths all the time then wonder why the load we carry gets heavy and burdensome. Only we can be complete within ourselves. We should be able to support ourself in life in every possible way. That is our responsibility to the life we are living. Then and only then, can we find an equal partner to share our life with. We choose to be together because we want to be – not because we have to be. Two people that come together to use each other's strengths might fit closely for a while because they compliment each other and for the most part they will feel better and happier than they have ever felt in their lives, but then the problems set in. These two people have become one – but they still have two heads, two sets of opinions, two sets of needs and wants and desires, so which head will be the controlling head? Who will be the winner and who will be the looser? It is an impossible situation right from the start. We like each other for our differences as well as our similarities, but once we are in a relationship together – we try to mould and change the other to our way of thinking. We suddenly feel that we own each other. Why should that be when it's precisely this that is the cause of the problem?

When we are incomplete before we meet, two incomplete people cannot make a compatible, balanced relationship. We will always be individual people with our own hopes, dreams and desires. We all want to find love, to feel needed and to be happy, but this seems so hard to find. When we meet someone we feel compatible with we fill the missing gaps in each other's life. A shy person will be attracted to an outgoing one, because they can be themselves and enjoy the opposite in the other. An outgoing person can always be so when the shy one is around because he can be outgoing enough for the both of them – while the opposite is said for the shy one. He/she is used to being quiet and so the outgoing partner will provide all the stimulation and enjoyment that is needed in the relationship. That is often the 'fun' side of the partnership. At first this can work well, but eventually the outgoing person will burn out as they feel it is always them that provides the entertainment and stimulation, while their partner will feel unnoticed and misunderstood because he/she is used to just following and unused to taking the leading role. This is a simple example of how what feels good at first will later become a burden. I, too, have experienced this, and I, too, had to grow and change myself. We experience both the same and the opposite to ourselves in this life. Ordinarily all will be well, but if we get stuck then we think the only answer is to break up the relationship. We are more used to breaking up and walking away than we are to staying put and fixing the problem. I, too, should know because that is how it was for me too! Life is the same for us all – only we don't often realise. We look at others and how happy they appear and wish the same for ourselves. We try all we can and when it doesn't work we wonder why.

When we are small we build up a picture of life, of our future, of the way we think these things should be and of love itself. We build up a fairy tale in our own way – and no one can tell us otherwise. But how could they when they can't see the workings inside that is mind? They themselves have done just the same at one particular time or another, so they too are looking for that fairytale ending. We wait for others to rescue us, to save us from the world and from ourselves, but they in turn need and wait for the same. They, too, are waiting for the pieces in the puzzle of their life to fit. Who can rescue whom – and how do we know? The answer is that we don't. We blindly try all the combinations we can, but how often do they hit gold and for how long before all feels the strain? This is the state of most of the world right now. It is a universal problem that is almost out of control.

Only we can make the pieces fit within our lives and we are the only ones who can straighten its balance. We become our impressions of love through our thoughts as children. We interpreted the world that we found ourselves in and put together a picture. This, combined with all that happened to us along the course of time (whether we were young or old at the time) is how we derived the finished article. The way we perceive love is completely individual and frankly it often bears little resemblance to reality at all. It can be so tall and out of date that is it hardly any wonder that those who come into our lives can't reach it. We look to others to fit a specific role or model that in reality does not exist and even when we are lucky enough to find it, or the one who can put us together, we forget that they are human too. They are susceptible to the same doubts and flaws that we have. Of course when we first get together it is wonderful. It is supposed to be. We are in love. Whether it is for the first, or last, or for the hundredth time, love is still love. It is still wonderful as it resonates with your soul. For a while the love we feel is all consuming. We can't think, can't eat, and can't function. We live to be together each time we are apart and so it goes on and on and on, but then reality sets in, regardless; it has to. Life goes on. We are still in love, but the feeling drops to a more realistic level. It does not matter how soon or how long after we met this occurs, the point is that it does. We come back down to a quieter – more usual kind of love; the same love that was always there throughout our life. The same love that has always sustained us, only we don't recognise it any more. Because of the ecstasy of the high we've been on the difference is too great to realise. Love is

93

quiet. Love is strong. It is sure and it is always there. Always, and especially when we are in 'the love mode' anyway.

Only we can make the adjustments necessary to recognise the love that exists all around. We are used to looking, finding and drawing it from one another, but in reality it is here all the time, everyday. It is just much gentler than we expect it to be. The complete devouring, raging love we feel is like a torrent that engulfs us. It is the most wonderful feeling there could ever be, but it is just that; a feeling, and because it is a feeling, it is liable to distortion and misinterpretation from us. We have searched our whole life for this moment, this time, this person, and we have found it (or them). We feel - perhaps for the first time ever - totally at one with the world, totally complete, in every way. The quieter love from our family and friends dulls into the background as we enjoy the experience, the ride, the high. We have arrived at where we have always wanted to be; and it's wonderful.

We are the only ones who can know how true these words are for us. Only we can know the times we have lived through them and know the outcome of those periods of ecstasy and that all consuming love.

Only we can know what love means to us. Only we can know love as it is right now and only we can feel what it feels like for us. We are not at the mercy of it; we are not at the mercy of life. We are our own masters and we choose to love. We choose to feel what we do. The coming together of two people who care for, or are attracted to each other, is a gift in its own right. The feeling of euphoria cannot last indefinitely. It may come and go very frequently, but it will come and it will go; that is that point. It will find a natural balanced level all of its own, because that is the nature of life.

Many of us today are broken hearted, dismayed and confused. We find it hard to understand why once more the

94

love we thought would last – has fizzled out. Life gets in the way and we take each other for granted. We work hard, we play hard and we try to do our best, but often it seems that our best is never good enough; but here lies another key. Once more we do all that we can because we want to. We try to make all the pieces fit tightly – because we want to, but at some stage our wanting to do these things becomes a chore. The whole thing changes and becomes a burden that we carry, and by that time it has become hard work. We can sustain the pace for a while, but unless we feel that our efforts are appreciated, we breakdown. We change from complimenting each other, to relying on each other, to needing each other to fix us and this happens in such a subtle way that no one even realises. I, too, had to learn this, but not before I had hurt myself, and others in the process; and it is all in the name of love.

Love is good. It is kind and gentle, but it is also the thorn that pushes deep in our hearts when we don't do it properly. It is the birth of a baby, but it is the cause of a war. Love is as controversial as the day is long, and we live our own example – each and everyday.

Our lives are full. We work hard to live to the style we are accustomed. We get up and the day is busy, but when we are hurt in any way by love, the world in which we function falls to pieces. In reality it does not really, but we just think that it does. Love plays not so great a part in our daily activities yet it means the most. When our hearts feel broken, we fall by the wayside and fall apart. All other aspects of life dim by comparison and we almost waste away in sadness. What we do then is personal to us, but you can be sure that it hurts all the same. We march over events time and time again in our minds without ever knowing why. We feel we are bleeding to death - and in a sense we are. We are bleeding emotionally. Remember earlier we spoke of two people that joined together too strongly to complete each other's lives – well that is the reason. When those people pull apart neither one is complete any more. It is like having yourself ripped open. Jagged edges and broken bits lie everywhere. Only we can relate to how we feel, because to others we look the same. They expect us to function just as we did before, because in reality life still goes on the same, but we are not the same. We are broken and we are bleeding inside. We scream out in pain – but it is a pain that only we can know. It is individual to our life and our being.

The only way to ever stop this happening again is to become a complete and whole individual in our own right. It is lovely to rely on someone – to allow them to perform the tasks we don't like, but when we lean too heavily on that person, it becomes their burden. Only we can take love and turn it into pain. It does not happen by itself. I, too, should know, because I, too, have done this. I have been responsible for my own pain and that of others without even knowing it at the time. I, too, looked everywhere to find the love I needed, when in reality it was always with me all the time. I just did not notice. All over the world we do the same thing. We all look to others to fulfil the expectations of our heart, but we fail to recognise that those we find are also searching. They, too, look to us to complete them. They, too, need love to fill a void in their being.

Only we can put things right, but it will happen one small step at a time. The person you are with is still the same person they were when you met them. The only thing that's altered is time. Life has got in between and daily problems are blocking the way. They, too, will be hurting if you are. They, too, will be wondering what has happened and what has changed. Nearly every thought that you think it is likely they thought of too, and if they have not then that proves it is with you. All unrest we ever feel must first begin in us; in our own hearts, in our own mind. Even when we think it does not, it can be retraced to a change of opinion, or change of mind, somewhere along the way and the trick will now be to find it; and we shall.

Only we can know when we begin to feel unrest. It stems from someplace inside that gets bolder and bigger as time passes by. We cannot put our finger on the problem and we automatically assume it is the other person's fault. These feelings are compounded when we subconsciously need our partner to prove their love to us in all that they do. We are insecure and we place the fault at their door when it is very probably ours. This feeling stems from our own head, yet we imagine signs in the things they don't do that prove it. When we look for reasons we can make any number of things fit the bill whenever we want, but only a truth that is directed at ourselves will reveal the problems as they really are. Only love will wait quietly by until we sort ourselves out. That is the nature of its strength.

Only we can look within to find the cause of the pain. Only we can see the thoughts we think and the opinions we have. Did we have a true picture of this person from the start – or did we see only what we wanted to see? Did they hide bits of themselves that they did not like – and did you? Did you change or exaggerate a little of your own character to impress your partner – or vice versa? Did you see something other than what was there, or did they do the same? Often when we put each other on a pedestal our expectations are too high, or too unreal, and things such as these are hard to live up to. I, too, have been guilty of this. Most of my life I waited for my knight in shinning armour to rescue me and love me forever, but of course this just cannot be. A bill such as this is too hard to maintain. It is too much pressure to expect anyone to carry, especially if they are expecting and seeing the same thing in you, your self. If you both rescue each other and both aim to be what the other needs and wants (even subconsciously), filling in the missing pieces of life is a tall order. It will lead to trouble, disillusion and heartache. At the end of the day we

97

are all the same, with the same hopes, dreams, doubts and needs. We are all in the same boat, in the same water. We are people who need to be loved, trusted and respected, but when we *need* to feel *needed* the problems arise, and eventually the balance will topple from pleasure in fulfilling that role – to anger at the burden it causes, especially if it does not feel appreciated any more as it used to. Appreciation is the reward we expect to receive. We will move mountains and run to the ends of the earth for anyone, just as long as we feel that they realise and they appreciate the effort. It is how we feel important in their life, but when our efforts become expected as the norm, the rot sets in and we only have our own selves to blame. How do our partners know how we feel when we did what we do because we wanted to once upon a time? It is us that have changed the rules – not them, so it is up to us to set the balance straight, not all at once in anger, but gently, by giving them time to adjust. We need to redraw our boundaries again – that's all.

At the beginning of a relationship we are in a more flexible frame of mind. We enjoy taking the strain off our new partner – even if it means that we are over stretching ourselves. We are keen to over accommodate each other's needs, because it is a way of proving our love. We show each other that nothing is too much trouble. We cancel and rearrange appointments and commitments to suit our needs and this love is all that we live for. We have found the love that others speak of. We have found our ticket to heaven. For a time – even years, everything in the garden is rosy. Life has a purpose – a feel good factor all of its own, only it cannot sustain this level forever; just for a while. Once this occurs we come down (either quickly or slowly over a number of years again). Sometimes this happens so gradually that neither partner notices, they just grumble a little more often at each other and anyone else that might be around. Life is returning to normal and their relationship is feeling the strain. It can be over silly things, there could be huge issues, but whatever the symptom – the cause needs addressing, not ignoring. All problems grow a little at a time. When niggles are dealt with honestly and kindly – then nothing more will really happen; life will be fine. But when we bury our heads in the sand and go deeper into turmoil inside, than those simple niggly things, they will start to fester and grow. They become distorted and attract more problems. When we first meet we have found our fairytale. We have found the person who could fill our dreams and fill the gaps in our life. Often we see an illusion, because the love we are looking to find is an illusion. The feelings we have are real enough – but the things we think we see in a person – we see mainly because we want to. We don't always see the reality as it really is, and by changing each other's life patterns to fit – we move even more into that illusion. There is no problem with this, because it is all a part of love, but the problems arise when we rely too deeply on our partners to fill a gap in our own lives.

Only we can be truthful to ourselves, because the face we portray to the world, is what the world will believe. There is no point in pretending we are something we are not, because eventually the strain will be felt by all parties concerned. Be yourself, be truthful about the things you feel at the time you feel them. The beginning of a relationship – when the chemicals run high, can take the truth much better than at any other time. Only we know who we are and we know what we see in this other person. Don't imagine you can change this or that about them, love them for all of themselves as they should love you too. When you find you must hide this and that because your partner may not like it, already you are on the road of illusion and sooner or later, the bubble will burst.

It is exactly for these reasons that we should be whole and complete individuals within our own right before we meet a new partner. Like attracts like, but so do opposites. It is an invisible process that begins on an energy level, often before we even speak. Like two magnets that have no hope but drawing together because they are propelled to do so. Only we can stop the pain in our future by knowing ourselves better first, and this comes from within – not without. The way we look is barely important. It is the energy that's inside that calls the shots and it's this that we cannot control – once the magnetic pull is in action. We owe it to ourselves to put matters right – and we have already begun by acknowledging a few things in this book. Love is what makes the world go round – it is also the essence of man, but to do its stuff it needs our help – in more ways than we could ever know.

Only we can know ourselves. Only we can know what we expect from love and only we can know when we find it – and if we do. Love is an individual thing that means something different to each and every one of us. Only we can recognise it for ourselves, but we forget that we don't travel a one-way street. Our partner is looking to fulfil his version of love as well. He/she too has his/her needs and visions to fulfil. Love is a two-way thing that should compliment the life we are already living. It is not the be all and end all of who we are, but a part of who we are. It is just a slice, an expression of our personality and character. It is not the whole of the world, but rather a taste of it. Love propels us forward. It should never hold us back. Love is just what it is – in all that it is.

Only we can find the correct balance of love and life to live within, and it is a balance. Too much can separate us from the world about us – just as too little can harden us unnecessarily. Life is a mixture of love and survival and it is up to us to find our level.

Chapter Eleven

The Winds that Control

Influences and the effects they have

Only we can live our life, but many influences control the things that we do – from the time we are born. First, our parents and their parents, our society and culture and any religious beliefs that are apparent. Next we move to school and piers and then the influences of the greater world. We move to college and work and social events, and through all this exists music, television, newspapers, magazines, books and films. We are bombarded from the start and life never lets up. We are pressured in every direction to comply with life, yet we must also retain our independence and sense of fun. Life is hard for us all and it is different for us all. Even members of the same family will give a completely different account of their view of what life means to them. That is how it is supposed to be and the way it has always been, yet every now and again we throw a wobbly. We stamp our feet and glare at the world. We wonder why things turn out as they do and why we appear to have so little control over the life we are supposed to own. We are responsible for it – or so we are taught. We alone should call the shots yet often our hands seem tied at precisely the times we ought to be free. Only we can change this, but before we do we must understand precisely what makes us tick and what influences the decisions we make.

Only we should call the shots, but we need a realistic view of life to be able to do so correctly. Only we can say what we feel comfortable with at any time, but again that might even be a trap. From the time we are small we are led by the hand to do all that's required of us. We learn what is and is not acceptable by the response of the elders around. We learn to make judgements and to explore – again within the boundaries that are set, but when those boundaries are absent or too severe, it can hamper the love and experiences we shall find. When we feel secure and safe we are free to explore as we wish – as we should, but when we are too bold, or too timid, we over stretch, or hinder our lessons accordingly, together with our experiments. Only we can know in later life if our childhood was all that it should have been and this will depend on the support and opportunities we have had.

Only man has the ability to change his life around. All other species remain exactly as they were created. Yes they evolve over time, but basically they remain as they were. Man has the ability to change everything about his character, his look and his personality. He can be whatever he desires to be, he can do all that he wants and he can believe and think whatever takes his fancy. I, too, have become a new person since I began to delve deeper into the depth of myself. I am all that I was before plus a whole lot more besides. I have grown into the person I was destined to be by filling in the blanks that were really part of me all along. We all have this same ability. We are much more than we could ever imagine ourselves to be and we are capable of anything. Life is what you make it. Even in our saddest times we are not bound and gagged by circumstance, we are free to choose differently, to pull ourselves up and out of the holes that have been placed beneath our feet. We believe that others are in charge of our destiny, but only because over time we have allowed ourselves to believe it. We are master of our own life. Yes we might have commitments and obligations, but even those we chose at one point or another. If the load you carry is too heavy put it down for a while. Imagine a large brown sack full of boulders on your back. Swing it to the ground and sit down. Send your thoughts upward and outward to God. Whether you believe or not the result will be the same. Ask for help. Ask that your load may be lightened and your spirit uplifted. Ask that you might be shown a new way forward. Stand by all that you are committed to do, but begin to redraw your boundaries and obligations. If you make yourself too available to others and their problems are becoming your own – learn to say no sometimes. This is not an act of selfishness – but of love. You are a person too. By taking charge of others too, often you actually can do more harm than good. You rob them of the chance to stand firmly on their own two feet. Perhaps they are missing something that they too need to experience to lead them forward to their next step. Sometimes the pain we come through and the trauma is a necessary process of growth. I, too, have experienced this first hand. I, too, have had to change all that I held dear – because it was in my destiny to do so. We can say a million 'if onlys', but they are only illusion. The truth is where you are right now and wherever that might be – you will pull through. You will be all right, but for goodness sake ask for help. You only get what you ask for and if you don't ask you won't get. Talking to God, talking to your own guides and angels is like using a help-line. If you don't pick up the receiver you will never get through. The problems that we fret and worry about will stay with us because it is assumed we want to keep them, to struggle through them under our own steam, but this is far from what we really want. We want and we need help and that help is there for the asking. Don't feel shy. It is between you and your maker. The thoughts you think and the pleas you make are for you to pass over. Remember how silly you felt when you first spoke into a telephone answering machine, well now it's automatic. You can do it without even thinking of what you are doing and the same will happen when you send up your thoughts. At first you might stumble and stutter but soon it will be second nature.

You can do this process once a day or one hundred times a day, the choice is yours. Ask and you will be given, but you must ask in order to be given.

There is much more to life than meets the eye. We amble along on a sure course of action unaware of the forces that work with us or alongside us. I, too, have had to rediscover the art of paying attention to life. I, too, have had to adjust to not always being in the driving seat of control. I also felt the need to harbour fear and self-pity, but once again I learnt to let go, to view my life and the world about me through different eyes. Nine times out of ten the situations we are in are down to our own doing, because we have allowed things to slip. We become complacent and happy to let life trundle along when often we should pay better attention to the little things that pop up everyday. I, too, was guilty of this because most of my attention was focused too far into the future, or way back in the past. I, too, let the 'now' run automatically of its own accord because I did not realise what I was doing. Life goes past in seconds, minutes and hours, but my own days just appeared to fly – without my being able to stop them. Now things are different. A day is as short or as long as I want it to be and all I had to do was ask that it be that way. When time flies past quicker than you can handle – ask that it be slowed down for you, to enable you to use it as well as you would like. If time drags along too slowly, ask for your perception of it to be sped up, but remember to put it back to normal later or you will be at the other end of the problem scale by chasing your tail once more.

Only you can know what you need to do and when you need to do it. Only you carry the burden of the thoughts that you think. Only you carry the guilt and the fear of the things not yet done, so it stands to reason that only you can help yourself by letting these things go. Recycle them whenever you feel them in your chest or stomach, your neck or your head. The place you carry stress is individual to you – but the cure is the same. Recycle these feelings time and time again and concentrate on the job in hand. Only you will feel the benefit of such an exercise, but others will notice your stress free zone. I, too, had to learn this for myself and it wasn't always easy or automatic. The more you catch yourself thinking or doing things you should not, the more you will slowly let them go. It takes practise to stay focused on one thing at a time, but it is a job worth pursuing. Energy flows wherever thought goes – because thought is energy in motion. It becomes obvious that if your thoughts are all over the place all the time and not on the task you are doing, it will take twice as long and you will be drained in the process. How often do we feel totally washed out halfway though the day without ever knowing why? Again it is probably down to wasted energy in the form of stress and worry. These two things are like water down a plughole. Your energy will ebb away completely unless you learn to stop it happening. We can control these things, but again we must ask for help. Ask that your energy be replaced and that all unnecessary drains be severed. Ask for help to remain focused in the now until your task is complete. Ask that life will help you to help yourself and ask for peace of mind, for quiet thoughts and a peace filled day. When life about you seems to be crazy, ask that the hype be recycled and its energy put to better use. Ask for whatever you need – at the moment you need it, then forget about it and carry on as normal. By the time you have finished – look back and notice the difference, and nine times out of ten it will be clearly visible. You yourself will even feel calmer and more in control without having done anything really at all. You have only asked for help and allowed it to channel through, to the place and the time that it was needed.

We are all part of the bigger picture of life. Like pieces of jigsaw puzzle or threads in an ornamental rug, we each have a place and a function. It stands to reason that if we are all part of the whole then we each have a part to play, and if we each have a part to play then we need help to do it well. This life is not supposed to be struggle and stress, but love and enjoyment and fun. We are supposed to love the life we are living, not dread it. We are not supposed to have burdens and cares and woes, but dreams and fulfilment and happiness. Problems and chores are supposed to help us grow and change, not buckle, fall and fade away. Life is a gift, a gift that we chose to receive long before we came to live it. We each have a purpose and a destiny and until we realise this we will only enjoy a part of what we can be and came to do.

Only we can make our life work. Only we can make the necessary adjustments within ourselves. Time is irrelevant, it can be now or next month, but the point is that it will happen. We can make the necessary decisions now, or we can wait for life and the universe to do it for us, and if we do that we can be sure it will be drastic and painful. These things happen to us for our own good − even though we don't see it that way at the time. There is always an element of choice present during these times, but the messages you get will be loud and clear. Only we can know what they are − even if we don't yet know why. The universe always works in our best interest. The world is changing, sometimes slowly − sometimes drastically, but the changes are there none the less. It cannot wait for any individual, so we must keep up with it if we are not to be left behind. Only we can enjoy the life we have, so let's get on with it.

The place we are now

Only we know the experiences we have had and the opportunities we have taken up or passed over. The place you are now is exactly the place you should be at this moment in time. It does not matter where you 'could' have been and what you 'could' have done − the truth is that you 'are' where you are because along the way you made the choices that got you there, and those would have been right for you at the time, or you would not have made them. In any decision there are always two pathways with at least two options to choose between. Sometimes we go for the easy route, the easy option, or the quick fix. If that works then all well and good, but if it does not, we are forced to retrace our steps and choose again. The end result is often the same, but it takes longer to get there, so the path you tread is surer, more secure and definite. Sometimes we are led on a detour, but that is only because there is something else we should do or pay attention to along the way. Life is like that. The universe will take care of us if we can learn to let it, but often we are too impatient. We barge through life this way and that to get what it is we think we want, but when we get there it is not what we thought at all, so we change quickly to the next thing on our list. If we slowed down just a tad, we would obtain a much clearer picture of where we are heading. We would also allow the universe to play its part. How often does something land on our doormat at exactly the time we need it? Or are you one of those who gets that information after the event? How often do we think 'if only we had received this last week', or 'if only I knew that then'? Life will support us if we open ourselves up to its influence, but the trouble is that usually we can't wait. We are impulsive and impatient and we want what we want when we want it. To a certain extent that is human nature, but it is also a part of us that does not always work in our favour. This is exactly a thing that we can 'choose' to change about ourselves, and if we did we would notice the difference – in life and probably in our purses as well.

Only man has the chance everyday to do something different, or to get a job finished and out of the way. How many of us are self disciplined enough to do what needs to be done at exactly the moment it needs doing? If you are this way inclined then you are lucky. You have nothing around you to slow or weigh you down, but I, like many others have always a thousand things to catch up on. I am always chasing my tail. It seems that no matter how hard I work there is always more to do and more I didn't do. We need to learn to prioritise. Only we can judge what is most important on any one day. Life will always produce more than we can cope with easily, but that is the nature of life. There is a fine balance between too much and too little, but life goes on just the same for everyone.

Only man can make the necessary alterations to get his life back on track in a way that will work better for him. He alone knows his obligations and his challenges. He alone knows his commitments and the time he wastes in vain chasing illusions. No one demands anything extraordinary from him; he does this all by himself. He alone sets his pace and the distance he feels he must travel. Only he can set himself free of the chains that bind him, even though he might not agree at this moment. Only life that's rippled with pleasure and love will make him content and happy in his daily grind. Love combined with understanding and knowledge will lead him back to where he wants to be. Our whole life is lived in effort to strive forward, to better ourselves and to fit snugly into the niche that fits; yet often when we get there we only find disillusion and more hard work. Man has built his life to fit his image of contentment and tranquillity instead of looking deeper inside to reconnect the missing pieces of his self. Life is what we make it, not what we force it to be. When we feel at our lowest there is always a ray of hope to grab onto – to pick us up. We are never alone, but merely accustomed to the belief that we are. Man has every tool he could ever need within his grasp. He has everything his ancestors strived with their lives to achieve. Nothing is out of reach, yet he still feels lost and alone as he strives for more, but why? Why should that be? Why do we think we are lost and alone? Why do we want to be like others instead of ourselves? We are all basically good and caring people. We have the same hopes and desires, the same aspirations. We all want basic peace and contentment with the lot we have chosen, so why is this so hard to obtain? Only we can know the answer to this and it will come from somewhere buried deep down inside. We are who we are – not who we think we are and that is the difference. Many people rarely look at themselves from the eyes and viewpoint of another. They look at themselves through condescending and little eyes of anger. They judge themselves by what they have not done instead of all they have. They are much more tolerant of others than they would ever be to themselves and then they wonder why no one seems to notice them for the person they are. They see themselves in an entirely different light. Love must come in to soften that light now, or many of us will go pop with the effort it takes to sustain the role we are playing. Only we can help ourselves, but not with force or the downing of tools – only with a little more self-understanding and love. People can never know the effort it takes us to do the things we do, because they are not looking. They, too, are in the same boat. They, too, are pulling, pushing and stretching with all their might, in all directions, to make their life work and amount to something, but the measures we use are often way off the mark. We live by an illusion of what we think we should be, because we have learnt to be like this through the course that our life has led us. Often we live by standards that are completely irrelevant to the reality of life and the place that we want to be. I, too, can relate to this first hand and I, too, came down with a bump on more than one occasion. In hindsight I can see clearer the reasons behind the events, but at the time it is rarely easy and often frightening. It is scary to loose all that you hold dear and all that you have worked hard to achieve, but often what we cling to most is purely of cosmetic value.

109

We undersell ourselves without even knowing. We bind ourselves with things that we have been taught matter very much, when the truth of the matter is different. These things only matter because we have been told they should, because we witness their importance to others, so we tread the same path and try to achieve the same things. We measure ourselves against the opinions of others and belittle ourselves with our own. How can we expect to feel happy, safe and secure when our biggest trouble is ourselves? We love the world and blank ourselves while we wait for someone to notice the love that's pouring out. We wait for someone somewhere to appreciate the effort we put into our activities, thoughts and words every single day and we wait for someone to love us in the same way that we love them, but they never can. They are different as much as they are the same. They love in a different way and think in a different light. They see life in another way to you. Life and love are different for us all even though we think they are the same. Only we can know when we get to where we are going and only we can draw the line, both with ourselves and with others. Only we can appreciate the life we are given and the distance we have travelled in the process. Only we can be the judge and jury to our own efforts and we must learn to decide when enough is enough, not in a bad way, but in a realistic and truthful way. We are stuck in a mode of behaviour that once upon a time served us well. We are almost overloading ourselves, and the planet, with the effort it takes to sustain the life we are living. Extreme is the word of the moment and we push all existing boundaries to meet with it. Is this the way we want to move forward? Is this the legacy we want to leave to our children? Is this what our ancestors fought through the ages to give us? We think not! Basic human rights are the same for us all and should be available for all to achieve, but after that comes personal choice and do we consider the cost to ourselves, to others, the effort, to our purses, or to the resources of the planet itself? The time is here for us to take stock, to make our adjustments and to move forward in a different manner, before all that we know today comes tumbling down once more. We have a choice and all we need do is choose it. The rest will follow in its wake – courtesy of our God and Creator.

Chapter Twelve

The Winds that Sow

Only we can be who we aspire to be. There is no one like us in the whole of the world. We are unique, because of the person we are, our individual character and the experiences we have obtained. Whenever two people appear alike – they are not. Distinct differences set them apart and you don't have to look too deep to notice them. The part that you play and the place you fill is unique, especially for you, and without your being here the world that you know would be different. Only you can fill that void. Only you can fit within the life space that you occupy so you must learn to do it well. Nothing left undone will ever be complete, so the role that is yours is more important than you know. The human body is itself a great example. Thousands of veins, capillaries and arteries course their way through your form yet if only one was not connected as it should be we would bleed to death, or suffer some other form of illness. Life is little different, because we are each a separate part of the whole, when we breakdown or can't fulfil the life we have charge of, we leave a space, a void that no one else can replace. Only we can fill that place – no matter how we opt to do it. Only we can be the person we are and that is our purpose, our role, our function. We are vital components of the planet we live upon. Many might say that this is rubbish. "How can we – so small, so insignificant in the scale of this earth - possibly be that important?" But we are. Because we are conductors of the planets life force each outlet, each person is extremely unique and complex. Only we can conduct the necessary energy correctly between the earth and the sky, because we have trained for our whole life to do it. When

112

we fall apart, or fail to open up as a channel, it is another wasted opportunity, another incomplete life cycle that we regret when we return home.

Man chose to fulfil his role in the Earth's evolution. We elected not only to be here, but to achieve other things along the course of our time, and now the time has come to understand what that role may be. Take me for example. I am living proof of what you've just read. Four years ago I would no more have written a book than fly to the moon, I had nothing to write about, yet here it is. You are reading it. Somewhere inside every one of us is a purpose, a reason for being alive, even if it is to enjoy – to really enjoy and be happy in the life that you live. If you cheat in any way – it's only yourself you are cheating. You short-change yourself by your own actions. No one here might ever know – but you do. You know very well and you kick yourself for it. Today is a new day, a new opportunity to be who you are. The past is past. Yes there may be consequences, but stand up and take them. Put your life back in order – no matter how impossible that task might seem, and remember you are not as alone as you think. Ask for the help you need. Just ask.

Only you love yourself and your family enough to turn your life around. All through your time here you have been trying to be loved and liked for the person you are and only you know the price you have paid for that honour. Now it's your turn to be happy. You have earned it. We all have. The world about us is getting faster and crazier. People want and expect more than they have ever done before. This is just the way the world has evolved, but that does not mean its right, or the way it should be. When someone jumps off a cliff should we automatically follow, or should we form our own opinion, make our own stand? Only we know how happy or unhappy we are. Only we know if our life is as rich and fulfilling as it ought to be. We alone know the answer to these questions.

113

A perfect world

Once upon a time a dream was born. It was a dream of a perfect world. The dream can still be a reality if we want it to – really want it to. Many people believe this world is on a course of destruction and in a way it is, but just as equally it is not. Since time began there has never been such a cry for help as we are crying now. Life has never been so good – yet for many it has never been so bad. Only we can put a stop to where we are heading, and the changes must start from inside. Only we can do what is necessary to put balance back into this world and our own lives too. Only we can look around at the world we see and recognise that all souls mirror our own. They are just the same. They, too, are searching for input and understanding, for truth and for love. The turmoil around every one of us is just a symptom of the larger unrest that exists on the planet's surface. All illness and strife is its proof. More and more people are becoming sick with serious conditions than they are of general bugs and colds. We have mastered infection and sanitation, but critical conditions are spreading faster than ever. Once again this is a symptom of the overload we are facing, both of the planet and of ourselves. Only we can decide when enough is enough and *now* it really is.

We are fortunate that we have a chance to redraw the rules by which we operate. We can curb our spending; reduce our intake of food and the resources we require such as clothes, cars, house sizes, jewellery etc. These are but a few chips to the boulder that is blocking our life, our energy and our welfare. We work too hard because we spend too much. We spend too much because we want too much and we want too much because we have learnt to be this way. We are stuck in a loop that only we can break. Only we can change the mould by which we live, but to do so we must wake up to the part that we ourselves play and the world we have made.

114

Fifty years ago we had war and export famine. We had almost nothing that would serve to fulfil our basic needs, yet look at us today. The shops, our homes, our cupboards and our stomachs are overflowing with wealth and sustenance, with goods we don't possibly need, or even use any more than a few times. When something new comes to light we rush off to buy it – whether we can afford it or not, whether we really need it or not, because we feel we must have it anyway. This is how we have trained ourselves to be and we get better and sharper in the process. Only we can open our own eyes to take a truthful look at ourself. Is this why we work, why we love, why we are here? We know it's not. When we stand on a beach with nothing around, when we walk through the woods with our hands in our pockets, kicking the leaves on the ground, we know we have never felt happier. Do we really need to do all the things we do, or are those things merely the weights that tie us down? Are we living life to the full, or are we our own jailers? Who can answer the question except us alone? And who can choose to stop except us by ourselves once more.

Many people say "Why should I be the odd one out?" "Why should I do what others do not?" Yes, why indeed. Why should you work as hard as you do? Why should you carry the burden of debt and dis-ease on your shoulders, simply to keep going as you do? And ask yourself again – do you get the use out of the things that surround you that you thought you would? Like me you probably don't. We buy and buy with good intentions, but in the end is the price we pay worth the stress, the hassle or the worry? Only you can answer this once again for yourself, and probably that answer will be no as well.

Man has all that he needs at his feet. I, too, have all I ever wanted and more than I have ever dreamed. I, too, am doing things that I never thought possible, things that some only thought are fairy tales. Because we have no limitations

115

of any kind all we ever have wanted is at our disposal. We look outwardly to others and marvel at their talents. We explore avenues already taken by brave men and women. We marvel at history and imagine ourselves in its shoes, but how often do we really attempt to follow the dreams that we carry? We live the life we live and build it the way we do and think that that is our lot. If we are happily content then that is fine, but often we feel life has become flat or dull. We turn to our family and friends and live their lives with them. Again this too is good providing it fulfils its purpose, but often familiarity sets in and we find aspects of that we don't like as much either. Because we've become too intimate, the 'breath of fresh air' they used to bring into our lives becomes stale. We have joined too closely and intermingled as one instead of remaining parallel and free. We have grown into their life and they into ours and we now focus on them as we have learnt to focus on our own. Again this is not a problem providing it keeps you happy, but when friendships fizzle and arguments and niggles prevail then that is the reason. The life we are given is for us to live. We need interests and stimulation to keep it fresh, to keep it moving, and to keep it sustained. When friends live in our pockets and we in theirs that stimulation dries up. It becomes mundane and part of our normal daily routine. Step back a little and do something different – either alone or together. Create a new avenue to explore, something new to talk about, to discuss, to investigate and get excited about. Discover a new part of you. Push your boundaries a little and allow some change into your life. Don't throw away all you hold dear – but open a window and allow the fresh air to waft through. Any change is as good as a rest, because it takes you out of the norm, away from all you would normally do. You can step back into the pattern of your life whenever you wish, but you will see it with fresh eyes. You will enjoy it as you used to before.

We used to take a lifetime to build up our life, to get a home, a career and a family, but now we are able to have everything – in a relatively short period. We can chop, change and explore avenues whenever we wish, only do it properly, with care, with consideration and with love. All we ever dreamed is available right under our nose and not just materialistically. Anything and everything is possible for us to achieve and all we need do is look beyond our normal conditioning, beyond the things we usually would do.

Only we can move forward to shake ourselves out of childish habits and opinions. I, too, must do this regularly and it is not as easy as you would think. Everyday we get locked into moods and power struggles just because another does or says something that we don't like – little different to children fighting for the same toy, or for a particular role in a make-believe game. In reality few of us have ever grown up. We remain children until we die. People who we live or work with, will eventually learn the buttons to keep clear of, but in general life we allow a hundred things to annoy us everyday. We mumble and groan and stamp about in our private thoughts and this in turn affects the words we speak, the avenue of thoughts we think about, and the way we behave and interact. In fact our true feelings can be sensed for miles – even when we think they cannot. Only we can stop this behaviour by learning to recognise the times when we apply it. The more we stop ourselves in full swing the more our tantrums will die down and settle back to normality.

We are well aware of our thoughts and our temper, because we get knotted up inside first of all. The most trivial things then taint the whole of the day we are in. I, too, had to learn to let go. In the midst of my anger I had to learn to recycle my emotion. Sometimes it was hard and other times it was easy to get cross with myself for backing down, but the truth is that you will be empowered – not

117

weakened by this action. You are more of a person for standing down - even when you know you are right, than you could ever be by adding fuel to the fire. By keeping tempers aflame you feed the issue with negative energy. Like attracts like and there will be no winners - no exceptions.

Stress stems from negative energy and it will stay with you all day. Irritation gets larger and larger until your temper explodes at the slightest opportunity. We must learn to recycle anything and everything that does not fit within peace and a calm mind. We can choose whether we want to keep the worry and trouble that crosses our path or whether we will let it go.

Only we can ease the burden we carry with us each and everyday, yet nothing can be removed from our being unless we make a conscious effort to help. Nothing will change until we silently send our thoughts upstairs to ask for the assistance we need, at the time we recognise that we need it. Send out a thought of love and light to anyone who makes you cross. Ask that whatever aroused your negative feelings in the first place be recycled and turned into love and light. Ask that love and light be given to the other party, then quietly go about your business, or the task at hand. In reality you will have done nothing more than send out a few thoughts, but in actual fact you have done much more. You have refused to take on the mood as your own and you have asked for illusion to disappear to let truth and peace prevail. You have asked that peace surrounds you and you will have recycled the temper and some of the stress load from the other person. Not bad for a few seconds work is it? And we can do this anytime we choose – twenty five times in a row if we wish. It really does not matter – except that we do it. We can ease the life that surrounds and interacts with us with a simple decision to take it on board or not. We can make ourself a stress-free zone, but it will take practice. The thoughts we think do matter. They matter very much indeed.

Energy in motion

Thoughts are matter. They are energy in motion. Thoughts erupt from us like water spurts from a fountain. Our thoughts are a constant stream as they chatter around in our mind, day in and day out. From the second we open our eyes in the morning, until we go to bed at night – we think the thoughts that we think. For the most part they continue as they wish without our even noticing – let alone caring. We are brought up to believe that as long as we behave and live a good life, within our own four walls we can say whatever we like – about whomever we want. We allow our minds free realm and our tongues too. We believe our thoughts are our own and that they really do not matter – but how wrong. The thoughts we think are as loud as a tannoy announcement in the world of spirit. Every word we *never* voice goes forth to land somewhere, with someone. It always attaches to something. How could we be so childish as not to realise? The laws of cause of effect rule the world, they rule our life and all that we are, so how can we ever think we could get away with anything? Bad thoughts are like magnetised lead balloons. They stick to all those they emanate from. They stay with the person who thought them up and weigh them down in the process. This in turn keeps our tempers smouldering and our spirits heavy, so we stay in catch 22. Because we are heavy and cross we think more heavy thoughts and continue that way all day. It's easy to see now how recycling helps. It uplifts our spirit and stops this chain of events from taking hold. Because it changes negative to positive it enables us to remain clear headed and unattached to do all that needs to be done and then move on. Recycling helps more than you think.

119

The load we constantly carry within our minds is an added pressure to our psychological well-being. It keeps us out of sync with reality. The moment you are experiencing now, is the one you should be fully operational in, so other thoughts simply get in the way. Thoughts alter your mood. They will cloud your judgement and take you to places that in reality you have no need to be. Sometimes we can be locked for hours in a deep train of thought that is painful and makes us sad. We go over and over past memories that we bring forward as easily as clicking onto a document file. We think and rethink the things we did and all that was said when the truth is that 'now' it's probably irrelevant. Try to recognise when you become locked in this loop. Bring yourself back to the time frame you are in and take some deep breaths. Ask that the thoughts you were expressing be released from your mind. Ask that their hold be removed from you and that they be recycled. Ask that you be surrounded with love and light and ask for help to remain focused on the job in hand. Don't check that this has been done, or you will be asking for it back. Just forget about it now and get on with the day. By doing this you are retraining your mind to stop unnecessary wandering at will. It is your choice if you wish to go back to them later, but you probably will not want to. I, too, still practice this regularly, but even after a couple of years I still can get caught out sometimes. It's surprising how strong the pull of the past can be and if the past is where you spend most of your head's thinking time, then it can be hard to bring under control. The same can be said for thinking too far ahead. Your mind is like a young unruly child. It is used to doing whatever it wants, whenever it wants and now you are changing its rules. You control it – not it you, and what you want to achieve is peace and quiet within your space. Peace in your head.

Peace is a hard thing to come by, yet in reality it exists all around. It can be difficult to retain with a list of continuous jobs that shout to be done. Life stands still for no one and really it shouldn't. Life is continuous - that is its nature, and we just keep up. But because the world – our own personal world is so busy, so are we. We flit from here to there doing the things we must all day long. Our minds have little chance to take time out. Even in our quiet moments our mind is not quiet at all. It has almost forgotten how to be - so we must help it remember. All the thoughts we think take energy from our personal store and we use it in continuous flow. We need that energy ourselves for the task in hand. It should see us comfortably to the end of the day, or until we are able to replenish its supply. Yet even though I know better, I, too, still have energy problems. It saps away without my even noticing until I feel drained and tired and wonder why. I just drip it away without even thinking and I, too, must keep mine under stricter control, but it will take a little time to master. We have our whole lives to practice all the new things we shall learn and as soon as we start, we will see visible improvements - in all directions.

Only we think that the world begins and ends with us, yet we are at the start of a whole new existence. The real world is far greater than we could ever imagine, and it's all there for us to discover. Even if we never do more than acknowledge its existence, we shall be richer than money could buy. Peace and contentment would be second nature and stress a thing of the past. Only we can discover the necessary steps that will lead us there, to a place that's available to all. Yet even in today's free thinking society how many of us realise that someone is taking care of us at all times and that we need only stretch out a hand – or a thought, to make that connection join with our own. We are programmed too deeply into the belief that we must shoulder all that life dictates and throws in our path. It is not a case of digging in your heels and refusing to comply, the force that enwraps us is more delicate, gentler than that.

121

If we could only see beyond our scope of material vision we would be astounded. A whole world exists and integrates with ours and waits for us to notice. I, too, only glimpse it from time to time, but I feel its presence daily. I reach out to my angels, my guides and my relations, and they never fail to help. Day or night, it is never a problem.

Chapter Thirteen

The Winds that Blow Hard

Moving forward yet falling back

The winds that blow hard do so with force throughout our life. For every step we take forward we seem to move three back. No matter how well we research a project, something will always get in the way and because nothing is ever as easy as it would seem - that is a problem.

Just as the world is driven by cause and effect, it also needs the balance of time. Things must come to pass in the time frame they belong and no man could ever live otherwise. The world itself was made by these laws and nature could conform to nothing less. Man, too, must learn to read the signals and signs that are open to him. Just as the tides ebb and flow, so does general life. There is a time to go forward and a time to take stock, a time to sew seeds and a time to stand still. There is a time for harvest and a time to learn, a time to go slow and for hard work. The whole of life operates within these laws, yet to the majority they are as invisible as air we breathe.

Life is nothing more than a constant work in progress and each of us has a part to play; and play it we must to the best of our ability. Nothing is by chance. There is a reason behind every little thing that happens – whether we know it or not. Sometimes we never know, we never find out, but a reason exists all the same.

Man lives his life in the fast lane. He rushes here and everywhere all day long. I do the same, because that is how life has become. Everyone is in the same predicament. We are caught in a loop of having to achieve all that we can all of the time. Days pass outside - as we sit inside and work. Too soon a week has gone; a month, a year and we still

123

tread the same road to do the same jobs. At this moment there seems little we can do about life except keep up. Yet how many of us know that we are our own chains? We are the only ones who can change the pace we live by. We must learn to slow down and to utilise the time we have more effectively. By learning to focus one hundred percent on the task in hand we can get through it faster and easier and by keeping this up like a constant stream, we can gradually clear the back load that has built up. We can also ask our brothers for assistance. Ask that the time in your day – be slowed down so you may achieve all that you wish in the time frame you have available. When we do this we can very quickly see the results that such a simple act can bring, and the more we can do it the more we shall see how it works. The reason we get fed up is that we attempt to squeeze too much in any one slot and when we do not achieve all we intend, we think we have failed, but rubbish - we do very well. Combined with interruptions we endure along the way – we do very well indeed. So ease up on yourself. Instead of moaning or stressing, take a look at all you have achieved. If the opposite is apparent and you have managed little, then make the necessary adjustments to restore a satisfactory balance. The ball is in our court and how we choose to play it is up to us.

Only during the past century has life evolved to this speed and level, because of technology and the industrial revolution. Life has changed for man more in the last one hundred years than has ever occurred during the life of the planet. Since time began each thing has had its own evolution speed, its own pace and its own time frame. Man has broken all records and is set to go further, faster still. Yet the problem is not the speed he is travelling, but the pressure and stress he has placed upon his being. He is set to burn himself out in a short space of time, and this is not the way it was planned. He has the whole of life, the whole of existence at his disposal. He is capable of more now than ever before, and he has a long, long way yet to go. Pace yourself. Enjoy the ride. Enjoy each and everyday you are given and make it count. Make it count for you. The things you do and the steps you take need not be monumental, but take them each and everyday. Just one small change at a time can move mountains over a lifetime. Only we can wake up and now it is time to do it. We are at the beginning of a wonderful adventure – not the end of the world. We are about to enter an age that our ancestors would not believe, so let's get this world of ours in order and go forward to embrace it.

Many of us work all day and all night too. We seem to need to do this just to make ends meet. Life, a decent standard of life, has become expensive. And what makes it worse is the constant stream of consumer goods and valuables that are paraded, as though they will go out of fashion. We look at the things we have and we feel shabby even when we're not. We look at how hard we work and we feel we deserve better. We feel wronged by the life we have chosen, but that's the point. We chose it. And just as we chose where we are, we can also elect a new way of life; new rules to live and work and survive by. Only we can pull ourselves out of the place that we are in, not by more stress and struggle, but by a new resolve; by making and sticking to some new resolutions. Make some alterations in how you approach the day ahead of you. Remove what you don't need. Stop and think how much you need to do – what you are going to and make a slight adjustment accordingly. I, too, am at this place and I seem to have been here a while. The necessary alterations will not happen overnight, but if we keep up our resolve and work steadily in this direction with everyday we have, then slowly, slowly we shall see the changes occurring. Only you can be honest with you. Only you know if your life is working for you in the way that it should – or not and only you can see the times that you could have done things better, or differently than the way you did.

One day you will get up and the sun will be shinning, the birds will be singing and you will feel glad to be alive. Glad to be part of this lovely world that you see. You will realise that each new day is a gift and you will be sad that you have only a number of years left ahead of you. When you can get to this stage, you know that you will be all right; that your life will be fine – for always. Yes there will be worry and sadness and pain at times, but that too has its place in the scale of this earth, but you will get through it, you will get to the other side probably quicker than you would have done in the past. I have also been here and in some ways still am. Life ebbs and flows like the tide. No things can remain as they are. Growth and change can be hard, like the winter seems hard after the summer blossoms, but it is all necessary to planetary evolution. It is the nature of this life we are part of.

Only man is stuck at this moment in time and that is why we experience all that we do. It is necessary for us to go through turmoil to come out of the other side wiser than before. Only we can do this for ourselves and indeed we all already are. Don't think that you are the only one in trouble, that you are the only one who struggles from day to day, simply to get out of bed, to get through till the end of the day ahead. Don't believe that others don't have just as many worries and fears and doubts, because they do. They have just as many and maybe more. The state of your life at this time is a problem that's catching us all. Problems are merely symptoms of the planetary adjustments that are occurring all around. We are being forced to rethink our lives, our beliefs and our thought patterns. We have taken the stage we are in as far as we can go, so we are being drawn to the next phase of existence, and because of this we must all reshape our lives. That is really all there is to it. The world is in a mess, but it is a mess that's born out of necessity. Just as a room becomes untidy before it gets better as you clear it out, such is the state of our life. We are merely at a clearing out and redrawing stage, that's all; and we are not alone. Every person everywhere is the same. Their problems might be different, but in the scale of life, problems are still problems and we all have them. We are all in the same boat, rowing for the distant shore.

Man needs to step back and take stock before he can travel forward comfortably once more. Too much of the control of our life has slipped through our hands. Our life does not seem to be in our control. We are at the mercy of our creditors and our worries. We are chasing our tails and getting nowhere fast anymore, and this is what we need to rethink. We cannot continue further down this road of destruction – because that is what it is. It is a box of trouble that's waiting to pop – and when it does, God help us all.

The state of affairs in which we find ourselves today is the outcome of years of striving to succeed, of trying to make something of our lives, our society, and ourselves. The problem arises not because of what we are trying to do, or what we aim to be, but because through all this time we have mistakenly thought we've been on our own, alone with our worries and our problems. We have thought for far too long that we alone were responsible for making this world tick, when the opposite is true. We are players in a larger game of life. Yes we do have personal responsibility for all that we do and undertake, but in the larger scale of things there is much more occurring than we can understand at this time. We each have a part to play, a role to fulfil and it is this role that interacts with others as they, too, play their part to the best of their ability. All goes well when we each do what we should, but when we don't or perhaps can't, the system brakes down, like the cogs in a working machine. When well oiled and properly maintained it works perfectly, but when one part suffers more use or more stress than another, it fails to perform at its best. That in turn over stresses other parts and they seize or break up also. Eventually the whole machine grinds to a halt and is of use to no one until it's mended. And so is the health of this earth that we live on. The same state as us all individually, both within our own selves and our affairs. The time has come to reassess the situation and make some necessary atunement and repair. And there is no need to do it alone. All we could ever want is at our disposal to help us. Man needs to learn to trust once more, both in his self and in those who stand beside him in his hour of need. He only has to offer up his thoughts and solutions will come gladly back, not always as he would imagine, but a solution just the same. Remember life ticks past in seconds so the help that comes forth will also flow one step at a time. Follow those steps as they appear and slowly, slowly you will get to the end of the tunnel you are in.

Man is his own worst enemy. When problems loom he takes the first solution that comes to light as his guiding rope, but often this is not the real answer. If we take the trouble to step one step back, we can quiet our mind and think for a moment. It is always better to look at the bigger picture, slightly to the side of where you are now. If you take that quick fix rope it may solve your problems instantly, but ultimately is it not another chain in itself? Probably. The better solution might not be immediately apparent and it may take longer and be harder to achieve, but will probably be better for you right now. Life will always deliver all that you need – whenever you need it, but it's up to you to be choosy. Personal choice comes in to play to give you the ultimate decision. Find as many options as you can and take a little time to explore them all. Choose the one that's the most comfortable rather than the quick fix.

We are totally responsible for the life that we live and the decisions and choices we finally make. Peace of mind is hard to find and I, too, am learning not to take on board more than I can cope with comfortably. It will take time to retrain yourself when you are usually the helping hand to all who ask. It can also be difficult to see those you love and care for emotionally in worry and turmoil, but once you have done all you can do to help or listen or guide, you must hand it back to them. We can do no greater favour to those we love than that. Whatever their experience, it is exactly what they must get through to arrive at the other side. Within the turmoil is something that needs addressing, something that needs attention to get them to the next stage of their life. It may be small, it may be large, but whatever it is, try not to rob them of this experience. Ask for help to the powers that be, both to give you the strength to step back and to help them clear their path. Ask that all unnecessary rubbish be removed and that only the truth remains. Ask for help for your friend; don't rob them of the steps they need to go through to get there. Help might come quickly, it may take a while, but it will come. They are no more alone in the life they lead than we are. They, too, have all they could ever require at their disposal. They, too, must learn to read the signs as they present themselves to lead them forward.

Life is a journey that we chose to undertake. There are problems and pitfalls along the way that seem to harm, but really can only help. They are opportunities to reassess, restructure and take stock. Once we have passed their hold we usually can see a clear path ahead. This may be long term or short term, but each time we pass those pitfalls, life will be easier than it was before. We are lead and helped over every hurdle and by learning to recognise the signs we can make life simpler than it otherwise would be.

Only we have come as far as we have in this life and if we took a backward glance, then we would see just how far that is. We should be proud of ourselves. There is no shame in making mistakes, in getting things wrong. The point is that we are all human and human nature itself is fallible. We are not perfect and never could pretend to be. Nor should we. We each do the best that we can in any given moment. The decisions we made – even the bad ones, were thought to be best at their time - or we would not have made them. Man does not go ahead in the knowledge that what he is doing will fail and cause him harm. He believes it is for his good, so he soldiers on. In reality there are no bad decisions. All things have their place in the scale of life. A not-so-good move will merely lead to more problems and reassessments. We shall be forced to rethink and choose again – that's all. Nothing is ever for nothing. Yes we could have chosen better perhaps, but the next time we shall and do.

Only we can stop kicking ourselves for our downfalls, because if we don't – who will? No one would dare treat us the way we treat ourselves. We would not let them. Yet we do all that we can in terms of punishing and putting ourselves down. We let others walk all over us because deep down we think that we deserve it, but we don't. We are all (or nearly all) good hearted, kind individuals who just want a peaceful and hassle free life. We do all that we can do to the best of our ability and when life backfires once more it feels like a kick in the face. I, too, can relate to this. We all can if we are truthful. Only a few can ever escape the knocks that life has to offer. Only a few are completely at one and happy.

Only you can know the thoughts you think and the feelings you have. Only you know the things you do each day and the direction in which you are travelling. Only you can know if you are getting close to those directives or further away from them, and only you can alter your life accordingly. When we are young, we all have hopes and dreams to aspire to, but along the course of life they often fade and die as reality of day-to-day living sets in, but this need not always be so. Only we can take the reigns of life

130

once more into our hands, and we don't need force to do it; just truth, love, and a resolve to get there – wherever 'there' may be.

(I am I). **Only you can make your life count. Make it count for everyday of your life.** (I am I).

Chapter Fourteen

The Winds that Sleep

(I am I). Only people with love in their hearts can make their lives count for something. It is not a choice; it is necessity. All of life revolves around love, and love revolves around life. (I am I).

<u>High hopes</u>

Only we can live the life we have, but to do so we must wake up to the life that is us. Only we can please ourself and only we can bring the happiness that we desire into our own being. If we are sad or down, it is up to us to find out why; does it stem from the people around you, or does it come from inside of yourself? There is a difference, all be it subtle, but it is there none the less. Happiness starts from within. When we wait for others to make us happy we are deflecting from the problem. We are putting our hopes and dreams into them and expecting them to return the compliment. We forget that they, too, are probably waiting for the same thing, so in reality we are in stalemate. Neither party is giving to the other what they need, because neither is fulfilled within himself. Both will go through their day with something missing, because they were looking outside of themselves for what they needed. If unhappiness stems from inside of you, it is slightly different. It means that you are dissatisfied with your life, yourself, or others around you. It means that in some way you are unhappy with your lot, the life you have chosen. Take a closer look within to see where the unrest really lies.

We live our life according to our beliefs, our hopes, our dreams and our perceptions. A perception is the way we interpret the things we see, do, hear, and feel. An interpretation of the life we experience. Sometimes instead of seeing reality we exist in an illusional interpretation of life. We don't see the truth as it really is, but instead, the version of reality that we choose it to be. Illusion overtakes our train of thought and we are in a little world of our own. I, too, used to be this way and indeed many people are. Remaining in the truth of life is an art. It takes practice and time to become good at it. Anyone can say anything. They can do whatever they wish, but how many of these things bear resemblance to the life that really exists around them. I, too, have lived my fantasies, but at the end of them, life was still empty. I had been living a fantasy alongside my normal life.

Real life is the truth. It is always the bottom line; that which is – and cannot be changed, or altered, with any amount of words or explanation. Real life is the facts of life exactly as they are. They are immovable in the way they cannot be altered in any way at all. Illusion is anything that lifts us out of this state. It is that which we do outside of the things we should be doing. It is seeing the world about us, and the people in that world differently than they are. Illusion is reading into situations things that are not really there – but you have placed them there by your wishing it to be that way. By assuming what is actually not.

Only we can learn what makes us tick, what makes us think and act the way we do. We have no need to rely on others to give us the pleasure and happiness we desire. In fact the sooner we realise this and come to terms with the reality of this, the better our lives will perform – instantly. We are placing the ball of control back into our own court, to play the game of life, as we would have it be. By 'control' we don't mean badgering, bloody-mindedness. We don't mean stressing and pushing to achieve what you need to achieve by force, but instead use quiet resolution. Each day gather a little more back of what you have given to others to do on your behalf. When you take a look at exactly how much you require other people to do 'for you', you will probably be surprised. Life will have moved this way, without your even being aware and it will only be by stopping and taking stock of where you are, that you can get some order and meaning back, where it should really be.

Life has a habit of slipping through our fingers. It moves out of our control by stages. First comes something small that others offer to take on board for you, then more and more until you rely on them for huge parts of what you need to be doing. This is fine as long as all things work well and remain as they should be, but when they don't you can spend far too much time at the mercy and energy of other people and this is stressful in itself. Who likes to wait for others to do what they are supposed to have done ages ago? It is far easier to take these things back and do them yourself. You will probably find it more rewarding in the process. A person who sits around with little to do, is far more dissatisfied and disgruntled than he who is busy, but from his own labours. Life is a gift, but it is also a chore. There are one hundred things for each of us to do everyday. When we give too many of these tasks away we overload someone else, who in turn gets stressed and disgruntled and the whole process goes on and on.

No man should need to do out of necessity, more than is right and fair, but we often push ourselves beyond the limit and expect others to do the same. Only by re-assessing the situations we are in, can we see the areas that cause the most discomfort and stress in our lives, and these are the issues we need to tackle. Be careful that you don't pin point something that is merely a scapegoat for something else that you don't want to face. We hide all sorts of things so as not to look at them and we argue over the weakest, most insignificant details indeed. If you don't know for sure where your discomfort is coming from, do nothing.

Instead sit tight, but be vigilant until you *do* know. Life will always open up your problems and display their content to you if you let it. Simply do what you normally would do and send your thoughts up and out for someone to give you guidance. It will not happen over night, but in small steps and stages, so just deal with whatever arises at the time it does. Use only the emotional content that befits the occasion and remain calm in the process. Always ask for love and guidance to surround you at this time and do what must be done kindly and wisely.

I must also remain on my guard to not take on more than I should. It is easy to overburden yourself. It is easy to help others when you feel the need and indeed it is natural to do that, but it is equally easy to get tied up in their turmoil. When you offer yourself as a guiding light, try if possible to keep the controlling light in their court, because that way it leaves you free to come and go as you must. Life is an art of love and balance. Love is our essence and it is this that gives us the need to reach out to those in turmoil or pain, but balance is the necessity that keeps all things in their rightful place, as they should be. Balance is what keeps the world ticking over and it is also the law behind cause and effect. Balance is a necessary part of our everyday life. Balance is what keeps the world spinning as it does – on its axis. The law of balance is a universal one that in nature keeps itself almost perfectly tuned. We say almost, because of the influence man has on this subject, because man at this time is unbalanced, he in turn affects much of what he is unaware, not only in his own life, but in his mind and actions as well. Balance must come from within. It must start and end (as far as we are concerned) with us, all day and everyday. It should be as natural to us as blinking our eyes and living life itself.

Only we can find this thing inside. Only we can reconstruct the fibres of our life to incorporate the balance that is needed. Only balance can keep our life in the order

135

that it needs to be in and it is balance that will render us healthy, worry free and stress free. Balance in love is a must and so is balance in finance. I, too, once again am working hard to keep my life and myself in a perfect balanced order. It is not easy because everyone and everything is clamouring to be acknowledged at once. Life has a way of throwing itself at you – when you really don't need it to be that way, but a forceful resolution within yourself will help to see you through. Be gentle but firm, not too rigid, but firm all the same, and slowly you will begin to make progress. Remember that the place you are at now has taken you a lifetime to get to. It is only natural that full balanced order will take an equally long time to achieve. The days go past in minutes and hours, but within each of those hours an opportunity to bring something back into balance will occur. We can do anything we wish with this life of ours, anything at all. There are no rules or regulations. There is no guidebook, or a completely right path that we should follow. Life is made up of equally good and bad things, but it is up to us as individuals, to find the right mixture of both, that will balance our life in the way we need it to be. All of life must remain in perfect balance in order for it to function in the way that it should.

Taking stock

Only we know the true content of our life, so only we can keep it by the reigns and help it flow in the manner that it should. It is up to us alone to keep it moving in the direction that we need it to. Only we can make the choices and decisions that can take us forward to where we can find peace, balance and happiness. Stress and dis-ease, arguments and anger are merely signposts to warn us that all is not quite right. When we take heed and look further (probably within rather than without) we can find that often the culprit is a train of thought, or a belief that is out of sync with the truth of the matter. Only we can determine the cause and only we can work towards a favourable outcome.

We must also learn to keep our tempers at bay. Only we can reassess when anger threatens to engulf either ourselves, or the situation at hand. Anger is a trigger that goes off without warning, for those who fail to notice the signals that build up beforehand. They believe that their anger is justified and that it stems from the action of others around. They totally blank the possibility that it stems from within themselves, first and foremost. They are oblivious that they might have any control over their behaviour at all. Anger is like the valve on a pressure cooker. Slowly our tempers simmer until they reach boiling point, then poof, off we go like a rocket into space and there is no turning back. Once we let rip – woe betide anyone or anything that stands in our way. Even instant anger can be traced back to a mood, or thought pattern you were previously in. I, too, had to learn this lesson, but not because I was shouting out and directing my anger onto others, but more because I kept it simmering inside. I directed it at myself more often than not, without even knowing I was doing so. Only we have access to the thoughts that whirl around in our head. Others see only the little bits that we allow them to, and often wonder why we do the things we do. All that we are stems from thoughts and opinions that were first born in our mind. I, too, am a product of this and so is this book you are reading. Once upon a time it was a thought, which was part of a daydream. A little hope that perhaps one day I might like to accomplish, and look at it now. It is here in your hand; giving you the strength and encouragement that you need to take you forward to your next step. I, too, must realise the power of thought in action.

Balance played an important part in helping this book to come about, because without it, many things could not have been successfully accomplished. Each and everyday many things come into our path that threaten to take up our time.

137

In fact the harder we try to concentrate the more disruptions we have to face. I, too, could relate to this, every time I sat down to write, but when you are balanced you can still manage to do all that you intend, as long as you really desire to do so. An interruption is often the excuse we need, not to do what we ought. It is the reason we give ourselves to take a break from what we are doing. Interruptions occur naturally as part of the flow of life, but it is up to us to try to keep them to a minimum. I, too, am still in the throws of practising this and so far I am winning.

Only we can keep our life moving and flowing in some sort of order. Chaos is not order, but neither is vegetating. Life must constantly flow and change, move and grow, in order for us to feel fulfilled and at one with it. That part of us which is us, our spirit, or energy part, needs constant stimulation and love. It needs us to love the life we are living and it needs continuous feeding with new experiences and interactions. It needs us to live, really live and to enjoy every moment we are doing it.

Only you pay the consequences of the stress, sadness and worry you carry inside, because only you can feel it. These things stem from your being, because of thoughts and situations that occur within and without you. Worry is a product of the happenings you are experiencing. Life can never be problem free, as much as we think it should - it cannot. We have already discussed that problems have their purpose and their place, but we could not evolve as a species without them. Problems are brick walls. They are the end of a particular path we are following, and in order to pass them we have to alter something, to find the key to the solution. Problems are a natural part of growth and only we can decide what needs to be done to pass through them.

People will always interrupt our plans, because they all need our undivided attention, but what they don't know is the importance of your job in hand. Only you can know that. Providing you are true and fair, there is no reason that they will not let you continue, but again weigh things up for yourself. Sometimes it is better to stop for a moment to deal with them, than it is to put their issue to the side. Life follows you. It does not and cannot stop just because you don't have time for it right now. Instead of getting hett up, make an educated choice and deal with the moment, just as you must.

Only man can choose what he will do from moment to moment. All other species act on instinct. Man is the only one who can choose the direction his life will follow. Yet too often we forget this when we are tied up in the course of everyday life. We feel that we are at the mercy of the world itself. We feel that time and everything else is running against us. How often do we sit down at the end of a day and count the things that went right? Most of us would answer 'not very often'. We go to sleep on a negative note, thinking of what we must do the next day or thinking over the problems of the day just finished. Instead, why don't we thank our lucky stars for all the good things that have come about – no matter how small? Everyday a hundred things can go our way, but we are too tunnel minded to notice. It might be that you were on time for work because the traffic worked with you. It may be that a meeting or reprimand went better than you thought it would. It might have been that you finished the day as you began it, little better, but definitely not any worse. The things you can think of might be small or monumental in size, but they are still issues that went in your favour. Send your thanks out and be glad. I, too, find myself doing this everyday, and it's surprising how many good days you will find you have had.

People automatically take life as it comes, when they operate from within the time bracket they are in. There is no need to look either too far forward, or too far back. All that needs to happen to you will happen at the time it should, not before. It is easy to look forward when an event is approaching and we do this in anticipation of either joy or fear. I, too, catch myself whenever I can, because patience is not something we adults are good at. We forever tell our children 'to wait and see' or 'be patient for a while', but how often do we fall short of this ourselves? We can't wait for this evening, let alone next week, or next year. We want everything yesterday, then we wonder why life goes too fast, or the event is not as good as we thought it would be. It is because we just cannot wait. For ages our thoughts have been wandering and planning just how we think it will be. We build up a whole scenario in our heads then wonder why reality can bear no resemblance when the time comes and events take place. Each time we look ahead we think about what will occur. Thought is energy in motion, so every thought will place energy ahead of you in your pathway. If it is positive energy, it will be excitement and pleasant anticipation that you place ahead of you. Sometimes this will be fine and the occasion will be all it should, but at other times you will have built up such a crescendo, that the event can't possibly meet the expectations you have placed upon it. We can prevent this from occurring in the future, by quietly drawing our attention back to focus on the event we are in right now - on the task that you are now undertaking. By doing this as often as you are able you allow time to take its natural course, so when the event or issue finally arrives, you have placed no more than a normal balanced energy upon it. I, too, had to do this in the birth of this book and when you are excited it is no easy task. Over excitement is itself an unbalanced state, so ask for your excess energy to be recycled and bring yourself back 'down' to earth.

The opposite is true when we dread a task, a day, or an event that is looming ahead. It is irrelevant what the issue might be, or when, because the effect is still the same. The energy that we produce now is negative. It is this that we are placing in our path. It is this that stops our easy flow of life and instead places grey matter around the time yet to come. Every time we think a negative thought the energy that that thought produces is bound for somewhere. It will either attach itself to the life of the person about whom you were thinking, or it will cling to and gather around the issue you were thinking about. When we have a task that we really should do, we know it needs doing, but we dread it. It seems that the task looms larger and larger in front of us, and we dread it more in the process. We almost have to psyche ourselves up just to face it. Yet how many of us know that we have made it ten times worse by ourselves? Because of our dread of it, we have placed nothing but heaviness ahead. I, too, am a culprit, but worse still I should know better. I know that all I need do is recycle, yet sometimes even this cannot stop me from venturing down that negative avenue. It has become normal for us to behave this way, and because of that it is a habit. Habits can be very hard to break even when we know better, but the thing is not to give up. Keep on trying and sure enough we'll get there. We have the whole of our life ahead of us, so we have all of that time to practice.

Life is good and it can be fun. All we need do is re-learn how to live it. From the time we were small we stumbled along its path until we became who we are. It is now time to re-learn much that we already really know. We just need to remind ourselves how to do it.

Chapter Fifteen

The Winds that Clear Away

(I am I). Only man can clear the debris he has left in his wake. He alone is responsible for things both done and undone by his hand. Only he can go back and place the pieces of his life back into the order they should be. Only he can come home with a clean slate. (I am I).

We are the only ones who can forgive ourselves for the mistakes we have made in the past, both in history and in our own life. We can look back with a greater understanding to see that we were no more than children. This is not fantasy, but fact. From the moment we are born we follow. We follow the lead of anyone who seems to know better than we do. Sometimes we are forced to follow because that is the way life should be, and at other times we choose to, either by instinct or by desire. But who has taught the people we follow what they know? How do we know they know any better than ourselves? The truth is that we don't know really at all. We just assume. We assume they know better, because they are older, or happier. They appear to be better at life than we ourselves know we have been. Yet do they really know all that we think they do, or even that they think they do? The answer is probably no. They mostly know what they have experienced, or have been told along the way. They are neither better – nor worse than we are. They are just people, much like us. Yes, they have different likes and dislikes; their outside shells and lifestyles might be completely individual, but at the bottom line they are the same, exactly the same as us. We are born into this world and we leave it, but the bit in the middle is merely personal choice and ability. It is completely down to us how we fill our days. I, too, began to see this at a very early age. We are all the same whether we are a pop star or a pauper. There is no difference of any kind except money, and this would be a chapter all by itself.

Only we can know what makes us happy and it's up to us to sort our life out until we are. We are to make the alterations appropriate to the world in which we find ourselves. The people with whom we interact are looking for the same. They, too, are only trying to live life successfully in the only way they know how. They, just like you, are the products of their life experiences and the sooner we can see that, we can learn to see past the obvious differences in their personality. Life for them is the same as it is for you. They work, they sleep and they play. They might move in different circles and do different things, but they are simply doing the same as you. People are still people – all over the world. They are looking for the same personal reward that their life can supply. They spend money, they eat, they work and they sleep. They use the bathroom and they look for fun. They are happy, sad and inquisitive. They, too, are living for the easier time they imagine ahead and they too believe that a better place awaits them after the rigour and turmoil of life. But unlike you, they are probably not aware that they can take up the reigns once more of their life and change its course to a smoother path. Life can be what we make it. Those who ruffle our feathers and give us grief are merely stuck in their own problems. If you are the cause of their difficulty then the matter needs some attention. You need to talk together to find out where the problem lies, but if you are not, then understand that things will right themselves in a while. Send your thoughts out for help. Ask that justice reign on top. Ask that both you and they can be as small as a grain of sand. Ask that all illusion and negative energy be recycled and ask for love, light and truth to surround you

143

both – or all. You are asking for the situation to calm down and for the truth to come to your rescue. Even if you are partly to blame – ask for help in the same way. Ask that you communicate better. Ask for all that you need and you will get it. When you expect a row it will sometimes fizzle out into nothing. You will communicate on equal terms and a conclusion will be met – far easier than it would have done before. By asking to be made small you have been placed on equal footing. There will be no difference or distance between you. You will be able to communicate, as two people should, without fear of misunderstanding and wrongful blame.

All we need do is ask with our thoughts, for the help we require and it will come to our rescue. There are no requirements or restrictions that will stop this from happening. You should not feel silly or stupid, because the thoughts that you think are only for you. No other person near or around can hear them. Only you can ask for help when you need it, because now you know how to. We are not alone at any time. Help is always available to us, because that is our birthright. All we ever need is available for our assistance, but to access it, we must ask. Just as it is impossible to speak to a person in another city without first picking up the telephone, or making a computer link, all you are doing now is making a better connection to those who are about you. You are sending out your thoughts and connecting to that other part of yourself and to God. It is not a fairy tale, and it is not fantasy. Try it for yourself. Just because we do not see the air we breathe does not mean it's not there. It is. And so is God. God is not a person; he (it) is an intelligent energy source, of which we are all part. You are not your finger, yet your finger is a part of you, and the same is so with us. We are part of, and are still connected to, the whole. We are a part of the whole that is; whether we like it or not; whether we believe it or not. We cannot change that we are, because it is

144

unchangeable. Like a drop of water taken from the sea will always be part of it, the same is with us. We are energy and matter beings who are always connected to God. We can be nothing else; not ever. We were energy before we came into this life and we shall be energy when we return home once more. The part of you which is you, is merely in a physical body, having a physical experience in a physical world. We need our body to be the vehicle that helps us experience and move and live this life, because without it we would be spirit once more. This life is ours to live, to enjoy and to explore. We are here to live and have fun, not to live and worry and fear. Only life can fill the void in your being, but to live it to the full takes practice.

It is up to us to fix the areas that need fixing. We can come to terms with our life and the place where we now find ourselves and rearrange the parts that no longer fulfil their purpose or function. We are the only ones who can ultimately 'please ourselves' in a way that no one else will ever be able.

The life we have charge of is our own affair and the path we wish to tread is ours as well. It is up to us to take charge of our destiny once more and to live a life that we would be proud to own up to. The choice of how we do, and when, is up to us also, but the fact that we must is clearly obvious.

Chapter Sixteen

The Winds that will Show us The Way

There are times to go forward and times to retreat. There are times to grow and change and also to take stock. Which one you are currently in depends on you. It is up to you to find out. I, too, must learn to recognise the signs better than I do, but it will take practise. In the world today we are used to charging forward at all events. We are used to pushing and conniving to achieve desired results. How often do we sit down and wait a while to see what will transpire. It is more likely that we will want to rush ahead in case we might miss our chance. Only we can know the truth in that statement, because only we can know the thoughts and plans that while about in our heads. And it's no use trying to deny it, because we also cannot lie about things too deep for others to know about. We alone know where we have been, where we are and where we intend to be in the future. We alone know the course we would like our life to take. Everyday we look at the day ahead and we read it like a book. We know exactly where we shall be and what we must do, but in reality how much of those thoughts leave room for life to take over? How much room do we leave for life to open up and show us its colours? We don't. We do what we do, when it needs to be done and for the rest of the day we wear blinkers. We are tuned into what we expect to happen, instead of what could happen, or actually is occurring. We are on automatic pilot without even realising. I, too, am guilty of this, because of the things that I know I must achieve in any given time frame. Part of this is natural, because without focus we cannot hope to continue in the way we should. To be organised is a good thing, but it is also this that keeps us bound deep in the throws of life. We get too rigid and inflexible, so that when other opportunities arise, we feel unable to partake of them. It is hard to go with the flow, because the guilt of what we will not achieve in the meantime takes hold. Only we can help ourselves by staying on course, regardless of the hick-ups and blips that occur all around. I, too, am in the midst of this, everyday.

Only you can make up your mind, once and for all, to keep on going forward, even when the path looks blocked. It is human nature to despair and fear when we find ourselves in the midst of unexpected problems, pains and doubts, but it is at those times we are not alone. It is at exactly those times that we are being helped and lead along the way. We don't know the way. We do not know how to move in the direction that will serve us best, so it is at these times that we need a little more faith in the powers that work around us. We are never alone, especially when we think we are. There is 'always' someone who knows what the next step should be. I, too, have had to have faith in writing this book. I, too, have had to learn to sit tight – even when my instincts were telling me otherwise. We are used to solving, or attempting to solve our own problems. We spend hours, days; trying to get out of the place we are in, when if we had only stayed put for a time the solution would have presented itself. Just like children we must learn that when we are lost we must stay where we are until help arrives. Only we can help ourselves by allowing the help to get here.

We must re-learn the art of waiting for the correct solution to present itself. We are taught at a very early age to ask for help when we need it, and indeed we do. We ask anyone who will listen to us. Only in asking the people around us, we often make things worse. How can they help us? They don't know which way we are going. They know the way they have been and they have perhaps seen a little of ours, but the things that they have experienced were for them – on their own journey, not you on yours. The steps that you need to tread are completely different to theirs, even though they may look the same. In asking your friends for their thoughts you are merely taking yourself in a sideways direction instead of an upward one. You even know this inside, after the event of asking. How often do we feel that even though they did their best, they did not really understand where we were coming from? How often do we still feel alone, even after the advice has been given? We realise again, that at the moment we are to make our final decision, we are on our own. Yet we are not. We so are not. We just think we are, because we are unaccustomed to the influence that stems from within. At your most turbulent time – sit down in a quiet place and go within. Quiet your mind and wait for your thoughts to calm down. Only when we are still can we allow our thoughts to lead us forward. Only we can learn to listen to the ever ready influences that surround us.

Life must flow under its own steam, as a river must flow constantly because of the sea. Man is used to making his own decisions and then enacting them out by all means possible to him. Man has free will. This is his birthright. It is his by the laws that govern the planet, and because of this only he can ever make the final choices that he needs to make. If this right were removed, then there would be no free will of any kind. Man is bound by the very thing that offers him his freedom. He looks to others to show him the light, to lead the way, or to show him the guide rope. He looks to others, because he feels that at some level he needs reassurance, or to be given the next step to take. He looks to others for strength and support, when all the while all these things and more are within himself. The art of listening and hearing correctly are two different things, but neither of them are easy. Learning to be still in the midst of confusion or conflict, often goes against the grain of his nature. He is taught to stand up and fight for all that he needs, yet the opposite is more accurate to follow. This does not mean that he should be a doormat for all to walkover and to do what they will, nor does it mean he is whimping out. Instead it means that in the face of adversity, it is better to stand still and remain small, until the storm has passed. It means that two conflicting energies can only create havoc. Wait until things have calmed down and review the options available to you once again. It is up to you which direction you choose. All options are available for you to choose from, at any one time. All that you need to do will be acceptable in any form that you decide to achieve it. Life is yours for the taking, but you must be clear in the direction you wish it to follow. The problem is that too often we are unclear. We travel halfway down a certain path, and then the doubts set in. We doubt that we have made the right choice. We doubt because we allow others to sway us. We even doubt on our ability to see it through to the end. There could be one hundred different reasons that we change our mind and all of them as valid as each other, but the bottom line is that we doubt at all. Only we can ever make the choices that we need to choose and once we have we should stay put. Only then can the universe come to our aid.

Only you can access and reassess the situations and predicaments you find yourself in. There will be times that you choose upon a course of direction, but then the circumstances that surround you alter. I, too, can relate to this, but at these times the course we were set upon was only a stepping-stone, even though we did not know it at that time. It was not to be a permanent fixture, just a vehicle that took you from one point to the next. Again it is the gift of man to be able to access and reassess all things at all times. It is the only way you can remain on track. Life is like a long haul journey. We begin at one point with the aim of reaching another. Along that route are many highways, 'A' roads and little lanes. There are by passes, diversions and accidents to encounter, but once we begin we have to check and recheck the best roads to follow. We have to choose and rechoose once we hit problems or traffic jams, until eventually we arrive. We might be late, very late, we might be tired and fed up, but we always get there. We know we will and never doubt that, and the same should be likened to life. Life is a journey. It will not always be plain sailing. Sometimes it's easy and sometimes we get stuck. We get snarled up in stuff. Other people's stuff as well as our own, but stuff still the same. Only by standing still and taking stock can we see a clearer picture. We can rise above the place we are at and view the whole thing from another perspective, another angle. Only we can do this, because only we know the way it should be. Only we know the truths we are living and the illusions that pull us back. Be honest with yourself. Cut the maybes and could or should haves. Find the bottom line, the truth, and look at exactly where you are. Only you can do this, by yourself, for yourself. And for those you love around you. Don't wait any longer for anyone to fix your problems. Don't wait for anyone to give you what you are lacking. Don't push and shove to get where you need to go. Go within and find out how to do it properly, perhaps the harder way, but the only way just the same.

Only you can fix your life. Only you can bring the happiness back into your stride, because only you know that parts that are lacking.

Chapter Seventeen

The Winds that Protect

(I am I). Only man has been misinformed to believe the world starts and ends with him. Only he believes that he is alone on this earth and that all he does he does alone, by himself, under his own steam. But he is mistaken. He is not alone and never was. He is just a drop in a large ocean of life and activity. He is just the vehicle that keeps the world turning and its energy moving as it should. He is the manifestation of a physical being that is only a part of who he really is. Man is love and life in motion. He is capable of birth and of destruction. The story of his life is but a chapter in the history of existence and it is this he must come to realise. His life does not begin and end with his present form; it extends an eternity in either direction. He had life before he was born to his parents and he will continue that life after his breath has left his body. He is the manifestation of a living God, capable of all his desires. He alone has any power over the universe that is his life. He alone pulls the strings and plays the notes that he dances to the tune of. He holds more power in his own right hand than he could ever imagine in many lifetimes. He is all he could ever want to be. He is all God intended him to be, and much more besides. (I am I).

You are in charge

Only man can pull himself back from the brink of where he is. Only man is capable of all that he can do. It is up to him now to wake himself up from the dream he has been living. I, too, had to go through this, four years ago. The

151

world is itself in the middle of a major shake-up and the trauma we feel is our wake up call. The time has arrived for us to step out of the darkness and into the light that is waiting quietly to lead us forward. We are being lead by the hand to a smoother, calmer point in our lives. We have earned it through the pages of history until this day. We are destined to have the peace and contentment that we have until now only dreamt of. It is here for the taking and it is up to us individually to find and make that connection. The place that you are now at, is not a mistake; it is not an error; it is by design. We have been given the life we have lived to find out who we are not. It was the only way we could learn. Like parents who love their children must allow them to learn from their mistakes, we, too, have lived such an exercise. We have learnt that life is hard, that we must struggle and stress to keep it in control. We have learnt that no matter how hard we try – or how kind and good we try to be, life still throws stuff in our path. We move two steps forward and three steps back, as often as there are weeks in a year. Many of us look around and wonder what life is all about. What is its point? We have had enough and that is why the cavalry has arrived to help us. It is time to begin again - from the day you are in right now.

Each new day is a gift. It is a blank page waiting for instruction. It is a clean slate and a chance to begin afresh. All the things you have ever done – were part of yesterday. Today is a step away from that and it must all begin with you. With a clear mind and a decision to make life work for you. It can only begin with you because you alone hold the key to your life. It is yours to use in any way that you choose, because that is your birthright – given to you by creation itself.

Only you can rule your mind. It does not control you. Only you can control your thoughts. They also should not control you. You are the boss of yourself. You may have many bosses over much that you must do, but ultimately you control all that you ever will do. You make the choices that will take you from A – Z. You make your own decisions moment to moment. You alone are responsible for anything you will ever do, say or think. Man is master of his own life and his life is his own affair. That is the way it is. That is the way it has always been. Only fear can overrule our minds, but it is up to us whether or not we shall let that fear enter in – in the first place. People can only hurt us if we let them, and we only let them when on some level of our consciousness we think that we deserve it, when we believe that they rule us, or have power over us. When we think that they have the right to behave as they do – or we allow ourselves to be controlled by their moods or beliefs. Yet, the truth is not so. The truth is that we are all the same. No one man/woman has more importance than another does. Yes there are different levels of responsibility, but this is not the same thing. At the most basic level we are all the same as each other, so we should treat one another with the respect and trust that we each deserve. I, too, have had to learn this lesson, from both ends of the spectrum. It is easy to become locked into a loop where you forget the realities of life. It is easy to forget that others are human too, that they are not just there to do your bidding – however you choose to look at it. All people have wants, needs, opinions, dreams and feelings. All people perform their own function within the life that they live. They are pillars of their own communities, their families and social circles. All things might not look the same. Indeed on the surface all things seem completely different, but that is just another illusion, built of the life we live. We are where we are because that is where we chose to be. There is no more to it than that.

Only man can change his world around, by altering his approach to life. He can readjust each and everyday he is in – just enough to help it go smoothly. Gradually, as he does this, more and more things will begin to turn around

153

and change direction for him. Change is not always easy. In fact as others begin to notice they may question your intentions, but it is up to you to keep on going – slowly but surely. Ask for strength and courage whenever you need a bit of a boost. Ask for love, protection and guidance whenever you need some extra help. Ask for extra energy to see you through your day comfortably, especially when your reserves are depleted and ask for God to be in charge of your day. Ask that you may follow him instead of doing it all your own way. Open yourself up to the help that is at hand. It is yours so you might as well claim it. Because we are not alone - we should live our days accordingly.

Spirit is with us always, but we are always given privacy when we need it. Just as relatives pop in to see us from time to time, so do those we have loved and lost. They pop in occasionally to say hi, too. 'Seven Steps to Eternity' by Stephen Turoff (ISBN 1-902636-17-1) is a book that explains this nicely. It is easy to read and is written as a window of understanding and love. It brings back into your life, what many often wonder about.

Only you can open up your views to the truths that exist all around. The Bible is a book of fables combined with truth. It was written in the style of the time it was born, before newspapers, radio or television. Communication was at its lowest level and only a few could read or write. Only man can renew his understanding of the truths that are written within. Religion is not about Alleluia – Praise the Lord, but about love and understanding, peace and joy. We are born to be happy, not to struggle and strive. I, too, have had to re-learn. I, too, have had to alter the rules by which I live life. In recognising the truth of the here and now we bring to life a living God that is here, by our side, every waking day of life. He communicates by thought. He listens to our needs and he helps us every step of the way. He does not need our wonder and our awe. He does not need our worship. He only asks for love - for our

154

reconnection. We are to recognise that he is our friend, our provider, our caretaker. He is a living God that is not light years away on another plain, but right inside, beside us here and now. Belief is not an issue or a stipulation and God is just the name we know him by. He does not require devotion, only recognition. He does not need belief, because life will prove his existence. He hears all the thoughts we ever think, but often he can do nothing to help because we are closed. We are closed to all influence except our own thought. But how can a baby raise itself? How can a child know what is best. It needs an elder for guidance and so do we. We are children until the day we die, each living his own experience, his own interpretation of life. We can look back with pride, or we can look back with sadness, but we do look back. The help and the love we need is with us every moment, we need only understand it exists.

Only you can wake yourself up. Only you can now live your life as you would like to live it. Don't be sad or worry about what you did yesterday. We all make mistakes. We all do bad things. We have only made wrong choices and would a parent ever turn his back on his child because of the things he did before he knew the truth? A good parent would not. He would always give a loving hand to be taken. And we are just the same. We did what we did because for whatever reasons we found ourselves doing it at the time. Now we can start again. We can live each day as though it is our last. We have been given a clean slate to write upon as we wish. Don't waste this opportunity, this chance. Open up your life to allow the love that is yours to enter. If you don't it will wait quietly by your side until you can. Only man can find this truth that exists because truth itself can never be altered. Truth withstands the test of time and man's opinion of it. At this time in history the truth has never been so clear and obtainable. It is erupting out all over the place in every walk of life. Truth can stand

155

on its own two feet and cross-examination is unable to sway its evidence. God is manifesting himself more and more as the weeks go by, and each time he does he opens another doorway or avenue of exploration and wonder. Science up to now has adequately explained the 'hows' of life, but only spiritual investigation will explain the 'why'.

A long time ago it was decided that investigation and truth of the spirit and the after life should be left to the church to explain and to show us the way. It was decided that the only important truths could be seen and felt and touched. It was left to science to lead us forward and to explain all that we needed to understand. And so it was. But man is not only a mixture of chemical and substance and neither is the Earth itself.

Life cannot be explained by science. Its essence lies far outside man's understanding. Life exists in all things and all things exist to make life. Science has still a long way to go before it can explain the presently unexplainable and man's teachings have far to go too.

Only today has man ever had the freedom of free thought and speech that is widely evident, and even this is still localised in terms of the earth's size and scale. We have never been so able to source the reality of truth for ourselves, yet we have never been so lost and alone either. Only we can take the next steps that will lead us to a brighter and more fulfilling future, regardless of what that might mean on an individual level.

The whole of the life you have lived until now, has only brought you as far as you are, so it stands to reason that making it better will take a little while too. But don't panic and give up before you begin. Things are not as black as they would seem. Step by step, little by little, you will notice the difference. Almost immediately in many cases, but the more deeply rooted your problems the longer they will take to solve. Rome was not built in a day but it was built, and it still stands tall and proud today. Don't give up

– just slowly go forward to the future that awaits you and your family.

Only you can take the next steps, but to do so you need to know where you have been going wrong, or perhaps what you could do a little better than you might know right now. Only you can know your own truth. Only you can work to find the solution. No one else knows the thoughts you think (well no one here anyway!). You carry that load by yourself, all day and everyday. We are good at carrying problems from days to months to years, and because we do it, others assume we don't mind, that we are happy with the life we have. Often their first inkling that something may be wrong is when we become ill, or we blow a fuse from here to kingdom come, then they look up in amazement and wonder. Yet the truth of the matter is probably very different. We could have been on overload for months, even years in one way or another. People are simply used to seeing us the way we are. They don't notice the pressures building, because they are busy maintaining their own. Have you noticed that when disaster strikes everyone has the same symptoms? Everyone suddenly says 'it's funny you should say that because…!' We are all in the same boat, but we are good at carrying on regardless.

Only you can make the decision that enough is enough, whatever that decision may relate to. It might be in business, in finance, in love, or in family affairs, but whatever the subject we have reached the end of our line. Our children are so used to seeing us struggle that they believe life is really like that, or the alternative is that we hide these things away from them and they think life is easy. But it is not - for anyone. Problems and troubles are problems and troubles, no matter how we dress them up or how they are presented to us. Only we can break the mould by living in the light of truth as it occurs.

Only truth can set us free, but in order for it to do so we must recognise when we are stuck in illusion. Often we are

157

far happier living a lie than we are facing reality, so we bury our heads in the sand and wait for something to change by itself or through the actions of another. We don't like change because it makes us feel uncomfortable and we don't like confrontation either, so we sit and wait and stew in our thoughts and in our minds. We leave signals poking out all over the place that we think are as clear as day, but when no one notices we get mad because we believe they don't give a dam. We falsely believe they don't care and that they are unfeeling or nasty towards us, but again the truth is often the opposite. They have probably got their heads stuck in the sand as well. They, just like you are refusing to look at the issues they must, so now both of you are in stalemate. Both are snapping and moaning at each other, both feeling perfectly justified, yet both on completely the wrong ends of the stick. The only way forward is to talk, to recognise that you are both the same and probably want the same thing. Two wrongs can never make a right until someone puts his blame down. Just ask God that illusion may be recycled. That truth, light and love may prevail overall. Ask that the words you both need to speak be given to you and then simply watch this space. Very quickly, without effort, all will be out in the open and all you need do is speak kindly to each other and listen to the words being said.

In every conversation when two or more speak we fight for the same space. We are all fighting to be heard. Just speak one at a time and hear each other out. Often this is all the situation will need. If tempers start to hot up – walk away for a moment, go blow your nose or something, break the cycle, and when you resume, it will be on equal footing once more. Even if you don't agree with what is being said – mentally ask for guidance and help. Ask that love will prevail, even if it seems a long shot at the time. Ask and wait and see what happens. You may be pleasantly surprised. As long as you have spoken your truth, the truth as you know it to be, then you should have nothing to worry about. Don't retaliate with anger, because anger can only feed the problem with negativity, just as you can't put out fire with fire to gain a favourable outcome. Patience, truth and love are the keys that work best, regardless of the situation at hand.

Communication is a difficult thing and it is open to infinite interpretation and misunderstanding. Given the individuality of the population and the infinite thoughts and words available to us at any one time, trying to make a connection is a very tricky business. Man has billions of thoughts that cross his mind in every waking hour. These combined with the moods we feel produce the words and actions that we present. This is how we become open to variation and mistakes. Only by chance do we ever get the connection completely right. The law of the power of speech is infinite. The words we choose to select are totally dependent on our discrimination of the moment at hand and this is itself open to variation and debate. Communication is an art. It is an art that is born from infancy – providing the setting was correct at home. Many people are afraid to voice their opinions for fear of reprimand or reprisal. They are scared to go their own way and do their own thing. They find it far easier to follow the opinion of the majority or the crowd. They are used to following instead of exploring and leading themselves in their thoughts and the things they do.

Life for many is a game of follow my leader and providing this is your choice by option, then that is fine. Only you know inside whether you are a leader or a follower, whether you like to make your own decisions or you follow the route that others have proven first. You know if you are good at reading people and situations or if you prefer to shy away from the hustle and bustle of main steam life. Only you can make the necessary alterations within yourself to allow you to go your own way,

159

regardless of the opinion of the people around you. This is your life. You are here to live it – to the very best of your ability. Only you will stand alone to answer for the missed opportunities that you let slip through your fingers. We are not only responsible for the bad things we have done and caused others to do – we are also answerable for the good that we have missed. No one will stand over you with an axe to punish you: you will do that for yourself. You will regret the things you could have done – but did not. You will be sad for all the missed opportunities that came your way. No one will punish you. You will just kick yourself.

This life we have here is a gift. We chose to come. We came not only to live the experience as fully as we saw fit, but perhaps to achieve a few things along the way. We alone are responsible for the life and the time we have spent and for the loose ends that we leave behind. The world would not be a better or a worse place without you having been here, but the fact is that you are here. You are living in this space and you have a function to perform. Man is the manifestation of God himself. We are not meant to be perfect because we are human beings and it is in our nature to get things wrong. Being perfect is the function of God, but we should come as close to perfection as it is in our nature to be. Yes, your past is probably a mess, but it is what it is. A child without guidance would never become what it could – or should, and so it is with us. We have had free reign over our life and look where it has gotten us. Ask now for guidance. Ask for all the help under the Sun. But ask. Ask in the silence of your mind, with the love that is in your heart. Only you can feel the difference when you do. Ask and you will be given. Seek and you will find. These words are taken from the Bible but they are not without meaning. They are truths that have been buried for far too long. Only you can take the hand that has always been extended towards you. You need only recognise that it is there. You can make the life you have finally work for you. It is your right to be happy and all the powers that be will help you if you can learn to let them.

Now it is up to us to take the next step that is applicable to us on our journey because only we know the truth of the situation we are in. We can show any face we wish to the world, and nine times out of ten we can get away with it, but you can never fool yourself or your maker. The blue print of your life stays with you for all of your life. It is who and what you are. It is all you have ever been, but only you can grow into what you are likely to become. It is all up to you and you alone. It is here that all things must begin and end. It is here where the world we interact with is born. All thoughts begin and end in each of us, from the first one to the last, and it is because of those that we do the things we do. We are the authors of our own scripts, our own lives. I, too, am still in the throws of this lesson each and everyday. Life has a way of letting you know exactly where your failings are, and if we can't learn those lessons ourselves, we have to learn them through the interaction of others as we watch them suffer through their mistakes. Life places us exactly where we need to be at any given moment because there is more to it than we know.

Only man can make this world better by love and with greater understanding of the world both within and without himself. We have travelled through eons of time and science has explained a lot, but now it is time to look at a different picture. It is time to recognise and understand our part, the part we play on an individual level. It is time for us to pull all the pieces together - the way that was intended by God. God is not fiction. It is not some fantastical religious raving by a society of Bible Bashers. God is real and it does exist. Before radio waves and sound waves we did not know of such a thing. We could not see them until we suddenly could, and the same is so with God. God is just the name that was given to him/it. Buddha, Allah, Mohammed, etc., are all names that relate to the same.

161

There are many paths that go up a mountain, but there is only one peak. All paths take you there and they may differ slightly, yet they are the same. They are all routes to the top and will get you to where you need to be. And so it is with us. We are all parts of the same thing – the all that is. We are all energy beings in a physical form, having a physical life experience. Our bodies are individual and our own, yet fundamentally they are all the same. Our energies are interconnected with the planet and with each other. The air in a house seems different from room to room, yet where is the split? There is none. It is all the same. It is all part of the air in that house. And so it is also with us. We are energy beings in individual bodies, but ultimately we are all part of one big whole and can never be anything else. We are joined without even realising.

Life is not a game of chance, of haphazard events and blunders. It is for real. It is very much a piece of art in motion. We do not drift along in our daily events at the mercy of all and sundry, it is instead a well planned, well thought out affair. We are like symphonies in motion, where each word, each thought and deed must play its part in the weaving of the final picture. We are not disconnected and alone from each other, but very much a part of the whole thing. We interact together everyday of our waking lives. It has always been this way and always will be; only now we are learning to notice the rules.

In order to know the part we play, we must first understand one other and until we do, we shall remain exactly in the place that we are, doing what we always have done and being who we always have been. In order for your life to get better you must first understand where you're at and to do that you need to come back to reality. The truth is always plain to see because it is the bottom line. It's the 'what is – without question' in your life. You must take a look at where you are now from behind the scenes. Go to the bookshop, to the self-help section. Have a browse, see what takes your fancy and go home. Kick off your shoes, get a cup of coffee or tea and sit down and read. This book is not just a book. It is the start of a journey that will take you in words to discover who you really are, why you are here and why you react the way you do to life. It will begin to tell you truths about yourself that you did not even consider, and the best part is that it cannot argue with you – or you with it. Only you can understand the deeper meanings behind what you read and you will put away ghosts that have been with you forever. You will open up like a flower, or a seed in sunlight as understanding will course through your veins, and slowly, slowly you will begin to rebuild what years of hardship, and struggle, and unloving has stripped away. You will get back to the person that you really are and always were – only most of the world did not know. We have become so good at doing the things we do that we don't even know ourselves. Or perhaps we never did...

You owe it to yourself to take another shot at life. To start again with a better understanding of where we are, where we've been and where we would like to go. If you keep on doing what you've always been doing, you will always get what you've always got. For something to change – we must change, not outwardly in appearance but inwardly with insight and understanding. Life is what you make it, so unravel the chains that have kept you where you are.

Only we can make the decision to make life work with us rather than against us. It is up to us to take the steps towards a greater understanding of it. How can we expect to be happy when we give so much of ourselves away unnecessarily? We almost invite misfortune to our door, everyday, without even knowing yet how can we know we do this until we learn? How can we expect others to treat us with the love and respect we deserve when we are our own worst enemies?

163

Life will come to our aid but first we must learn a better way to connect with it. Force, fast change and panic are not necessary. Just do what you do as you always did, but in the meantime get some advice and learn about yourself and how others interconnect around you. Instead of picking up a chat magazine – read a book. Instead of staring blindly out of a window, read a book. Before you go to sleep for five minutes, read a book. There is no time we ever know all there is to know and we are never too old to learn. Life is ours for the taking. There is no magic formula. No quick fix and no easy rides. But there is a new day, a new page to write our life history upon. With a new perspective and knowledge gained we can make educated choices rather than haphazard guesses and mistakes, but above all we must never forget that we are never alone. Even in our gravest moments there is always help, strength and love standing by and all we need do is let it in through our mind, through our own private thought structures. Pain, worry and stress serve no purpose at all. They just make you irritable, miserable and ill. If you don't want to keep them any longer – then learn to let them go. Ask that all you don't need be lifted from your shoulders and recycled. Ask for love, light and energy to replace it. Just ask.

Life will not always be plain sailing, because that would be boring and make us stale, but with each passing day it will get smoother and it won't be your imagination. I, too, have had to go through this. It is hard – yet it is surprisingly easy. Once you begin just allow the changes to happen. You will be helped if you ask – and only if you ask, every step of the way.

Only man can help himself. So it is written and it must remain this way throughout his life.

Chapter Eighteen

The Winds that Live On

Man is a physical being. He is also an energy one. The two must combine to produce life within the body of matter. The physical body is grown in the womb for this specific purpose. It is the same for all things on the surface of this planet. All things grow into the final shape that we see and all things have their purpose, apart from decoration and existence. Man is not different. He, too, has a purpose upon this earth and it could not be otherwise. Man is designed to be keeper of this planet. He is the only species with intelligence beyond that which he was born with. He is capable of lifting himself far above his original birth state, to become anything he could possibly imagine. He is king of the world he surveys, not by presumption and greed but by design. He was made specifically to fulfil this role. That is his reason for being here.

Each and every man is the lord of his own castle, ruler of his own affairs. He has intelligence and free choice. He is master of all he can wish to achieve. He was born to live a physical life and experience any part of that life he could wish for. There are no rules, no boundaries and no regulations that can starve his need for growth. He alone is capable of anything his mind can imagine or desire. Everything in his life up until now has first been wanted or desired by him, first as a thought, then as a dream, then as reality. This, too, is the nature of life.

Only he can pursue the route he would like his life to take. He can make a million different choices and he can try them all, but only he can have the final say in the actual direction he settles upon to live. He has done this many times already along the course of his own life. He can see the evidence all around him. He has lived it through the years he has been here already. But the question that faces him now is whether or not he is happy with his choices. Is he happy within his very being, because if he is not then he needs to reassess the situations his life is currently living. There is no reason that he should not be content given the fact that his life was his choice, but how often do we make those choices and regret them later? How often are we disheartened and unhappy with the life we have worked hard to achieve? We believe we are at the mercy of others. We blame them internally for the fact that we are where we are. Only we forget that nine times out of ten we chose it at some point for ourselves. It is not their fault that things are not as we expected them to be and vice versa. You cannot be blamed for the unhappiness of another, providing you are not directly responsible – but that is another matter in itself.

Only we can stand our ground and work steadily towards what we believe. It is up to us to stand up for ourselves and for what we think is right – but not to the point of nastiness, butchery and war. None of these things are ever necessary. They themselves symbolise all that we are stepping away from. They themselves represent nothing but a total lack of self control and respect for fellow men. Only love and kindness can take us forward to the place we now need to be. Not the sissy 'flower, wimpish' love, but the solid love with respect and kindness that stems from a place deep within us all. Only we can tap into this connection. We are the only ones who can do what it will take to get us where we need to be, which is to find the peace of mind and contentment that is ours for the asking.

Only you can find the truth and the happiness that exists within the locked chamber of your heart. A long time ago you shut those doors tight, to keep you safe from the harm that you came across in the outside world. It was when you were young that you learnt that the world was not always a kind place to be in. You learnt very early through survival and self-preservation, to keep part of yourself locked away for safe keeping, far out of harms reach. You learnt to read situations and people that you found yourself interacting with. You learnt what to show to the world and what not to, for the sake of peace and quiet, or for the sake of your own self-respect. Only you can know the truth behind those statements because only you know the different parts of yourself that you have placed out of reach, out of view from the world and yourself. The problem is that we are who we are. We are all that we are and we cannot remove any part of ourselves without affecting the person we have become. We are all that we are because of the past and the life we have lived. Any part that we would not have experienced would make us a completely different person. All we have been throughout our life was a necessary part of who we became. We cannot be perfect because we are not God, but we are human and it is our nature to be both good and bad at some time in our life. I, too, have been my fair share of both, but we learn our greatest lessons from pain and sorrow, tears and anguish. Life will lead us in many directions but it is up to us individually to discern which has the best outcome for us.

Steps in time

Life comes to us in stages. It is built up gradually, little by little, and stage by stage over time. There are distinct patterns that can be visible when we look to find them. Only man can decide if he has been fulfilled over these phases or not. Only he can honestly state if he achieved what he sought to achieve, or if when he got there it was flat and empty. Only we can know. Only we can be open and honest as we look back with an open heart and mind. Only we can decide if we made the best choices at the time it was necessary to make them. Only we can answer these questions and more besides, to determine the truth from

167

within and to understand that all we have been was so by choice - by our own permission and decision. Man is the only one who can pull himself out of the pits he has dug for himself whether they be financial, emotional, character, family or friendship based. Life is not over. It is not even half way through. From this moment in time we can begin again with a new day and a new frame of mind. Only we can make this change and this choice. Only we can do it once and for all. Make the difference that your life is crying out for – even if at this time you are not sure how. Do not worry any more, just calmly pull yourself up and out of where you are at this moment in your life cycle. Take charge and recognise this chance you have been given, so make it work for you. Be quietly resolved to it and don't do the things you would usually do that keep you where you are. There are other choices open to you at all times providing you go out to look for them. All is not doom and gloom even when it looks that way. Place your trust in the help that surrounds you on an unseen level and ask for guidance to come. Don't be too rigid in your expectation of what that help will look like, remember you are open to suggestion and new ideas. Sit tight for a while and allow life to unfold a little before you decide on the next step. Only you can do these things for yourself and to the majority even this will be a huge transition.

Man was energy before he came to birth here on Earth and he will still be energy after his time is spent. That part of you which is you is not in your arm, nor your leg. It is not your hand or your head. If you were to loose a limb you would still be the person you are, you would still be all that you are. You might be incapacitated but you would still be yourself. That part that is you is your consciousness. This is your life force, your soul. This is the essence of who you are and it is everything that you are. That part which is you is made of pure energy. It cannot and will never die. I, too, am such as this, as is every living creature on the planet. We are all living energy. We are all part of a living whole, a living Earth. Because of this only you can fulfil the part that you play along the course of your life span. You are individual. You are unique. Throughout the world there is not another soul such as yours. There is no other who has the same intelligence, life experience and expectations, no one with the same past, or the same destiny. Only you can fulfil your space in the scale of time. Only you can make the choices that will now take you on, further towards your destiny, your future and the rest of your life. You are an individual Son of God but you are an important part of the whole, the all that is and ever will be. Only you can come back to find the peace and quiet that awaits you in the corners of your own mind, the peace and happiness that you have searched a lifetime to find.

Now you can decide to find out who and what you are. You can look forward to where you want to be, but you should look back as well to better understand where you came from and to recognise the strengths you have obtained along the way. Even when you believe that your life was total doom, gloom, sadness, pain and hardship, you will be able to find surprising hidden strengths that you gained because of those circumstances. You will be able to read the past differently and with greater understanding. I, too, can relate to this because there were many lessons that today have stood me in good stead. Life is not all that you think it is. There is a host of activity that is invisible to the naked eye, and it continues in a constant stream of movement. You can begin to see this for yourself when you decide to open up to the truths that lie before you. Nothing is ever for nothing. All things occur for a reason, either for you or for the other person/people concerned. There is no such thing as a chance meeting, a chance conversation or a chance decision. Because life is a symphony in motion all things occur at the time they are destined to do so. Not before and definitely not later. You are at this point in your life because at this moment in time it is where you are supposed to be. Only with our wish can the creator change anything at all, so to instigate a much-needed change in our outlook to life we must plug into the whole once again. We must unblock the places that are blocked in our life and we must open ourselves to accept life's flow once more. This is not a fairytale, but necessity.

Only we can decide when we have had enough of the life we are living and in doing so we are not giving up – but instead quite the opposite. We are opening ourselves up to attract the help that we need. We are asking to be thrown a lifeline, so we may use it to bring us back to reality. We are saying that we have had enough of life, of the troubles and the strife. We have had enough of all the .... (rubbish) that is placed at our feet and we are saying we want out of the rat race that we presently call life. The life we have is often no life, but mere existence, and we have reached the time to sort ourselves out.

Only we can step off the merry-go-round of daily monotony to return to the basics, the reality of our life. Peace of mind, happiness and love have never left us – but instead it is us who have distanced ourselves from these things. We have herded ourselves down a one-way street and we have reached the end of our tether. Is that where you want to stay for the rest of your life, living hand to mouth, week-to-week, year in, and year out? Is that to be the sum of your achievement, the result of your hard life's labour? Only you can decide for yourself – by yourself. If you have had enough, then down your chains and get off the cyclone. Climb back to reality and look at where you are and what you are left with. Make the choice to find a better, easier way to live your life, to be your whole self and all that that entails. This book can sew the seeds that will start to instigate a change. It will give you some tools that will help you, but then only you can put in the time and effort that it will take to get you where you need to be. I, too, have travelled this road and since I did I have never looked back. Life is good. It is a joy to be lived everyday but first you must remember how.

You have to be open and honest with yourself, because you will have to be – to be truthful. Only you can know whether you wake up with a spring in your step or if each day is a chore, if it's hard going. Then you can decide if you want to stay where you are, as you are, or if you have now had enough of the pressures that surround you. Only you know if you want a happier, lighter life, where your perception of time will slow down and you can learn to laugh and have fun again. Only you know if you want to feel the love that is directed at you instead of the pain and negativity of others all the time. Only you can make the difference that your life is crying out for, but not with suffering and anguish – just love and a new way of looking at and responding to life. We have been stuck in a loop of behaviour and reaction, and it is now time to break free – for us all.

Only man can make the necessary connections that he needs in his life. Not outwardly but inwardly. He must reconnect his self with his own inner dimensions. He knows the world about him – inside out, but knowing and approving of his self is a different story. He knows too well all the times he has let himself down. He often forgets the many good and courageous things he has done along the course of his path. He connects far easier to the negative side of his personality than to the positive. It is far easier for him to take insults on the chin than compliments. He believes on some level that he deserves all he gets, but the truth is opposite. He deserves a good clean break in his life - a lucky streak. He needs to reconnect with the 'all that is' – to help his life run smoother than it presently does. Life is good. We should be glad to wake up every single day. It was not designed to be the chore that it often is.

Only man can love himself enough to allow a new day to evolve. I, too, must make a conscious effort to do this everyday. I, too, offer my day to new experiences, to new beginnings, to new opportunities and developments. Instead of rigidly sticking to the things you must do, categorise them and allow a little chance to take over. Step back just a pace and see what happens even though, because we are moving against the grain, it will not always feel comfortable. I, too, allow this to occur. When you begin to stress out over something, hand it up. Silently hand it over to your guardians that surround you. Ask that they recycle the problem and give it back in a way you can handle. Ask that you yourself be made as small as a grain of sand (so that all unnecessary energy fluctuations bounce right off you) and ask that your day may work better. Ask for the negativity and stress to be removed and ask that peace and love control the situation instead. Almost immediately the knot that was building up inside you will disperse. If another person is involved, quietly ask the same for them too. Ask that all things be as they should and quietly get on with your day. Often you will then forget about what you just did, but when you look back later the effects will be apparent. Life will be sweeter the more we had it up for help. I, too, do this twenty times a day when necessary. We can never do it often enough. The help that waits quietly by our side is ours by right of birth. It is up to us now to make use of it.

At the time of his birth, each and every person is designated a guardian angel – a spirit protector. This is someone who has previously lived his own life here on Earth and has proven his worth as a trustworthy character. This is not the same as a higher realm angel, but is instead your life long companion. The two of you will travel your time together until the time comes for you to separate. They are neither judge nor jury nor instructor to us in any

172

way because the life we live is ours by free will and choice. The guardian we have is merely our protector -our friend.

Man will need many helpers and inspirers during the course that his life will run. These and more are beings who have also lived their own time on Earth. These are beings who have gained valid experience in their own specific fields of knowledge and understanding. These beings will come close from time to time on man's right hand side to inspire and help in his times of need. They are the inspirers that will help only when their help is required or when it is called for. This is the work they have now elected to undertake and it is through their input, combined with mans that new inventions and ideas are born. It is a combined effort that will take man forward to a more balanced future and a more peaceful existence.

Man is energy in motion. His thoughts have more power than he can ever imagine. He will see the difference that recycling the negative stuff will make to his mind. He will notice how situations and arguments will be greatly reduced when he purposely brings his mind back to peace. The endless chatter and turmoil that we usually allow to churn over in our head will slow down and we will remain more in the truth of the present. Only we can do this for ourselves because only we know the thoughts that we are thinking. We alone must realise that our mind is like an arena. It should be clear of all except what is occurring right now. The rest is superfluous to requirement. Recycle your raging thoughts and bring yourself back to peace. Peace with your mind and peace with your day.

Man is the ruler of his life. Very often it would seem that he is a victim of circumstance but that is not strictly so. The circumstances that tie him down are regularly born of his own lack of attention in other areas. Usually he is given many signs that all is not well, but very often again he chooses to ignore those signals. I, too, am guilty of this but it is easy to bury your head in the sand and continue as you are. Putting something back into its rightful order means that we must stop what we are doing. We must reassess or excel our energy in another direction, but again we choose to wait, believing that tomorrow will be just as good. But often it is not. How many times do we wish we had tackled something yesterday because it would have stopped an issue coming to a head? I, too, have done this many times. It is not always easy to keep on top of life, especially when life is busy.

We must bring our focus of attention back from where it was, to operate fully once more in the time frame we are in. We must aim to do what needs to be done at the time it should, to get life back into order. Life is precious. Time runs through our hands like running water. Once it is spent, no amount of wishing can bring it back. We are so busy that we are missing life itself. It is not always easy, or convenient to take time out of a busy schedule, to do something a little different, something for you. It is easy to work and to work hard, because the work still will keep coming. It is harder to prioritise and keep a little time free for life itself, especially if this is something you normally would not do. Don't let it be that you look back in old age to see all the missed opportunities you could have had, if only you had taken the time to grasp them.

Only you can rearrange your schedule to allow a time slot for living. Man is used to there always being a tomorrow, but it is today that counts the most. If we learn to make today work for us, our tomorrows will suddenly free themselves up. That backlog of stuff that stands in our path now will be gone. I, too, am guilty of leaving things until tomorrow but tomorrow holds its own challenges and it would be nice to greet them with an open mind.

It is easy to slip back into past patterns of behaviour, especially when you must live your life around other people. It is hard to realise that they themselves are probably stuck too, but you are one step ahead. You can

174

choose to free yourself up because you are realising that there is a problem. People will always place demands on you, both in work and pleasure, but again it is up to you to stick to your guns, even when it makes them mad. At these times ask for help – mentally. Ask to be helped that you may achieve your objective. Don't be too rigid, but instead try to remain as flexible as you can. Be able to do what needs to be done but remain aware of the needs of others. Follow your inner guidance systems and you won't go far wrong. Providing you keep yourself small when you get up each day, you will not feel the onslaught of anger and negative emotions that others emanate. At all times keep yourself balanced and protected. Close your eyes and imagine a large old-fashioned set of pendulum scales in front of you. Look at them for a moment. They represent that state of balance inside you. Notice whether they are level or lob sided. Place the necessary brass weights upon its scale until it rests in perfect balance. This exercise should take only a few seconds to do, but immediately you will have centred yourself once more. Now carry on with your day. You can check from time to time that the scales are still level, especially if you work in a stressful environment. I, too, should do this exercise a little more often than I do. To remember to calm myself – especially when I become 'snappy' towards others. Being out of balance or out of sync with yourself, can happen at any time. You could start your day very well, then for no apparent reason things can change and the world will clamour all over the place about you. It is also easy to revert to over aggressive tendencies in retaliation, but don't give up. As soon as you recognise the fluttering of anxiety inside your stomach or your chest, simply bring yourself inwards once more. Imagine yourself as small as you could be and check the position of those scales.

Because we are energy as well as physical beings we are susceptible to the fluctuation of the moods of others around. We have already said that in reality there is little difference in the air from room to room in a house, it is all part of the same, it is joined. There is no break off point. Well, the same is said for us. Man is pure energy - housed in a physical body. It is the energy part of him that houses his body, not the other way around, as we would imagine. The part of himself that is energy extends at least a meter, if not more, outside his physical shape. It also enters the inside of his being. The part that is energy is merely denser inside his body and gets finer as it splays away from his form. It is like a gobstopper. The little black seed inside being man's form, while layer upon layer of energy exists round about him, in different colours and varying thickness. Man is walking energy and that part which is him is the blue print of all that he is, all that he has been and all that he may become. It is like a black box on an aeroplane. His energy is the record of all his movements, everywhere, all through his life. It shows where he has excelled; it shows where he became stuck. It shows his state of bodily health and his state of mind. It shows just how far he has progressed along the time that his soul has been in existence.

This energy has no boundaries or barriers. Just as the air within a room is not contained by the room, so it is with the energy of each one of us. It, too, has no definite cut off point. Like the clouds in the sky have their own shape, they also become part of the whole sky as they intermingle with each other, so it is with us. We are joined permanently with every one and everything. We, too, have no defining line other than our bodily form. As our energy pattern moves further away from our physical form it gets finer and finer. It blends into the surrounding space. Only we think that nothing exists in the space that we see between people, objects and all other matter. Only we think that what we can see with our physical eyes is the beginning and end of all that there is. Man can create anything. He can now grow bodily organs and complete beings at will, but these things can only operate with the divine energy that is a part of us. Only we think we control all things around us.

Only we think that all life begins and ends with us. We think we alone control all that we do, but this is not so. We are part of a much larger scale. Only we believe that we must scream and shout and badger our way forward to get where we need to go, but this is just the way we have grown accustomed to thinking. We believe all we have been taught to believe by people who in this respect knew little better than us. Throughout the history of man we have been taught to believe in only what we can see. What can be explained and touched and felt. We have been punished for believing that other things could and do exist. Only we can make up our own minds, because the truth is plain for us all to see and that is why man has been searching for the meaning of his life – through all of his life. That is why nothing has really sustained him, because deep inside his being he knew there was more. Man is much more than he can even begin to grasp. This is not a 'pie in the sky' statement; it is truth. This is also not a reason for man to become full of his own importance. It is a simple statement of the truth that is. Man little understands the role he must play in the scale of the universe.

Man is used to running his own show. He is used to making all decisions for himself, by himself. He thinks that he alone has control over the things he says or does. Man is not a pawn that the universe plays with, but a part of a larger picture and the things that he does are timed to perfection. No things will ever be completed before their time is right. All things must occur in order, and we do not always determine that order. A greater force, a greater help than we can at this moment comprehend, leads us.

Only we think that we alone are capable and responsible for all that we do. To a certain extent we are – through personal responsibility, but that is in itself a completely different thing.   We are completely responsible for the things that we personally do, both to others and to ourselves, but we are not completely alone in the tasks we undertake and the routes we choose to follow.   We are part of a greater whole and once we have decided upon a course of action, it is then that the universe collaborates to help us achieve it.   We get help from all sorts of directions and until now most people have been totally unaware of this fact.   Man is not the be all and end all of all that is; he is an integral part in the workings of this planet.   He is a cog in the workings of a well-run machine.   Only he can fulfil the place that he has just by being alive.   Only he can be all that he is supposed to be in this lifetime, just by being alive.   I, too, have had my purpose in the greater scale of things and it is not over yet.   Only we can fulfil the part that was allotted to us before we were born, before we were even a twinkle in our parent's eye.   We can fulfil our destiny, whatever that destiny might be and wherever it may take us, but one thing is certain, because only we know what our deepest hopes and desires are, only we can take up that challenge to complete the cycle of our being.

Before we are born we exist as pure energy.   We return to that energy state after physical death has occurred.   In between, we are energy having a physical experience.   We each came to Earth with the outline of a life plan that we would hope to achieve.   I, too, had mine and hopefully this book is part of it.   Many are part of a larger life plan as well as their own individual one and that is why some seem to excel more than others.   We are here to experience life in all the ways that we can, to enjoy everything that this world has to offer.   We are here to look after the planet and the things that fall into our pathway.   We are here to do all that we can, in anyway that we can, both for others and for ourselves.   Only we can know what that will entail for us. It might mean nothing more than the fact that you love and look after your own family, but for others it can mean a lot more. There are no limitations upon the things that we can do or be, but there is the problem of us getting stuck, before we even get to that part.

Man is stuck in a loop of behaviour that no longer serves his purpose. I, too, have been here and in some ways still am. It takes years of focus to undo all that we have become so good at doing automatically. But then we do have the remainder of our life to work these problems out. We are not perfect and we probably never can be (not in this life time anyway). I, too, must remember this because I, like many other people, am often far too hard on myself. We have already said that we are far more tolerant of other people than we are of ourselves.

We need to set the balance straight once more, but it will take honesty, time and patience. It will also take practice and focus. Life does not control us, it responds to us. We send out thoughts and unconscious signals every time we allow ourselves to think. That is another reason we must learn to control thoughts that chatter uncontrollably in our head. I try to practice this as often as I can, but again it is easy to forget and to slip right back into old habits. Aim to catch yourself out as frequently as you are able. The more you do the more you will focus upon the tasks and decisions in hand.

You can control your thoughts, although they are not as private or as silent as you think. It is only here on Earth that words are necessary; everywhere else thought is used for communication. Generated thoughts are heard like tannoy announcements on the spirit plain. Nothing remains wasted or lost. Only you can curb what you transmit, and perhaps now that you know that others hear your thoughts, this will begin to help you. It may be just the ticket you need to wake up to yourself, to the truths that surround us and always have. Don't just believe in that part of life you already know, go and search out the truths for yourself.

Today we have never been so free and able to find out whatever we wish. We are not punished for our beliefs or for the things that we do. The world has never been so tolerant about the individual needs of the people. We are free to move in whichever direction we choose, and in this country virtually nothing or no one stands in our way. The time is ripe for us to explore deeper the mysteries of the universe. Not in a historical, scientific sense but in a deeper, truer, spiritual one, and all our journeys should commence from within. Until we can learn to understand and accept ourselves, we can never achieve a true understanding of the rest of the human population.

Once we can begin to trace the truth of our evolution and understand it better than we do now we will trace the course of our individual unrest, right back to infancy and beyond. We have been brought up on patterns that run distinctly through our family trees. These patterns are forms of unconscious behaviour that have been passed down from generation to generation. Most of this we would deny given the opportunity but history can plainly show us the opposite. We cannot deny all that is plainly seen throughout the human story. The time is here for us to begin a new, not in a materialistic, technological way but in a gentle more understanding manner. Are we willing to see where this new opening will take us, or should we close our eyes and our ears? We can choose to stay exactly as we are. We can deny things as much as we like by burying our heads in the sand, but the world will still keep on turning around us. Sooner or later the universe will give us cause to catch up. The world cannot and will not stand still just because we might choose not to play ball. I, too, have learnt this many times along the course of my path. I, too, must watch and understand every step I take – to get me safely where I will eventually be. Life comes in stages of fluctuation – of clearing out old habits and beliefs that no longer serve their purpose. We are in a period of new growth and all that we see around us is a mirror image of this fact.

Only you can live your life, so your needs must be rearranged to fit you better. It is not for us to run away from our responsibilities and obligations but for us to live up to them in a more realistic light. We are simply taking off the blinkers that we have worn since our childhood, and in many cases, that have been handed down through generations. We are weeding out that which we no longer need or want and we shall feel a lot better for doing it.

Chapter Nineteen

The Winds that will Lead Us On

Only man can decide that he has had enough of the pain and turmoil that surrounds him both in his personal life and in the world at large. Only he can decide that the time has arrived to instigate some much needed change. It is time to move forward to the next level, we have exhausted this one. The only thing left for our children in this stage is to take all things to the extreme and as a society we can already see the effects that this will have. It is time to give back a little of what we have taken out of this world, not in monetary terms but in understanding, love and knowledge. It is time to learn about things that really matter and we owe it to ourselves as well as our children to learn all that is waiting to be learnt. The truths we shall find are not new. They are the truths of the universe that are as old as the planet itself. Yet to us they will be like diamonds. The truths we shall find will overshadow all that we have previously held dear. We shall wake up as if from a sleep and see the world the same, yet differently. We shall see others and ourselves without the masks that we have learnt to wear. Nothing will be hidden any more. People will not be able to cheat each other. They will recognise the truth at a glance. All things will be different, yet the same. We are about to grow up and out of the old ways that have held us down, ways that no longer fulfil our thirst for life.

Man is not born to live and then die. It is not for him to struggle in pain and sadness forever. There will be no finger pointing at him and his failings at the end of his days. There is no final chapter.

Only he can make the choice for himself that he wants to know more, because until he does he must carry on in the ways that he has. If the life he has suits all his needs, if he wakes up each morning happily fulfilled with his lot, then let him carry on. He will wake up when the time is right for him. Perhaps this life might not even be his time. But if like most of the world he is fed up and bogged down with the stress and pressures of his life, then it is up to him to find the alternative. The universe will help him in any way it can, once the decision has been made, but before then he has his free will. It is up to him to make his own choice. He has been given this life to live in any way he sees fit.

Only you can decide if you want to go on as you are or not, but remember that the world will not stand still around you. You are not being forced to make a decision. All things are entirely up to you. This is your life to live. Only you are responsible for it. If your life serves you well then keep it as it is, but the very fact that you could relate so well to this book indicates that all is not as it should be. All is not quite as you would wish it to be.

We can change our surroundings at any time, or our work, our home, our partners and our life, but we can never run away from ourselves. We are stuck with all that we are until we learn to look deeper, to find the flaws and errors that keep us exactly where we are once again. Only we know the truths that lie within us. We know the hopes and the dreams that we aspire to. It is only fair that we find the happiness that we deserve. Life is good. It is not supposed to be a chore that hangs over us for all our born days. Only you can decide if you must look at the way your life is going or if you will choose to stay as you are. I, too, had to make that move. I, too, had to look at what was keeping me —or drawing me back to stalemate once again, despite my efforts to alter this. I, too, found it necessary to put my life on hold. If you break up, what will it mean to others who depend on you? You are probably the main pillar of strength in your own corner of the world. If you fell apart would it serve any purpose? I, too, had to address these

183

thoughts and more besides. For me the best course of action was to do only what I needed to do for a while, to keep my life in tick over. When we have responsibilities to others it is necessary to meet those requirements, but after that use all your free time for study and growth. I, too, was bumped onto this road. I was handed my lifeline – one step at a time. I, too, was held by my hand, but not in a way that I knew at the time. All the help that I had (or most of it) came from an invisible source, at a time I did not even know it existed. All my help came from those who love and protect me. Only you can help yourself, but once this decision is made the universe will run to your aid. This thought seems somewhat pretentious, but I can assure you it is not. I am no more special than the next person. The help and kindness I received was no more spectacular than would be given to anyone else. I am not an angel. I, too, have lived my life to the full and have made more than my fair share of mistakes. I have unknowingly hurt others along the way, just as we all have. But I, just like you, am still worthy of being and finding happiness. It is our birthright. Once we can understand and accept this we can open ourselves up to allow the help that is waiting by our side to come in. The life we have lived is living proof that we don't always know what's best for us, even though at the time we would swear that we do. But there is always someone by our side who knows us better than we know ourselves. They have been with us our whole life. They are our guardian angels. They are not myth. They are fact, and more and more this is being proven.

Tuning into some help

At the time of our birth an angel is assigned to protect and guide us. They do not make any decisions but instead try to help and support us through the journey that lies ahead. This is not an angel with wings, as we would imagine, because after this physical life everyone who has

184

ever lived can be known as an angel. There are many, many ranks of angels, all with their own jobs and assignments, just as there are many people with different professions and roles here on Earth. The person assigned to us is chosen for the job before we get here. Not necessarily by us, but for us, for the properties that they have to offer to us. Depending on the route our life is to follow they are chosen for the skills they have. We are put together because we are in harmony on some level. Either they have the skills that we will need or we are able to help them advance along the course of our own life. This is a labour of love, of choice. If you don't grow – neither can they. If you grind to a halt, so do they. It is a two way relationship that has stood the test of time.

Only you can decide if you believe it or not, but then belief is not a necessary requirement. You cannot alter the truth by refusing to acknowledge its existence. Your angel will always be with you whether you want him/her there or not. There is no other alternative.

He/she is not there to judge you – and never would. Your life is for you to live in any way that you see fit, because it is your journey, alone. You are here to do all that you want to do, to be all that you want to be and to achieve all that you would like to achieve. You are here to experience this life in any way that you choose, but when you go back home you will have cause to look back to see where you have been along the way. There is no good and no bad. Only what is. Only what has been. You alone will decide if you have lived up to your own expectations, if you have lived up to your own requirements or not. You will decide if you fulfilled your objectives – or if you will come back someday to try again.

This is one of the reasons that *The Winds of Change* is so important. It will give us a chance to wake up in this life. To remember who we are and to try again, before we get back home. We can choose and re-choose the things we wish we had done better. Man does have a chance to try again, perhaps not with a completely clean slate but at least with an empty page. Each new day will bring forth new opportunities and new choices. We can continue along the path we are already on, or we can dance to a new beat, a new rhythm, and we hold the key. Instead of being dragged along by the flaws of his past, man can choose to step off the merry-go-round. With new understanding he can make new decisions, better alternatives. I, too, have been here and have come out the other side. When you are hurt or sad the world can seem a pretty cruel and scary place, and the people closest to you appear to have the sharpest talons. It is up to us if we let this continue, not just for their sake but for ours too. Without knowing how, we allow all these things to beat us down and it is only by better understanding that we can change the mould.

At the back of this book you will find reference to few of the many books that are available to help you. Pick a selection from those that grab your attention, and then notice what else comes into your view. Within these books are references to other books that will take you off on a course that is right for you. Don't forget that you are not alone on this journey. All you will need will be placed in your path, but in order to get it you must help yourself a little too. It is impossible to catch a lifeline without first extending your own arm. Only you can begin to see the life you have lived in a slightly different way. It is easy to feel like the victim of others but do we always recognise the lead we take to get us to that point? If we are always falling victim of others then somehow we are giving our own power away. Do you know how you do it? If you did then you would not be in that predicament in the first place. Life is not always against you, even if it may seem that way most of the time. During the course of your days you probably miss many signals and signs that could help you along, but because of your frame of mind they go

186

unnoticed. Life is not your ball and chain. It is not given that you may suffer and stress. Wherever you are now is where you are supposed to be – good or bad, but where you go from here is up to you. You only need the tools that would better serve your purpose. Books that you might read are just one way. They will place truths in front of you that family and friends could not. They will reach buttons and switches that have not been flicked for years.

When you understand what has happened to your own life, you will find the strengths that the traumas have left you with. Wisdom born from pain is the strongest lesson of all and if you can get past that, then life will unfold at your feet. Be ready and be able to read it correctly when it does. Don't wait for others to lead you, because most probably they don't know how. They, too, are looking for the answers to their own life's questions. They, too, wait for the time that their own boat comes in.

Only now are we evolved enough as a race to see behind the surface of human behaviour. Only now do we have the flexibility and ability to be our own person. Throughout history man has been more in tune with material success than he has with his feelings. He needed the chance to gain all he could before being able to see that it did not bring him the happiness he thought it would. Man needed to get where he is now, to come out of the other side. He needed to experience all he has, to better know who he is not. You cannot know where you are going until it is clear where you have been. You cannot give something up that you have not had in the first place. Only when what you have and where you are, no longer serves your needs, can you leave it gladly behind you. Only a rich man can give all he has away, because a poor man has nothing to give away. And so it is with most of us. You can't be who you will become until you are clear of who you are not. Life will always have cause to challenge your ideals, regardless of whether you want it to or not. By looking at life in a different way now – you are calling the shots. You are saying that from this point on you have had enough. You are picking up the reigns once more for yourself, by yourself. There will be no one else who can. You are the pillar of strength in your own life and probably in others too. I, too, had this made very clear, but not at the time by choice. Because this book needed to be born, the depths of my challenge was like water breaking free of a dam. I had no choice but to hold on and keep going forward, and it might be the same for you. Who knows what your destiny is, but you can be sure it will be a happy one.

Take the next few weeks and months out of your life to do a little soul searching and you will never look back. It is worth more to you than you could ever believe possible. You cannot switch your life to pause, but you can use all the free time you have if you believe it's worthwhile. If you think it's not, then you must be happily content with where you are. Then you are lucky.

Only we can put this world we love back in order, not by barging, pushing and conquering eachother and everything, but by understanding better the role that we alone play in it. I, too, have had a part to play, but by far the most rewarding is seeing my mountains of pain disappear. I have learned a softer smoother road to travel and it will only get better for the rest of my days. I have nothing that no one else has. I can do nothing that another person cannot do. There is no order of difficulty in a miracle, just the ability to recognise they do exist and to then let them in.

Man is already deep in a period of flux. He is caught up in the crossfire of all that is occurring around him, at work and in the world at large. Only he can now take charge of his kingdom. Life seems to be out of control, everywhere and for everyone. Only he can undo what is happening about him, but combined we can stop life from over loading. We alone are responsible for the future of the planet we live upon.

In the beginning the world was created. It grew up and developed over billions and billions of years. It was good. Man was also made, and over many years again he has progressed to the point he is at today. Man has now the role of God. He has superseded and over taken all that ever was. His boundaries are pushed to the limit. He is in the middle of a technological explosion. The world was created in the way it was. All life was balanced and in harmony. All things lived together – not always peacefully, but as they were supposed to be. If we look around us now we can see man's world. Man has made the world what it is. Because of free will, man will take the world forward to whatever heights he dares to climb. He alone sits at the helm of all his creations. He has forgotten that there is another side to life that needs consideration. Life is neither good nor bad. All things are simply as they are, but is this the way that given a choice we would want our world to be? The world is losing its life force. Man is draining away all its resources; all that helps it function in the way that is has since it began. It does not matter whether you believe that it was created by God, (the name for its original intelligent energy source), or whether you think it happened scientifically. The point is that it happened. We are living proof of an intelligent energy at work. All we survey is also living proof of the capabilities of this living energy force. Science merely explains the 'how' of creation. It is not the life force itself. You know the how of your own life – but you also are the life force behind it. Not your arms, nor your legs, but that part that is you - your soul. You and everyone else in the world are living proof of the existence of God. What more proof can we need? Are we so inconceivable that we are unable to see beyond our own bodies, our own world that we own?

We are living, breathing works of art. We are living, biochemical machines. This planet that we live upon, combined with God, has created what until recently we could only make in metal and wood. We are better than the highest technological, mechanical construction that we could ever dream of. We have spent decades attempting to recreate robots that can perform the tasks that we do naturally. We fail to see just how wonderful we are. Life is our oyster. We have simply lost our way.

Man has a lot to live for. He is up against the world, but more so − he is up against himself. He is his own worst enemy. The one who instils the most fear, doubt and negativity in his own being. He knows full well the things he has done wrong, the things he could have done better. He knows his failings and shortfalls inside out and he never forgets to remind himself of any of them. If he gains a compliment, he shrugs it off. If he does something well he believes he could or should have done it better. He can look at others and sing their praises, often from the heart, but when he looks at himself his eyesight begins to dim. He can see a million things that he is not happy with. All the days of his life will be spent dragging those things behind him unless he can stop long enough to shrug them off. Not dump them, but learn to let them go. He is the only one that needs to learn to forgive himself. God his maker and all that exist around him have seen past those faults long ago. They see him in the true light of his colours. They know the person beneath the behaviour and activity that is on display. We are who we are and the bottom line is that we are all the same. We were made that way.

There is nothing I can do that another cannot. The world we see is the same world that we all can see. Yes we might move in different directions and circles, but the world is structured that way. There is little and large, fast and slow, intelligent and no so intelligent in all things. I, too, fit somewhere in the middle. I am not stupid but I am not so cleaver either. I am all that I am but not yet all that I can be. I have the rest of my life to go the distance, but I know

I will. Yet many will not. They are totally or blissfully unaware that more exists apart from their daily strife. They are not happy but they have resigned themselves to the fact that they probably never will be. Their shoulders are drooped and their days are long and heavy. If only they knew the truth. If they only understood that they hold the key to their own happiness.

<u>Finding your way</u>
Only those who are willing to learn will find the truths they seek. They will find them according to their needs and beliefs. There are many paths up a mountain as we have already said, but they all will eventually reach the summit. The content of our findings will be tailored to suit our needs but at the bottom line the truth is the truth and no amount of coloration can change it. Each person has his own preferred way of learning. Some will read, some will listen to music or watch films. Some will merely walk and think. But along each route triggers will be met and you will be guided along the best path for you to take. Nothing is for nothing. There is a reason for almost everything. Only we can fit the pieces of our life into a slightly different order. Only we can make this life work for us – in the way it is supposed to.

Children grow and learn everyday. They learn of the past as they look to the future and live in the present. They can see the world as it is now better than we can. They can listen to stories of the past and shake their heads at the stupidity of it all. They will embrace the future with their own ideas and ways of doing things – just as we did. But wouldn't it be nice if they did not become as bogged down as we have? Wouldn't it be nice if by clearing away our own rubble – they could go the distance? Life is crying out for love and understanding, peace and normality. I, too, keep getting caught in the crossfire of events that are occurring all around, everyday. It is time to slow things down so that we ourselves might catch up on an emotional, spiritual level. Not spiritual as in 'Alleluia, Praise the Lord' but as in a realistic down to earth sort of level. Instead of racing through life with our feet on fire we should learn to walk once more. To enjoy the little things as they occur, before we miss the lot. Life is short and we shall be a long time on the other side of it wishing we had used our chances better.

Many moons ago a wise old man told of a dream he had. He told of things yet to come. He told of things gone by and he told of the bit in between. He told of bridges and of ladders. He told of mountains high. He saw the shape of things to come, but first he told of our ability to get there. We are a race of intelligent beings. Nothing is too tall or far or deep for us to cross. We can do the distance if we choose, but choose it we must, for ourselves, by ourselves. There is no knight in shinning armour coming to your rescue, only plain old common sense and a new way of thinking. This new way is not new at all. It is as old as the hills, but we have simply forgotten it. We have forgotten our roots, our origin. We are so good at striving forward, of achieving all we want that we have forgotten to look if we have got there yet. The start/finish line was crossed by man a long time ago. Our race has been won. All we need do now is to find ourselves once more.

Only we can slow our pace. Only we can relearn what we already know ourselves to be true. Only we can break the cycle that we are caught up in, but we are not alone. On some level or another all of humanity is locked in the same boat. We just don't know how to get off.

If we are sincere in our efforts we shall get back on track. The world seems to be falling apart, but we can stop it if we want to. At this moment in time many of us don't know how. We are fighting for our well-being – holding on for dear life. We are not quite sure where it is going to end. I, too, am at the same juncture, but I am lucky. I already have

192

hold of my lifeline. I already know where I am going. And you can be the same – if you only try.

Only you can shake yourself out of the place that you have nestled for years. Your life might not have been working properly, but you, too, have played your part. You have been happy to stay there, even though you didn't realise. How often do we rather face the hardship we have grown to expect rather than face the uncertainty of the unknown? How often do we moan and groan but still do the same things over and over again? Only you can step out of the habits you have acquired, but to do so you must first recognise their existence. Don't make any rash alterations at the moment. That is not what this exercise is about. It is more about waking yourself up to the little things you do day in and day out automatically. It is about recognising how you help to keep yourself exactly where you are. We all do it and our parents and grandparents probably still are too. Just because your life has dealt you a rough ride does not mean that you have to curl up and take it. You are probably not living to your true potential. Life has a habit of moving you slowly into positions you would rather it not. Life is not a game and we are not its pawns. We are the masters of the life we have, not in a commanding, domineering way, but in a quieter, more refined way. We have a new page to write upon everyday and whatever we choose to put there is up to us.

Only we can decide where we go from here. Perhaps this book has engaged a sleeping connection within you. Perhaps you have an unexplained excitement waking up. That is only normal. You are being shown a window of opportunity - a new lease of life. At this moment in time probably nothing has changed in your life at all, but you have. You have already begun to change the way you look at it. Perhaps you could use this newfound freedom to search deeper into yourself. If you keep on doing what you have always been doing, and thinking the same thoughts, you will soon be right back where you were before you read this book. You will just get what you have always got in the way life operates for you. Don't waste this change that you can feel inside. Take it onto the next step. Keep on going forward. Don't slip back into old patterns as you normally would. Be more aware of the things that are going on within and around you. Take time out to read a little, to explore new depths that until now have merely been sleeping within you. I, too, have been here. And I, too, am still going forward. I am the same person I always was, but with a little or a lot more besides. The life you are living now is probably not your full lot. Find the keys within yourself and make the difference that only you can.

There is another twist to this too. We have lived until now in the best way we could. All our lives we have tried our best to please others as well as ourselves. Only you can know if your efforts have paid off, but what about our children? They only know what we have taught them and what they have seen and put together for themselves. By not removing the baggage we carry around we are also pilling it onto the shoulders of our offspring. How many times do we hear the expression, 'The trouble with you is that you are just like your mother/father'? We repeat patterns that we have been subjected to, even when we try our utmost to stop. This is the way it has been for generations, all the way back along our own family lines. As each generation grows up they are either the same – or the opposite of what they have experienced for themselves. Then as the next grows up they, too, choose the same or the opposite. Eventually we get back to where we were. We are stuck in a loop of behaviour and response that we are oblivious too. The only way to break the cycle is to make your own changes from choices that are born within. By learning more about yourself, you can make more of a choice in how you now respond – not react to the world - to your world - the one that you live and operate in. You can

194

make educated choices instead of worried, frightened, hurried ones. You can drop your haphazard approach and work out what is really best for you. Only you can make the choices and decisions that you come across each day. It is not for our helpers to make those for us. The life we are living is our life alone. We have a free reign over every word, every thought, and every action we undertake. We alone must take our life forward to the next stage that waits for us. The choice is ours. We can stay as we are for all eternity if we choose, but the point is that this is not necessary. If we are true and kind in our dealings, in our hearts, then there is no reason that we should remain in pain and hardship until we die. The lessons that we have not learnt here simply await us as we cross over into the next life. Yet there is no next life – only continuation of this one. We can never be what we are not, so we may as well use this opportunity to grow here and to retake some choices that we have passed over before. In allowing ourselves to put our life into better order here, we are also helping each other. The more we open up the more open people can be with us. There are no holes barred. Life is ours for the making – not the taking. Only we can make the choices that will take us to where we need to be, but to do so in a new light we must first relearn the basics. And by doing this we will have a better chance of re-evolution. I, too, have been here. It is surprising how your thoughts, especially misshapen ones, can falsely colour the things that we see, hear and feel. We do not always hear things in the way they were meant. We sometimes see what we want to see rather than the truth as it really is. And our feelings, how often do these get mixed up from bad news, sad films and music etc? How often are the things we feel overwritten in an instant by the deeds of others? How often do we fly into a rage at the drop of a hat and let it spoil something we have been looking forward to for weeks? Which of these senses shows us the truth? None of them do. They <u>all</u> depend on far more than we give them credit for. I, too, have made many mistakes and have hurt myself as well as others, simply because I was following my feelings. Our feelings are capable of taking us a million miles out of reality, without us even knowing. We are simply living a truth that does not exist – except in our head. How often when we are confronted by the truth are we ashamed? How often can we hardly believe the things we have done, simply because we saw life in one way and not another? We are being given an opportunity to begin again, on a surer footing. Yes, there may be repercussions for some as they let old behaviours slip away, but what about your own peace of mind and your own self-respect? How much does it mean to you to sleep soundly at night? To know that the life you are now living is to the very best of your ability. How much can it mean when you are being offered a new way forward? I took it, because I was fed up of hurting. Life was cruel and I wanted it no more. There were people who needed me too and who depended on me, and I knew that if I cracked up then it would also affect their world too. I felt that I owed it to them as well as myself to pull myself out of the place that I was – inside, not outside. Life should never make you feel worthless. It should be a pleasure to know that because of you this world is a better place. And it will be.

Each of us has a special function - a theme that only we can fulfil. We do matter and the way we feel matters much more than we know. Only the conceited could ever think that they know it all. We can never know all there is about ourselves, at least not in this lifetime. The more you learn the more you realise how much there is yet to learn. We are all in the same boat.

Only you can learn to see that all things are not always as they may seem, that all of life does not flow as effortlessly as we believe. There is a book inside us all, perhaps not like this one, but one that will share experiences that are unique to you alone. We are all works of art and we have not been finished yet. Do you want a say in the finished article, or are you fine with others and life calling your shots? When you stand up in front of your maker will you be pleased with the result, or will you try to hide most of it? No one will judge you. You will do that for yourself – by yourself.

When we are children we make mistakes because at the time we don't know any better. Then when we learn we stop doing those things that we did. But when we grow up we are still often as children. We have not learned by our mistakes and still repeat them over and over again, even when we know better. At what point in our life do we grow up? And who determines what we have and when it will be? There is no trumpet call. There are no exams to take. It is just assumed that we know how to look after ourselves and so we do. Little by little, if we are lucky, we grow and learn along the way, but only in the directions we come across, only if we are open to the experiences that cross our path. For the rest of the time we continue as we are, in the way we always have, until we meet a hick-up. Then we pass it in whichever way we can and continue as we were once more. How do we ever know when we have finally grown up? The answer is that we don't. Many people are still like children until the day they die. They have the same tantrums, the same moods. They have the same likes and dislikes and will do – or not do the same things. As a race we don't welcome change very easily. We prefer to stay with the devils we know rather than face new problems of those that we don't. It is hard to see past a looming obstacle. It is hard to know which path to choose for the best, but a little more understanding within ourselves, will always point a clearer picture. We can learn to read the signs from another viewpoint, not just the way we always have.

With a little time and effort we can make the difference that our life is crying out for. Not by blame or by force, but by understanding how and why we are back at this point. Why others behave as they do and what are the motives that are driving them. What they say is not always what they mean, just as you yourself colour your words to suit the understanding of the person you are speaking to. The signals we think we are giving are not always as clear as we intend. They are often completely misunderstood and we wonder why. I, too, can relate to this nearly everyday – even now. But unlike before, it does not pull on my emotional cords. I am able to see and hear better the truths that are being told.

Only you can look to see if all is as it should be in your life. Do those around you appreciate you as they should? Do they understand all you are trying to achieve? You can only be who you are, but do others see that? Do you let others pull your strings and push your buttons? Do you dance to the sound of your own tune or are you caught up in theirs? Only you can answer these questions and more besides. Are you true to yourself? If not then it is time to explore why. It is time to know better how you got to where you are and then how you move away from there. Life is full of as many positives as it is negatives. Which do you attract? Do you know how or why? The answer for me was that I did not know. Life was calling more shots than I was, and I was always on the not so sweet receiving end. This is no more. Yes life is good and bad as a mixture, but the lows are never as deep as they were and I can pick myself up far easier when the need arises. We don't always have to be so brave, but we don't always have to scream and shout either.

Looking within

Only you can look into the workings of your head. I, too, had to do the same. During youth we set the basic behaviour modes that ordinarily will take us safely through life. We learn how to act and interact around others. We learn how to behave and how not to behave. We put together all the building blocks that will help to make us who we are. But even in a loving family environment mistakes can be made. I, too, should know this. Each member of every family will view the world in their own way. Even when children are treated the same, the very fact that they came in a different order will play a huge part, much larger in fact than most of us give credit to. Parents ordinarily do their best to give their offspring all the love and support that they need, but once again we have never been trained for the job. Mistakes are made left, right and centre. Out of love we do the most things wrong. Out of love we hurt each other without realising almost everyday. So how do we stop? How can we find out where the mistakes are being made? Most of us don't, that is unless we are lucky. Most of us have to live with the result, whatever that may be, through adolescence and early adult life.

Only we can ever love our children enough to find out the mistakes we are making. Is it fair to simply try our best and then leave our children with our mistakes? It is they who must learn to live with them, or to painfully put them right in adulthood. Only people who love their children will go out of their way to source and correct any problems that exist within themselves. Many of the things that go amiss lie in the way we view daily life; in the way we act and react with it. Children not only have to face their own lessons in growing up; they live through their parent's baggage and emotional crossfire as well. They spend a lot of time ducking and diving the moods of the adults that surround them. Is this completely fair to them? They love us, and because of this all-complete love, are led in many directions that they really have no need to travel. The sincerity of their desire to please takes many forms and it is up to us to channel that to the best advantage for the child itself, but how many of us as parents realise this? How many times do we use this desire to our own ends instead? Our children, just like we, are moulded into little versions of the adults they look up to. Is this what we want for them, or would we prefer that they grow up into complete individuals within their own right, to follow their own dreams and creativity? We owe it to the children we love to get our parenting techniques and ourselves in order. We all make mistakes. That is part and parcel of being human, but it is up to us to find how deeply these mistakes lie and put them right. Only we can do this for ourselves, for our own peace of mind and for our own futures.

Life as we know is not always as straightforward as it may seem, or indeed as we would like. Even when we are ourselves in order, it is easy to get knocked back off course by the troubles and anxiety of others, especially when those others live closely with you. I, too, can vouch for that, nearly everyday. It is difficult to remain centred; especially when fear and anxiety are knocking their loudest to come in. I, too, am here more often than I care to be, but you cannot stop life from turning around. The only thing we can do at these times is to remain small and attentive to that which must be done. Try to let the storm pass as painlessly as possible, especially when it is not really in your nature to do so. People have the right to come and go through your life as they will. Sometimes they create havoc around you but if you remain small and calm – against all the odds, you will not be caught up in their wake. We know inside if we have contributed to their distress or not, but in all cases we must ask for help. We must ask that it may pass as easily as possible for all involved. Ask that all negativity is recycled and that it be replaced once more by love, light and understanding. We are the only ones who can do this when the need occurs, and it has more effect than you realise.

In times of stress it is easy to let the strength of our emotions take over and toss us onto a wild and turbulent sea of fear and worry, but this is itself perpetuating. We fear because we are worried and because we are worried we feed on our fears. Notice when this roller coaster has you in its grip. As soon as you realise, try to get off, try to calm the storm that's raging within and bring yourself back to the moment you are in. Try with all your might to let go of these thoughts. Recycle the issue and once again face the task you are supposed to be doing. Ask that your worries be lifted and ask that they be returned if necessary in a way you can handle. Ask that the solutions be made clearer to you in the next few days or sooner if possible, but above all try to keep yourself in the love mode. Ask that the worry be lifted from your shoulders and that you may continue as you must.

Negativity is a powerful force. It engulfs all the unsuspecting. It can take an otherwise ordinary, perfectly fine day and turn it upside down. It can rip you to shreds along with your confidence and your peace of mind. Negativity is a product of the Ego. It never fails to let you know how indigenous you are. It tells you - you are useless and stupid. It tells you that you are being used and that you are stupid to let it happen. It tells you a multitude of useless negative thoughts that have no use other than to feed your doubts. The Ego is what keeps you down when in reality you need to be uplifted. You need to be helped out of where you are, not pushed further into it. Recycle all these things as soon as they arise that you may no longer be held captive by those chains.

The truth is quieter, less obvious. You are where you are because at this moment a few things need addressing. If you sit down quietly with an open mind, if you stick to the task in hand, slowly the thoughts that can help you will filter through. No one is deliberately pulling you down. You just need to reassess, to redraw a few of the things you do. Perhaps a few things are out of date. Perhaps a lot of things are out of date. But you can be sure that something needs addressing. Stay in the love mode and it will become clearer, faster, than if you stayed in the stressed one.

The future stems from the present not the other way around. When we become fearful, it is because we are looking too far ahead. We are worrying about what might happen and trying to fix it before it occurs. This in turn sets the present amiss, because we then alter what would have taken us to a better point had we not altered it. When we worry and fix things before they arise it is like trying to set a bone before it is broken. We are doing something that does not need doing. We are interfering with the flow of life and are chasing our tails for nothing. We cannot get to where we are going until we get there; and before we do many more steps need to be taken in between. Life does not go from A – Z in one foul swoop, it takes days and weeks. By trying to pre-empt a problem before it arises we don't always take into consideration natural progress and growth. Things alter with time and it is easy to forget this. Yes, there are specific times when it is necessary to plan for time further ahead, but in these cases that is obvious. When we keep on changing our goal posts because of fear, we alter a whole array of things that will actually draw us closer to that which we fear. In all probability if we had left things in place, natural progression would have taken us close to where we needed to be. All things cannot occur before their designated slot in time. Because we are running so fast to keep up we forget that time must take its own course as well. As a nation we are trying to run before we can walk and we are upsetting the apple cart in the meantime. In order to put things right we must slow down the whole process of life a little. We want everything fast, but this just does not work as it should. All things in life must take their time to manifest, and our greatest role model is nature. Nature has perfect timing for all things, yet even that we are altering with science.

Be positive

Only we can bring ourselves back into step, back into line with the universe, and that must begin within our own selves. If it does not then we shall never get any further forward than we are right now, and right now the world is in crisis.

Only people who are positively balanced can take on a new lease of life. Those who despair will only drag negative energy with them wherever they go. Life is for living, for enjoying the experience. I, too, must take each day as though it were my last and live it to the full. Sometimes it is necessary to make mistakes in order to get to a point that you can get past them. Life is a gamble. It is not always a sure thing. The news everyday merely confirms this fact. The world is a big place. Each person is on his own path. Some will be stuck and some will not, but ultimately we all have the same potential for happiness and contentment. There should be nothing else that matters.

God is with us all. He/It cannot be anywhere else. God is the body that we live upon. His is the intelligence that is part of us all - everyone. It is up to man to pull his self out of the place that he has fallen and it is a very necessary exercise. Only we can begin to make our lives work for us. No one can do it on our behalf because they do not have the correct combination of answers to fit. They are in the same predicament. Each and every person – no matter who they are, is trying to make his/her life work, to meet his own ends. Only we can bring all the pieces of who we are, where we have been and where we go from here – back together. Only we can complete the final picture of the life we have lived, and whatever we miss we pass automatically onto our children. We are giving the world we have made to them in their innocence – to clear up. We expect them to do what so far we could not. Is that fair? Is that why we invite our children into this world?

We need to look honestly at ourselves; at the things we do, have done, and at the world we are creating, not just for now, but also for the future. You must be completely sure that the person you see yourself to be today is the person you want to take with you to the next level. Only you can decide. Only you know you and you will live with your regrets for a long time after this life is over. If you can put yourself back together it will automatically affect those around you. Lead by example and you won't go far wrong.

If man were completely alone, the things we have yet to accomplish would be a scary prospect, but we are not. Once a decision has been made we shall be helped every step of the way, providing we are open enough to recognise that help. Only you can take that step. You know if you are happy with where you are now, or not. If you are, then fine. Well done. But the majority of us have done our best and are still failing fast, not necessarily because of our own mistakes, but because of circumstances that seem out of our control. Yet they are not out of our control. We have simply given our power over to them. We can get it back whenever we wish. We can stand up and start to rebuild, but from within. We need to understand better how we always get back to the same place, or we shall end up here again in a few years time. You can change the world, your hair, your job, your home, your partner, but you will always be the same, attracting the same things, until you do not any more. What makes you do and say and go in the directions that you do? Only you can answer this, but you must be truthful with yourself. If you cheat you are only hurting or kidding yourself.

Only we can make the most of the life yet to come. We could carry on forever as we are if we choose, or we could try to make better use of the time we have left. I, too, have some corrections of my own to perform. Just like everyone else I am far from perfect, but these things will take time and patience to perfect. It does not matter how little or how much we can achieve in our time here, but the point is that we shall have started to make an effort. We will have begun what others will continue in their time. I, too, must play my part – as should we all. I, too, have little desire for my children to be left with the world as it is today.

I, too, must take my time. All things that need to be done, as urgent as they are, must be done slowly, precisely and with care. I, too, have tried to hurry when I should not and this in turn creates more turmoil. A job cannot be finished before it is destined to be complete. All things have their own time scale. As important as the task of setting ourselves straight is, it will take an equal amount of time, patience and self understanding to complete. The universe will place in front of you exactly what you need – at the time you need it. In actual fact you will find that you need look for very little. As you open yourself up to the truths that surround you, all that you have learnt will be put into action. All you need do is face the issues that confront you and make your choice depending on the thoughts you will have at the time. There is little more to it than that.

We are to operate fully within our present moment, the one we are experiencing right now. The past is past. Each day, each hour and its minutes will bring you all that you need to address. Don't go spinning in directions you have no need for right now. All things will present themselves at the time necessary for them to do so. Life is not a game of chance. It is well thought out. Every instant has its answers and its questions. Every word we say, every thought we think and every deed we do will have its connection somewhere for someone. We are constantly feeding others as we feed off them. Life is a stream of energy connections. It is always on the move. When we are stressed or worried we are like live wires that have broken free from their connections. We are like main line cables that wave frantically in the air from side to side. We flop about in all directions and unsettle others in the process. This is not good. In itself it means that for those moments we are out of control. We have been knocked off balance by circumstance or by life. The first thing to do is to find balance once more and to bring yourself back down to size. By flopping around we have blown out our energy field and we are interfering with everyone elses. Bring yourself back to the size of a grain of sand. Imagine you can get that small. It will help you feel more secure in yourself. You will stop attracting adverse attention and you can settle your problem in the peace of your own mind, not out in the open for the world to see. It will be easier for you to think with less interruption. I, too, bring myself to this point whenever I feel anxious inside. Once you are practised at it then you can work out if it is your own anxiety you are feeling, or someone else's. It is surprising how much garbage we collect in the form of other people's stresses in the course of a day, especially when we work with the public. Life in our own circle can be fine, then for no apparent reason we become grouchy, because we have picked up on someone else's negativity. Always recycle what you are feeling. Ask that it be lifted from you and from the person who owns it. That way you have killed two birds with one stone, so to speak.

With patience and practice you can get so far in tune with yourself that you will begin to feel things you never felt before. You will be able to talk with a person or walk into a room and feel the energy that is at play. You will feel comfort or negativity. You will feel warmth or adversity. You will know if someone is working with you or against you. You will know if someone is happy or sad, pleased or mad. All these things and more are very much at work everyday in our lives on an energy level, but presently the majority of us are oblivious to everything. We think the day holds no more than the little we see, hear and say. But how wrong is that!

We are the only ones who can learn the lessons that matter, the things that really make us who we are, not by how we look but by the person we are inside. We are used to changing our clothes, our hairstyles, our whole outside life, but the changes that will make the most profound differences are inside, and these can only be accessed with a will to learn. I, too, had to learn this and I went through many tribulations before I did, and in some ways I still am. We have already said that we can never know all there is to know, at least not in this lifetime.

Only we can lift ourselves up to the heights that await us. Life is changing by the day as it gives everyone a reason and a chance to reassess the situation. Rubbish is falling down on everyone, everywhere. It is up to us whether we give up and drown or stand tall and fight. Not with words or fists, but with knowledge and a greater understanding of how we got into this predicament in the first place.

Stepping back

Many things come to try us in life, but it is how we handle these times that determine our strength of character. I, too, can vouch for that. Life is never smooth for anyone all the time. Trauma helps us keep our life in good working order. It usually pre-empts a period of change, of alteration. I, too, am in this place even today. I work hard to keep my life in order but then something happens that throws the whole thing into chaos once more. Actually not the whole thing, but it seems that way to us. Usually a problem occurs in one specific area at a time, but we automatically feel that all the good work we have done for months was wasted again. This is not always the case. I, too, have problems that seem earth shattering. If we looked down from a higher level we could see that much of our life would be functioning normally. Problems usually occur in one place at a time and it is a clear indication of where your attention needs to focus for a while. If we look at a car engine that is broken, once any part is broken it renders the whole thing unusable until it is mended. We are lucky that that is not the case for us. We can still function, and indeed most of our life continues to tick over quite nicely during those times. The largest problem lies within us in the way we over explode. A problem whether it is large or small can throw our equilibrium balance all over the place. We think our world is falling to bits and forget that things have a knock on effect. We must clear our heads of excess worry and deal with the situation at hand in the way that it dictates, at the time that it arises. Problems are merely areas that need special attention. They need attending to. They highlight things that are not functioning as efficiently as they need to be. They show areas of life that need updating for whatever reason. That is all. There is no gremlin making your life hard. Problems do not arise because your life was made to be difficult. They are more the result of a lack of care and attention, not always your own but other peoples too. It is easy to let fear take over and allow your emotions to run riot but it is precisely at these times that we must look to God once more. Make yourself small again, and keep that way until the storm is over. Ask again that all illusion and all negativity be recycled. Ask that you may be helped through this situation in the best way possible for you. Ask that you be surrounded by peace and love and light. Ask that you may be given the strength and courage that will get you from where you are - to where you ought to be.

The solution may be clear or it may take a little time to find the right one and put it properly into place, but the point is that you will. In the meantime look at areas in your life that are working well for you and draw strength from those. Look at all things around you that you have achieved and take pride in those too. Life is not a battlefield. It is a well run body of cause and effect. It is a game of survival.

Only the fittest and the most vigilant will come through with flying colours. Not the fittest as in health but in our minds. A good frame of mind can overcome anything. It is our mind that needs attention at this moment in the Earth's history, not our bodies. Our bodies have never been so pampered.

Many of us just don't realise the power of thought and what it is capable of in terms of doing, achieving and attracting. The mind is the most powerful force in our body. It is that that can raise us high above the mountains or can bring us crashing deeper than the ground. It is this that is the cause of world wars, death and destruction.

(I am I) Man was given a mind so that he could experience and enjoy all that he surveys, all that he masters and experiences. He was given a mind so that he could know himself and his function, so that he could be more than his wildest dreams would allow. It is his mind that can take humanity from strength to strength, to heights far greater than the original symbol of Adam and Eve. Man has superseded all expectations in every way, but to all intents and purposes his mind is still closed to much that it can do, and much that it has yet to achieve. Man does not realise that it is the collective mind that he controls as well as his own. Each thought that he ever thinks has a knock on effect somewhere, especially the negative ones. Life really is a struggle over darkness and light; the dark being negativity and the light being positive. All the worry, stress and fear that he produces, not just individually but collectively, has an effect far greater than he can imagine, and it is this that keeps him often where he would rather not be. It is this that is the driving force behind war and turmoil. The more things go wrong the worse he feels. The more he worries and stresses and fears. It is this

once more that adds to his load as it attracts even more negativity towards him. He gets pulled deeper and deeper into his own worries and doubts. Positivety has the opposite effect. It immediately repels the negativity and allows him to operate within a clearer area. It serves to keep him energised and motivated, that he is able to go forward to seek the solutions that he needs. Positivety is what both man and the earth are crying out for now. It is this that is the central requirement for life. Man is more responsible for the condition of the world at this time than he knows. It is time for him to wake up not only to his own self but also to the effect he has in the larger one. He is not alone in the things that he does. Because he is joined to everyone and everything the negativity he produces has a knock on effect. Collectively it is this that is making the world unstable. It is this that is attracting much of the bad that is occurring. It is not the hand of God because he gave man free will. It is the hand of man that is the cause so it is only by his hand that things can be corrected once more. This is the turning point that this Earth is crying out for. This is the whole point of this Book.

Man has gone as far as he can in many ways at this point in time. He is living the life of a king by many standards. Everything he could ever want or need is at his disposal. He is the ruler of all he surveys, of all his wants and of all his dreams. He alone is responsible for his state of life right now, if not individually, then collectively. He is not alone in any way, shape or form. He never has been and never will be – ever. He is a living breathing, bio-chemical work of art. He is far more advanced than any machine he could ever make. Even the computer – mans favourite toy, has not the living capabilities of man. He is life in motion; energy in motion; intelligence in progress. He is the thing that

will either take this world to its next stage, or he is the tool that will destroy it. The choice is up to him, not just individually, but collectively. (I am I)

It is so easy to get bogged down with chores and responsibility that many people have forgotten how to have fun. Yes, there are always things we must do and places we should be, especially when others rely on us, but sometimes we forget about ourselves. We forget that we should allow some free time for us – just to be. I, too, need a gentle reminder every now and then. I, too, forget the importance of this life I am living. Time is the most precious thing we have yet we allow it to run through our fingers like water. We forget that each minute spent is non-returnable. We are also experts at wishing it away. We long for things to be other than they are and fail to notice the space we are in, in the meantime. How many of us are creatures of habit without even realising? How many of us can honestly say that we make the best use of each and everyday? Not just for work but for pleasure too. How many of us take our work and our worries home with us and spend much of our free time worrying about this and that? I would like to say not many, but in reality we all do. It is a habit. Only we can learn to empty our minds and bring them back to peace – the way we empty our bins at home and the bins on our computers. I, too, have had to master this, but even now my old ways try to come back. It is habit born of a lifetime of worry. It is the fault of us forgetting – or in some cases not knowing that we control our mind. It does not control us. How often do we allow our thoughts free reign to wander ceaselessly wherever they will, then when we try to relax – we can't. We are too busy trying to quiet our minds. We get stuck in a loop, when the only way out is to hand those thoughts and turmoils up to those who can defuse them. We should hand up and recycle all that we don't need at the moment we are in. Our thoughts will always come back to us when we need them, and that is the

211

nature of man, but there is no need to churn them over and over again before or after an event. The only time that truly matters is the moment you are experiencing at the time of its birth. All the rest belong to past or future.

We are lucky to be able to look forward and back. We are lucky that we can plan and practise a little way ahead because it can be beneficial to set things into place, but sometimes we forget that the time of the event is its most potent. The time of an event is the only time that we should get things in order. Each moment we experience is the one and only of its kind. It is these that we should pay more attention to, even if it means learning how to enjoy them more. How many times do we wish we had spent more time with someone or on doing something? How many times do people say the same thing to us? We have built a world that is so fast and so needy that our time gets eaten up before it even gets to us. At this moment even writing this book is difficult to fit in to our busy schedule of life. But we are managing.

Pace yourself

Only we can pull our time back down to a more realistic and usable level of pace. It seems incredible but all we have to do is ask and it is given. Ask that your day be in the hands of God. Ask that you may achieve all that you need to do and ask that it be protected by love and light. Ask that your perception of time be slowed as much as possible so again you may achieve all that you wish. Ask and it will be done. But you must ask first – before it can be.

Only we can bring our lives back into a better working order, one that works better for you. And as soon as you realise you are not in it alone the more help you can open yourself up to receive, but it must work the other way too. Not only is it good to open yourself up, but it is also necessary to close yourself down properly as well. Every night once you are in bed you should do this in your mind. Snuggle down first then you can begin.

Imagine you can climb a ladder (perhaps only a few steps high), but this will vary with each individual. Close down the roof hatch tight and pull across the bolt. Climb down the ladder. Imagine now you will take a shower, but as you begin the droplets are not of water but of a pure and brilliant light. Imagine this light washing over you and as it does - slowly from your head to your feet, the stresses of the day simply drain away. You yourself are transformed into a vibrant light, a much brighter shade of your normal self. Imagine a towel being lovingly held open for you to step in. A white towel, that goes from your head to your toes. You don't know how but you have been gently carried onto your bed and a breathable glass dome has been lowered over you and shut down tight to keep you safe. Inside the dome are little glittery bits of colour that sparkle and shimmer in exactly the colours you need at the moment. Rest down and go to sleep. You will be safe and sound until morning, having slept like a log and completely refreshed. Wake up slowly and let the day come gradually back to you in your usual but 'calmer' fashion.

Man is in need of a lift. He is tired and emotionally drained. All his time is spent doing what he ought until there is little left for the things he needs to do for himself. If this is where 'you' are, begin to notice when you are granted the extra time you need to achieve something. Ask that your day be slow and send the thanks you feel out towards God. I, too, must learn to recognise the little things that help us out each day. It is too easy to be channelled into the ordinary instead of noticing the extra ordinary. Little things come to clear our way often but the more we keep our eyes open the more we will notice.

When we wake up to things that occur ceaselessly around us we can recognise that we are not alone in our daily tasks. Those we have loved and lost are with us much more than we know. Life is not just a struggle but more a tool to help us grow. Our friends, relations, guides and helpers actually smooth our way. As soon as we really need something they bring it to our aid. They are not here merely to prove their existence, but to tell us that they are with us, loving, helping and supporting us in all that we try to undertake, especially when it is for the good and furtherance of others.

(I am I). I have made a promise to mankind that I will honour always. That promise is that I will never leave his side. I will help and watch him grow and I will never judge him harshly. The words that were written in the Bible such a very long time ago have put the fear of God into Man for far too long. They were written by men, who a long time ago felt the need to install fear into man for his own protection. I will not hurt man. I gave him life. I am his life as he is mine. We both need each other for survival in this physical world. (I am I).

Only we can learn to recognise the truth behind our existence. It is as though mankind has been in a long waking sleep, but the time is ripe for him to now wake up. This waking up has always been a requirement of our being, but it is only now that it is necessary for our own happiness and self-esteem.

(I am I) Man was given free will so that he could use it in whatever way he chose to. The time is here for him to extend that free will in other directions. He must choose those directions for himself. I can give him the means and the support but only he can reach out his hand to take it. This is not a dream, nor is it a fairy story. I am real and this book is living proof, as are others that I have also had my hand in. These are given as truths to help mankind back onto his own path of 'self' discovery. Man has exhausted much of the material world about him, but all is not lost. By turning ourselves onto a more forgiving, loving path we can put

214

back 'in energy' that which we have taken. We can pick up and live the life we have chosen rather than to live in sadness, sorrow and turmoil. I shall be here to help him every step of the way, but first he must recognise that I am. He must wake up to the choices that surround him everyday of this waking life. (I am I)

Man is on the brink of a new wave of life. All his dreams are about to fruit, but just like a gardener; he must weed out the parts that do not belong there any more. Over the years it is easy to collect excess junk and baggage. This means mental as well as physical. As we grow we change but how often do we clear the corners of our mind or refine the way we behave? How often do we continue doing what we always do, simply because we always have? A new company boss is apt at looking around and removing what is broken, dysfunctional or out of date, and we too need to approach ourselves in this manner. It is easy to weed out your kitchen cupboards, but do we easily do the same with our wardrobes? We cling to the things we like in the hope that perhaps one day we might find use for them again, but in reality, do we? Instead we buy and buy new things. More and more we accumulate until our cupboards are crammed. I, too, was the same, and I, too, find it hard to let go of things that I love, but we must if we are ever to move forward and on towards this new beginning that is promised.

Only we can look at ourselves in the truth of light. We know all our quirky habits inside out. We don't need anyone to tell us more, but it is exactly these little things that hold us back and keep us where we are. The older the habit the more the energy surrounding it pulls us down. The more the energy pulls us down the more tired and lifeless we become. Man is energy in motion. All that he does has an effect somewhere. If he is not operating to his full potential then slowly the air around him looses its vibrancy. Others will not feel the strength of a positive

215

connection when they are in his company and slowly, slowly he will find that he spends more and more time on his own. The harder he tries to combat this, the needier he will appear in the unconscious minds of others around. The only thing then to do is to clear his energy field once more and this can only be done by hard work, not in the way he is used to - but on himself, in understanding his ways and his habits. By clearing the thoughts that he automatically thinks and by affording himself a new and fresh outlook to life, he will think that nothing has changed. Indeed the material life he leads may still be the same, but his mental blocks will have altered, and because of this the life force that surrounds him will begin to flow once more. People will again enjoy being in his company and he in turn will benefit from theirs, and the energy that they bring along with them.

Only you can choose your path and what you choose is up to you. Only you know what lies deep in your heart and you know if your life is all you need it to be to make you happy. Life is short. The older we get the quicker time seems to pass. It is supposed to be a pleasure, to live – to create – to experience and to love. Love is the strongest emotion we have. It can move mountains, but it can just as easily tear us apart and burn all our bridges. Love is the essence of man and that is why he searches to find it his whole life through.

Only you can live your life and the choices you make are only a part of it. The rest is building and labouring, or reaping and sowing as the bible calls it. Life is the whole package and it is basically the same for everyone. Some may be rich (materially) and some may be poor, but we all strive to find the truest essence and meaning of our life. That is the part we play in the scale of the Planet. We are all part of the same thing, the same Earth.

Chapter Twenty

The Winds that Bring Hope

(I am I). Only man likes to believe that what he builds is permanent. It is how he has learnt to judge himself – by his achievements. He has grown beyond his wildest expectations. The majority live like kings while the rest still struggle for the basics. Life is a balance and at this moment in time many things are off balance. The answer does not lie in finance and materialism. Nor is it in technology. Instead it lies in quality of life and in state of mind. Only we can bring peace back to our inner selves and at the end of the day when our life is said and done, it is only this that we can take back home. All we have ever built will fade away with time because that is in the nature of this Earth. It will always reclaim itself. Man is beyond that. He is eternal in nature. He cannot and will not fade into nothingness. All that he is he will always be, and still much more besides. (I am I).

The essence of man is pure energy. **(I am I). He is made of the life force of the planet. (I am I).** I, too, am energy. I, too, am eternal. All that I am I shall take with me and all that I can be, I am not yet. I, too, am still a work in process. I, too, am still in a state of transition. We all are. The person you are now is not all you can be. It is not all your final lot, unless you choose it to be that way. This does not mean you should rip your life apart. Nor does it mean that you should throw in the towel and run away from where you are right now. Instead you are being given the tools to climb to a greater height. To change the parts that need to be altered and to move forward and on to a plain

217

that you might be happier. Worry and stress are not the requirements of God. Instead they are the result of choices we have made in our past. They are signs that all is not as it could be, so they are areas in our life that need to be addressed. Only we feel the stress we carry around - unless we pass it by anger onto another, so it is only natural that it will fall to us to redraw these areas. I, too, have been here – but not so often now. I, too, am still picking up the tools that I need to take me forward and out of the grey areas of life. Happiness is for all who wish to attain it; it is not an impossibility, but a promise.

Only we can make the life we are living run smoothly. If there are things that need to change then do them gently and with love. Don't change anything in the spur of a moment. Be sure first, and the only way to do that is to learn a little more about yourself before you do. Open your eyes to the truths that surround you. Not the version you want to see, but the bottom line. Look and learn. Get some advice from books or from others who have been there. Not necessarily your friends, but professional people. Always search within, before you change without. You are like a baby who is not sure of what life will hold. It may be necessary to re-learn some of the things that you thought you knew. You are not at the end of your life, but at the beginning. This is your fresh start, your new page, and how you choose to approach it is up to you. This is your life.

Only we can take our family, our life, our society, and ourselves, out of the place that it is heading. The chaos of the world is a sign of the times. It is a symptom of a deeper unrest that is causing through the veins and the thoughts of man. There is much negativity in the form of debt and fear and pain. Many people have dug holes so deep that they pray things will not change in case they will topple. They fear everyday and every delivery of their post. They fear they will get ill. They worry and fret their lives away, all in the name of progress. Is this what we really want? Is this what we have lived and worked our lives to achieve? Only you can know your own answer. Only you know where you presently are and what the truth of your life is like, so only you can scale things down once more to a realistic and suitable level. A life without hardship is no life at all. We need to reach our parameters in order to realise that we don't need as much as we thought we did. Life comes without promises, but it is up to us to find a happy balance. It is necessary to reassess again and again.

Only man can grow into his future. It is not pre-written, although many things would appear to be so. The world is our oyster. It is up to us where we take it and how we get there. The only person we must answer to is our conscience and ourselves. There is no such thing as good and bad. There is only what is. All things are simply as they are and that is the bottom line. All of life has always been this way. Could haves and should nots are irrelevant. It is up to man to set his own level of standards and then to stick by them. All things are as they are for whatever the reason, but it is where we go from here that counts. The choices we make from this day forward, to the end of our physical existence.

Only people who are fed up will want to search within. Those who are happy with their lot will simply continue along their chosen path, until they choose to do otherwise. God gave us all the right to learn and to grow. He knew that when we search things out for ourselves, even though the going might be hard, that we would value them more. He gave man the will to survive, to stretch past his limitations and to fight back against all odds. He gave man the will of self-preservation. He gave him instinct and intelligence. He gave him the essence of himself that he could take life forward to his highest expectation. He gave man the ability to choose and to re-choose when the life that he chose fails to fit. He gave us the power of determination and of love.

All we are, we have chosen to be. I, too, am the product of my past, both good and bad, but given that there is no such thing as bad, I am simply all that I am - that is born of my past. I am my mistakes and my triumphs. I am born of my mother as she was of hers. I am the present in a long line of blood that goes back further than I could ever trace, but my spirit is unique. I alone have access to that. Nothing from anyone could be blamed for the person who is me. I have lived my life according to the choices that I thought were best at the time that I made them. The same is true for us all. We are the product of our own life and our own destruction will be no less, unless we choose to re-look at and rethink the route we are following. There is no one in our past to blame, even though we might believe otherwise. There will be no one in our future. We are the result of all that we chose to do along the course of our own life, and that is all there is to it.

Only I can make my life work. People can say all they want to say. They can try to help me, or try to hold me back, but only I have the final say in the outcome of my time here on Earth. Life will always be tough. That is in its very nature, but out of the ashes the best roses can grow. When we think our life is over it can be then that it really begins. Stay with it wherever you are and learn to see past the events that engulf you. Look for the meaning within and beyond the difficulties that face you. Realise that stepping-stones will be placed at your feet and take each day, each decision as it comes. Don't look too far ahead because fear will always be there to engulf you. Stay calm, stay focused, stay small and stay in the moment. All other things will fall back into their proper perspective and place. It is the very fact that you are not alone that will help you. Try to remember this as often as you can and look for the light that will show you the way. Always.

Only you can bring your life back into a well-balanced order, especially when things are not quite as they should be. I, too, still struggle with fear as it sends doubts and criticism towards me. For many it is far easier to accept these are true, than it is to accept a compliment. We tear ourselves apart for no reason. We point the finger of prejudice at ourselves far more than we realise. Only we can retrain and redraw the thoughts that we think onto a kinder, more forgiving level, especially when they are directed at ourselves. There is enough criticism and opposition already apparent in life. We don't need it to seep from us as well. Life is not always easy, especially when the thoughts we think are coloured by illusion or doubt. I, too, must be more aware of when these things pull me astray, especially when we can make them fit so readily. I, too, must have more confidence in the things I do.

The seeds of doubt take root from a very early age. They are hammered home extremely well during the course of childhood and adolescence. Even as an adult we still dance to its tune. Only we can learn to recognise when we are criticising ourselves, and whether those criticisms are just or not. At any time we make a decision we always choose the best choice at that time, yet we look back at that instant and beat ourselves up later. We wish we had chosen better, but we chose what we did for good reason at that time.

In any decision there are always two options – or there would be nothing to decide between.

(I am I). I, too, had decisions to make at the beginning of creation. I, too, could have beaten myself to pulp because of the way history has turned out, but I also must stay in the love mode. I must have faith in my own creation. I must believe that in the end all things will correct themselves and that the planet will be revitalised. I, too, could let the seeds of doubt and pain take root, but if I did it would not take long for negativity and fear to take over. Like running weeds in

221

a garden the bad thoughts we have are all consuming, that is the reason for the seeming original split in the Garden of Eden. In actual fact there has never been a split at all. I would never and could never separate myself from you because you are myself. I am myself and I can never separate from myself. There has never been a separation between man and God. Man just allowed his own mind to enter the bin of fear and doubt and negativity. Man lost confidence in himself, because he believed that he was completely alone. He thought that struggle and stress were a necessary requirement to life. But they are not. Problems help you grow, as they require your attention to check certain areas of your life that are malfunctioning, but that is all. Problems are not given to break the confidence of man. They are merely signposts that will lead you on to a smoother runway once more. Problems highlight trouble spots that need to be sorted out. Whether it is a pain in your body, a spot on your face, an industrial dispute or the stirrings of war and unrest, problems need attention to stop them escalating further. (I am I).

Only we can bring about the changes that we desire. There is no one else that can. Only you can take the leading role that leads you back to happiness, harmony and success. The point is that you are not just stuck with your life. You do have a choice. Maybe just a few or perhaps many, but each one will take you closer to your destination of a happy future and life. All you have ever been is not all that you can be. The real you might be in a completely opposite direction from the one you are following now, but don't worry and don't be afraid. Take life as it comes – day by day. Take each decision one step at a time, even if it seems to take you off course for a while. Detours happen day by day but we always get to our destination eventually, if we persevere. The only thing you must stand by is personal responsibility.

Only you can turn yourself around. No one forces you to do the things that are making you mad, sad or irritable. The life we live is far too short not to live it well, and if we do come back it may be a long time in between. Everyday we have here is precious. It can never be repeated, never be copied. That's why we should make the most of them. Use each one as though it were our last. Only we can get ourselves back into order, and that includes our emotional closets. Only we can dump the rubbish that in many cases we have been dragging around for years. The old stuff is past. It cannot hurt us anymore. We just have to learn to not let it. Every time we dwell on something painful we are feeding that pain with our thoughts. We are keeping it alive. It is possible to drag old issues through a complete lifetime if we don't let them go. The pain you still feel surrounding them is brought forward by your attachment and can become even stronger over years as you can't seem to let go. But now you can.

(I am I). I can take it away. I can lift all you no longer need off of your shoulders. This day you are in should be free of all that does not belong there. Choose to let go and go forward. (I am I).

Only you feel the hurt that you keep locked inside, and it is because it is locked inside that you feel it. Pain from the past can come crashing to the present when we least expect it. It can bring us thundering down and ruin a perfectly happy occasion.

(I am I). There is no pain or negativity that we cannot let go of. All these things serve no purpose other than to keep you under their control. I, too, have let mine go. But before I did, in many ways the past ruled my life. I was beholden to it even though I did not want it. I had to let go and step forward, or I would have lost my battle. Life is for living, not for regrets. I, too, have had to learn this, and those lessons are rarely sweet. All that we are, we are because of our past, but buried within

223

that past and the pain are the strengths that can take us forward. Find those strengths. Find all the positives that you can, no matter how remote, and place them under your belt. I can help you let the rest go. Recycle all your litter back to me. Imagine you could wrap the whole issue in a blue sack. Tie it up tight and allow a large hook to come down and lift it for you. The roots may dangle deep from its base but they will pull up easily. Let this parcel go now. See it drift away into nothingness and know it has finally gone. Don't check because you are inviting it back, but instead just know that it has. Fill the space with a warm bright light, the colour of your choice, and sit down for a moment and enjoy the tranquillity. Open your eyes and continue with your day. Only you can let go of a past that no longer serves its purpose. (I am I).

Only we can learn to control our mind and its thoughts because only we have the ability to be in on the action. Only we have the brains to catch our thoughts when they go spinning off on a tangent and the more we learn to catch ourselves out, the quicker we can stop those thoughts reoccurring. Only we can know at any one time what is rattling around in our head. We allow out only a fraction of what actually occurs at any one moment. The thoughts we think depend on a feeding system that links in with what we see and hear, taste and smell. Our thoughts depend very much on our senses and feelings at the time.

Only we can put ourselves back together again because it is up to us to find out how. Life should hardly ever be automatic. Each day should be a day in its own right, so by remaining too rigid we loose out on spontaneity. How can we judge in advance when we have not been there yet? Yet most of the time we do. We judge future events on the experience of past ones, of similar situations we may have been in, when in truth we should take each day in its own merit, under its own steam. Only people who love their life

224

can be like this, for the rest just follow the leader. Only you can break away from this circle of behaviour – by living completely in the moment, by focusing on the job in hand and not worrying about past or future until the need arises.

Only people who care about themselves will ever begin to look deeper inside for the answers that are needed in their life. Those who believe there is more for them will reach out their hands to attain it. Where you are is probably only a fraction of where you will be before your life is over, so if you can believe in yourself – then go for it. Do a few of those things that you always wanted to do. Don't let your work, or stress and strife rule your life. I, too, am still here far too often, but then I have had a lifetime of practice. It will take patience and time to form a new way of thinking, but every small step we take along the way will bring us closer towards our destination. Start by putting small things in order first. Life will present you with more soon enough. Just take each day as it comes and look for the sun that will start to shine through.

Man is not used to staying in the positivety of the love mode. Most of his life he has lived in fear, even though he does not realise it. It is natural to wonder about the future, but more often than not we worry about it. We worry about our own failings, about our short falls. We worry about things that should not be worried about. We worry when we don't have anything to worry about. I, too, am here even now about this book, so I must again hand it up to the love and guidance of our Father God.

(I am I). I have made a promise to help man in any way that I can. I shall stand by that promise through all eternity, but he must allow me a look in, in the first place. I can do nothing without his approval and his consent, because I would be violating the very gift I gave to him - his free will. Many times I watch life from the wings and I wish someone, somewhere, would invite me

225

in, not in an alleluia manner, but as a person - as his friend. I am real. I am here. I am with each of you everyday of your life. Not judging, but just with you. I can never be anywhere else. I am you. You are a part of me. This is your life, your time – to enjoy. I am here to experience it with you. When you are stuck in pain, in sadness, in doubt, or in negativity of any kind, you separate yourself from me. You stand alone and you carry these things alone, like burdens on your own back. Only you can let me in, into your life as a confident, as a friend. I can recycle much of the things that burden you down, but not without you first giving them to me.

I have made a promise to do my best. I will stand by you your whole life long and I will bring you safely back home after it is over. There are no exceptions. Would a mother disregard a child for making a mistake; even many mistakes? She would not. And neither would I. I have given you free will so how could I admonish you for then using it?

The atrocities that occur on Earth are driven and fed by the hand and the mind of man. They are not of me. I will take you home and place you where you can do no more harm, to yourself or to anyone else. Each man has his own pathway to follow. There will be many opportunities to do bad as well as good. The path he will travel upon is his own choice. It will never be too late to begin again, to change course onto a better route. I have given him free will to choose, to use and to go forward on a surer foot. He alone is in the driving seat. He alone is responsible for the world. For his own world even more than the larger one. He alone is responsible for the thoughts he thinks and the deeds he carries out. I am here to help him whenever he chooses. This book is proof. But he must first choose to allow me to guide him before I can. I am here. I am for him. But first he must realise that I am his friend, not his judge, nor his jury, and definitely not his executioner.

Only man can help himself but first he must recognise the opportunity and the need to do so. All that we achieve here goes to help us in the next level, on the next plain of existence. This life is not all there is, neither is it a school or a firing zone. It is a world that was created for love and for life and it is this that he is crying out for. He is love. He is the essence of love itself. All he surveys was made by love. I am with him now – and I ever shall be. (I am I).

Man is his own boss. Whatever he decides to do with his life – he can. There has never been anyone standing over him, directing him, except in his own imagination. From the time of infancy adults and superiors have welded their rods of iron and rules, but when he grows up he can choose which of those rules to keep and which to stand by. He can work out for himself, which rules were useful and which were hindering. He has the intelligence to make his own decisions and to stand on his own two feet.

Only those who believe in their own self worth will ever push beyond the boundaries that were set either rightly or wrongly in childhood. During infancy rules are put in place to keep you safe or to teach you right from wrong, according to those that set them. Rules keep the world in some sort of order, but too many can lead to rebellion and the need for extreme behaviour. Sometimes rules hinder rather than guide. Sometimes they bring happiness and sometimes they lead to heartache, but whatever they do it is up to us the individual to work with them or through them. It is up to us in adult life to make our own finished article. When we stand in the next life, what are we going to say? "We couldn't because... because so and so said no... because I didn't know I could... because I thought I could only do that..." The list is extreme and endless. This is your life, so live it in a way that you can be proud of, that your ancestors can be proud of, that they would be pleased that they are associated with you. Make their struggles of the past worthwhile by taking your own life on good note into the future. Make everyday count for something, even if it's only something small; even if it's only the fact that you were completely focused on your actions within that day; even if you only had a smile on your face and was happy. No one can do that for you – except you. You have all that you will ever need to draw from – inside of yourself. No one will rescue you. No one knows better than you. Others can talk, listen and advise, but at the end of the day all you decide to do is your choice.

Life is full of people who are searching for their own answers, their own way forward and their own happy ever after ending. But no one can give us these things until we first find our own peace of mind. I, too, was here about four years ago. I, too, had to put my life on hold while I did some soul searching. I, too, am finding my own self and it's not over yet. The person we become we do so over the course of our whole life long. It is not possible to shed all your ghosts in one foul swoop and neither would it be good for our health. Time itself must play its own part but we must be the leader in its direction. It falls to us to put the past and its lessons into a perspective that will work better for us. To find the strengths that have been afforded us by the experiences we have had and been given or subjected to. Life is not a bed of roses all the time for anyone, and if they say it is then perhaps they are not being as truthful as they would like to believe – to themselves. Life is full of pits and snares as much as it is full of music and love.

(I am I). I am here with you to carry you when you need to be carried. I have the strength and the ability. I can only do this if you turn to me - if you let me in. I can laugh and I can cry. I can experience all that you can, but I cannot override your decisions or your will. I

**cannot step in and stop what is the cause of mans
sorrow before he stops it himself. I can move
mountains but I cannot interfere in the laws of cause
and effect. These are driven by the will of man, not by
the will of me. (I am I).**

Many years ago man was born. He knew very little. He
learned how to eat, to drink and to grow. He learned how
to dress and to find and build shelter. He learned how to
make a family, a community and how to band. Little by
little his knowledge about himself and his world grew to
the extent we have evident today. He learned what he
needed to learn to live and function as he does today. He
knows his history and his roots. He lives life to the full and
he takes advantage of the situations he finds himself in. I
have taken advantage of a situation or two myself, but I
have never hurt anyone in the process. I have even done
things that I perhaps should not. I am human like everyone
else here on Earth. I have been to breaking point and back,
but I came through it. I have been broken by life and by
circumstances that were beyond my control, yet as I look
back it seems like a distant memory. Life has been tough
but I came through it all. There will always be things that
will bring you down but there are just as many to lift you
up high. Life cannot and should not be a smooth ride for
anyone. Life needs its challenges, even if we can't always
see that at the time. We are human beings – not mechanical
machines. Just as the tide must ebb and flow for all
eternity, so must life for us.

Only you can look at your life, both past and present, in
the full light of truth. Only you can judge your actions,
your responses and your decisions, not to punish but to
learn and to truthfully assess. Only you can see where you
were one hundred and ten percent correct – or completely
and utterly wrong. Life is able to show its colours better
through hindsight than it often can in the moment we are in.
Only we can look back at the tracks we have made and

decide if they were worth it – or not, and are we pleased with the outcome? Are you proud of the part you have played in your lifetime?

This is not about guilt. Nor is it about reprimand. It is more about recalibrating and redrawing your life's plan. It is about fine-tuning and taking personal responsibility for the deeds that have occurred and either taking stock or changing your route altogether. I, too, have been here, and not always by choice at the time. I, too, have made decisions that perhaps in hindsight I should not, but I have learned to view life from a different perspective. Things are not always what they would appear to be at the time. There are many angles of approach and consideration. Often we see through eyes of illusion and doubt rather than truth and reality. The thoughts we think and feelings we have at the time play a huge part in what it is we think we see and hear and understand. I, too, have been here, so I know what I'm talking about. I, too, have had to redraw the shape of the thoughts that I produce and in the process have learnt much more than I ever thought possible.

Life can never be a bed of roses for anyone, at least not without and before some growth and pain, but there is always a way out of all situations. There is always a time when enough is enough and that time is now. The rubbish that is happening in your life is not unique to you, even though it seems that way. Everyone everywhere is going through a shake up of some kind or another. The circumstances may vary, but pain and trouble is still pain and trouble, whatever label you care to stick on it. Everyone everywhere is being asked to reassess, to take stock and to account for the total of their life's achievements. Not in material gain, but in emotional satisfaction and happiness. We are being asked to look at the sum total of the being we are. We are to assess ourselves and look at the person – not the situation. We are to look within to see what will come home with us when the time will come. We are to look at the life we will leave behind and the legacy, not financially, but emotionally, we shall leave behind. Only we can see if we shall leave peace and harmony, or stress and worry. Have we lived life to the advantage or to the disadvantage of those who have crossed our path? Have we been an asset to this life, or have we been a disadvantage? Do we weave flowers or scars into the time we possess? Only you can tell because only you can see the life you have lived, not from an external viewpoint, but an internal advantage. Only you can look at yourself in this manner and now you don't have to wait until you die to do it. We are able to do it now. And with everyday that will now come before you.

It is up to us to make a stand, to stand up for ourselves - within ourselves. There is no need to cause a rumpus, nor is there need to moan. I, too, must remember this. Life will always try to lead us away from the place that we think we need to be, but if we stick to our guns it will also help us out. It is completely up to us whether we go with the flow or swim against it. No one can know what you have in mind to achieve, nor can they know what it took for you to get there. I, too, can relate to this. I, too, still struggle against the tide more often than not, but there are also occasions that all seems to flow as it should. Life needs our attention everywhere in equal bursts. When we do not comply as we ought, life has a way of ordering our attention. When we recognise this, we can move beyond those obstacles quickly and smoothly, but when we do not, we tend to get stressful. Stress is a negative emotion that only serves to feed negatively, the commotion that surrounds you. The sooner we can learn to recognise this, the sooner we can let it go and get back on track once more. All of life will not stand still and wait for us to catch up. Instead we must catch up as well as keep on top of the life we live. Only we can look at the full picture and make our life work accordingly. I, too, must juggle and strive to fit in all that needs to be done to keep things ticking over, as they should. Even the people who are helping me write this book find that they must do the same. There is no point in getting cross when things don't work out as they should. It is far simpler to get over and past it as soon as possible. The less fuss we make the smaller the obstacle, the quicker we can get on with what we should.

(I am I). Even for me things get in the way before a project is complete. Even I must contend with life, and not necessarily in the way I would plan. Life is like a roller coaster. It takes you up, but it brings you back down, sometimes a hundred times a day. But it is up to us to try our best to keep a balance within ourselves. Anger is as natural as laughter, but only in the required dosage. Too much of either at the wrong time can cause a problem that soon escalates out of control. Negativity attracts further negativity and the opposite is true for love, light and happiness. The vibrations that surround us have a knock on effect always. It is up to us to make ourselves small when necessary, especially when the going gets tough. It is up to us to recycle the negative stuff when we think the situation calls for it, and it is up to us to ask for love and light in return. It is up to us to balance our frame of mind and to make the most of the day we are in. (I am I).

Only few will ever attain total peace and harmony within themselves. For the rest the best we can hope is to remain relatively happy within our chosen field, but stress and unhappiness is not an option for choice. People accept it too readily. Many forget that it is they who control their mind. Many forget that they have a choice. It is easy to become so busy and bogged down with life that you forget more exists besides in the world. Only we can bring ourselves back into the life that surrounds us. Don't let time pass you by, as you miss the little things that matter. Man is stuck in a loop. Because we think we need so much

232

in our material life, we must work hard to maintain and feed the demand. Then because we work so hard we feel justified to treat ourselves to whatever we think we want. Even when the purse says a definite NO, the head overrides its decision. Credit is more a problem than a lifeline. Again it serves to keep us working and providing beyond necessity. The only way to stop is to stop. Take a look at your life. Is that the reason you live? Do you really need to buy and replace all that you do? Man gives away more new things than ever before. Hardly anything becomes worn out. The charity shops are brimming so high that they too throw much away. Only we can step off this merry-go-round, but the decision must start within, before it can filter without. Only we can alter the course of this trend, but not with an idea that we are being heroic and will deprive ourselves. This will only serve to feed the illness at a later stage, when you think you have been good for long enough. The only true deterrent is to wake up to reality and look at how you keep yourself where you are, working as hard as you do. I, too, have been here and I still wrestle with myself. We are combating a habit that for many has stemmed from a lifetime of wanting.

(I am I). Man has all he wants and certainly much more than he needs. Man is like a computer programme that is locked on a course of action. (I am I).

He and only he can break himself free of this. He and only he can decide that his buying has reached beyond the normal scale of necessity. This does not mean that we buy no more but it means that we wake up to the truth. Everything we have – we want more. All we do we do to the extreme. We buy all the necessary equipment before we have even mastered a task. Then before we even get going we change our mind and quit. The dumps of man have little to do with rubbish but more and more to do with dumping.

233

(I am I). The earth is my body. Why do we treat it as we do? Is it because we don't realise, or is it because we really don't care? The truth is probably because we did not know. But now we do.

Man is my creation. Whether you believe this or not is irrelevant. You cannot change that fact. Only he can learn the truth of this existence and alter the course of his life accordingly. This is not a command, but a natural outcome of the truths that are here to be discovered. Only he can look at life and learn to see beyond what his eyes relay. Only he can engage his own power of deduction. He does not have to wait for the majority to lead him. He is capable and able to do his own research. He has a perfectly equipped mind of his own. Finding the truth that lies all around does not take major intelligence, but an open and truthful mind. (I am I).

Only we are responsible for the little corner of the world that is us. Only we have to answer at sometime for the life we have known.

(I am I). I will not stand in judgement, but perhaps more in sadness, just as man does now when he looks about himself at the real world he can see. What he does not see is the part he plays himself in keeping the world exactly as it is. He is just as guilty for not seeing the truth, as the man is that does it deliberately. Man can never be a saint, but he could live his life better than he does now. (I am I).

Only we can look through our own eyes, but we do not see beyond the surface. In truth we don't always see at all. We see what we choose and want to see. The eyes are not capable of sight alone; they rely on the brain to transmit. They see only what the brain tells them they are seeing. Learn to look beyond and behind the shop window. Learn to look at reality instead of what you usually do. Only you can do this for you. Only you can wake yourself up from the automatic state of existence that is normally apparent.

(I am I). I gave man life so that I could experience physical life myself. It is only in solid form that I can know all that you do. (I am I).

Only we as individuals can turn this life around. **(I am I). Each man does matter. He matters more than he realises. (I am I).**

Only man can make the changes necessary within his own life. Only he can make the part he plays more functional and positive. I, too, must reassess continuously otherwise life would become stagnant and stale. The nature of life is to keep moving in forward rotation. This same pattern applies to most living things, so it is only natural that is should befall on man as well. Because we have become locked into our ways and habits, we try to keep things as much as possible as they are. Many of us have learnt that change is sometimes a bad thing, so we try not to rock the boat unless we have to. We prefer to remain safe but stagnant instead of carefree and unsure of what the future will hold. This is the way life has taught us to be over the course of events we have lived through, but without risk there can never be any growth. We have already said that sometimes it is necessary to shake things up to allow the dust to settle in a different order.

(I am I). I also can verify this. There have been many events throughout history that have appeared to signal the end of a cycle as we knew it, but clearly as we look back we can see how far we have come in its wake. (I am I).

Only we can look back upon our own life to see the distance we too have travelled. The world has changed ten fold in my lifetime alone, and it is not over yet. Periods of time need periods of change and rest in between. Only we can make these into positive or negative experiences, and the choice is really up to us on an individual level. Each person really does make a difference, because collectively we make a force and a force is a power to be reckoned with. The choice is with us on where to take our lives. Only we can learn to be proud of ourselves once more.

Only we can take this life on a positive note into the future. This does not mean that we abandon all that we did before, but more that we learn and understand why we did what we did, on a deeper lever. We need to find the scars that are buried deep inside and lay them to rest once and for all. No one can take away the experiences you have lived through but we can pick ourselves up and move forward 'despite' those things. We know clearly what we are not – so let's go and find out what we can be. Everyday is a new chance.

(I am I). As the sun rises, so it must set. What man does in between is his own affair, but he must understand that it is his own conscience he will wrestle with when the time comes for him to do so. It is up to each individual to be the very best example of a man he can be, again 'despite' his history and his background. He lives in a society today that welcomes freedom of thought, speech and action. There has never been a better time to come out and live for all you are worth. Man has never been so free yet so stuck by his own life. Take each opportunity and live it in the best way you know how. Find out more about the workings of your own mind. If parents are but children themselves, how can they ever be parents? How can the blind lead the blind? They cannot. (I am I).

Only we can step down from the treadmill of excess and indulgence, from over work and over stress, from living automatically to living in light and happiness.

(I am I). Only man can come back to a more realistic level that will be kinder to him and to this Earth he lives upon. While he continues to indulge in excessive obligations then he will continue to drain the resources

of his fellow man. The West is bleeding the East dry, while the Middle East is killing one another. Balance can only be restored one step at a time and whether we realise it or not, this balance <u>must</u> come from within each one of us at home. It will have a gradual knock on effect that will reach far beyond anything we can imagine. (I am I).

Man has come a very long way in his evolution. In fact he had come further over the past fifty years than he ever has before. He has left behind animalistic senses of greed and barbarism. He has grown both mentally and technologically, yet emotionally, in many ways he is still a child. He has the same wants, needs and expectations that he obtained while at home with his parents. He still thinks that the world owes him a debt. I have also had to shake this belief from my own psyche. I have also had to wake up and grow up as well. We look to others to feed us with the love and fulfilment that we need, when it is really in our own emotional banks inside. How can another give us what we are looking for? How can they share what they have yet to find themselves? Again you can see how easy it is to be stuck in a loop of behaviour that you don't even realise exists.

Man has become apt at providing all that he needs for his material survival, but as far as his emotional self is concerned he really does not yet have a clue. He still has much to learn.

Man was equipped at birth with a brain and a heart. The brain is to keep the body functioning and to process his experiences in a way that he can comprehend. The heart was to pump his life force around his body and to experience all that it could in the name of love and emotion. Man has gone extremely far with the use of his brain but if in infancy misinformation and misplaced emotional building blocks were apparent then his feelings will lead him astray. The heart can feel love and pain – in an

237

emotional fashion, but it is the brain that transmits what those feelings are. Very often misinformation is transmitted and the heart does not know, but because man is used to reading his heart, he can follow behind on a wild goose chase. Anxiety can be mistaken for fear; fear can be mistaken for love. Love can be disguised in any number of means, but the point is that these emotions have become muddled. How can we follow what has not been labelled correctly in the first place? How can we go forward when our emotions are misleading us and are pulling us back? We can travel all over the place when in reality what we are really looking for can be right under our very noses. How often do we realise things when it really is too late? How often do we wish we had seen more clearly both the negative and the positive aspects of life? How much do we allow ourselves to take in the name of tolerance when really we should have pulled in the rope months ago? All these things and many more are the direct result of our emotional mix-ups.

How can we tell if this is happening to us - if we are the victims of our own illusions? It is easy. Just look back over your shoulder at the life you have lived until now. Is it a happy one? Are you living your 'happy ever after'? Is it even in sight at all? Are you as understood as you 'think' you deserve to be? Do your parents fully know and understand you? Can you communicate both professionally and personally as well as you think you can? Or do you find yourself in unwelcome situations again and again without really knowing or understanding why or how? Are you giving life your best shot and is that best shot providing you with the peace and happiness that 'you think' it should? Again, all these questions and many more besides are indications, signals, signposts that all it not quite as it should be in your emotional life. Your physical, material life may be functioning quite nicely. You have probably got that down to an art, but your true emotional self is a completely other ballgame.

(I am I). Man is clever. He is intelligent and he is resourceful. He is apt at taking his life and moulding it into whatever he seems to need. But how often when he gets there does his expectation fall on its face? How often does his life measure up to his tall order? It is easy to pin anything we wish onto a future event or date, but again how often does it fall short of what he 'thought' it would be like? The new millennium is a good recent example. Up to the event man was building himself up to a crescendo. He had his life practically wrapped up in expectation of the good it would herald. He knew a change was coming so he placed all his unread dreams and hopes and desires onto the forthcoming event, but when it came and went like any other new year, he almost felt cheated. He soon saw that not much was to really change at all. His balloon – built up of months of expectation -deflated. The changes that he desires are possible. In fact it is up to him and him alone to make them into a reality. The date is just the day; the time is just the time; but in himself, now and always, is the potential to do and be all he could ever dream to be. Instead of pinning these hopes onto events and other people, the time is now ripe for him to instigate these changes within himself. Not without as he learnt in his childhood.

From a very early age man has looked to others to fulfil his expectations. Indeed that is the role of a loving and caring parent. But somewhere along the course of his life man should make the switch. He should wake up to the fact that really he must only rely on himself. All he ever needs in courage, strength and love is in an overflowing abundance inside. At this moment in time it will possibly be hard for him to believe because he must learn to access it, to tap into this resource. If it were easy he would have done so already and the world would not perhaps be as lopsided as it is today. This is a skill he must learn to acquire. He must first understand that there is another side to life, another lake of tranquillity that he can tap into. He must learn that he is not as internally alone as he thinks, that his thoughts and his heart are an open book to another level of life, of existence. He must understand that the struggles he sometimes must face are not always the course of providence, but his own lack of correct understanding. He must learn that he is not struggling against the world, completely alone and he must learn to open up – not necessarily to others yet, but to himself, to his own self understanding. Life is falling at his feet but often he just does not notice. (I am I).

Only man can look at his own inner voice. Only he can look at his life in the true light of what really is, in the moments that he is completely alone with his thoughts. The majority of the time we can feel fine. We can ramble through life quite nicely on automatic pilot, but every now and then we have cause to ask ourselves what it's all about. Why we live the way we do. We ask ourselves if it is worth it, worth all the sweat and the worry. We ask whether we are reaping the joys and the rewards that we deserve. We wonder why life is flying ever faster. Why there is so much turmoil and sadness around us, even within our own social circles. I, too, had cause to re-examine my life and the route it was taking. The sun would rise and then set once again without my having seen it at all. I was not locked up in a room but I was so involved with my life that the outside world just passed me by. Days would role into weeks and it was nearly Christmas again. I, too, had to check that I was using my life to its best advantage, or whether I was simply allowing it to pass on. This experience was not unique to me. Many others experience it in one way or another. Some more, some to a lesser degree, but it is a symptom that is widely spread across the moral world. It is a state of mind that is instantly recognisable when you are busy and concerned with the necessities of life. Many of us squeeze so much into our waking day that we can forget to also take time out – to rest. **(I am I). Even I had to take time out for a rest. (I am I).**

The human body is not like a mechanical machine. It requires periods of waking rest in order to keep it uplifted and in full waking order. When we push ourselves too hard all we want to do is sleep. It can be an effort to go out to have fun. Without fun, life can quickly become a chore.

Man must uplift his self-esteem. He must not do things always to the extreme as he does now. Is this the lesson we want our children to follow? They will copy our examples long before they heed our words. At this time they do not necessarily have a good track record from us to follow. Again it is up to us to reassess and to put things once more into a better waking order.

Life must be balanced in almost every direction for it to work smoothly and efficiently. We can do anything we want, whenever we want, but the rule is that is should be balanced.

(I am I). I must also keep the world in balance and given today's erratic behaviour by much of the human race, this is not always an easy thing to do. (I am I). Balance is not always a word that sits high in the human vocabulary. We rarely think of it at all – other than in our finances or perhaps our dietary requirements. Balance is a word that is too often forgotten. Yet it is perhaps one of the most important.

(I am I). At the beginning, the world was made in balance and harmony and light. Man fitted perfectly and the role he was given was to retain that balance. Even in our own state of health a state of balance must be maintained. (I am I).

Life is pulling mans attention in too many directions at once. He must do too many things at any one time to give each task his full attention. This is not necessarily bad but it does not give rise to a good sense of balance either. As long as he can keep on top of the chores that are raging for attention, all will be well, but when he becomes tired or distracted, his lot begins to crumble. It is hard going to keep up with the juggling of life. Only we can prioritise our time and our attention.

(I am I). Only man can look at his daily timetable and adjust it to a more flexible level. (I am I). I, too, have commitments, but it is surprising what you can achieve when you live and focus your energy as and where it's required. This book was achieved in such a way. This book is a miracle all of its own.

Only man can bring his life back into the reality of the present. I, too, practice to achieve this everyday. Sometimes I win and can remove a heap of backlog, while at other times I seem to get nowhere fast, despite my efforts to do so. It is necessary for us to 'bend like the willow branch'. If we can bend and flex we are less likely to snap under the stresses of life - at all times try to remain flexible, not physically, but mentally. Whenever something or someone drags you off course, come right back to it after the event. Life will not stop and wait for you as you attempt to sort it out. Instead it will continue to march forward and all we can hope to do is to keep up and sort it out. Life does not wait for any man. It must keep on moving because that is the nature of the planet's survival. Only man gets stuck and stagnant for a while, so it is only he who can free himself. But first he must learn to do so.

If you can learn to keep an open mind, during the next few months you will be given ample opportunity to begin your own voyage of self discovery. It is not boring, nor is it hard. Once you set your mind to it all things will fall together into place, piece by little piece. I, too, am still in

242

the process of working through my history. I mean the 'since I was old enough to have an opinion and make my own choices' sort of history. I, too, am moving forward but am clearing my path at the same time.

Only we can choose whether we wish to be happy and content with life or whether we want to stay exactly as we are – at the mercy of life and all who cross our path. This voyage of self-discovery will stop others from taking advantage of us any more. We can stop them in their tracks instead because we shall see them coming a mile away. In learning more about yourself you also obtain a better understanding of other people. You will spot the things we all unconsciously do to get life to flow in our favour. You will recognise things that have been going on for years, invisibly, for everyone. Life will present its colours to you in a completely different dimension, just like a child who suddenly wakes up to a new way of thinking. We shall do the same. We shall wonder how on earth we did not know these things before.

Only we can learn to see beyond the vision of the eyes, beyond the feelings that lead us astray and beyond the words and actions of others. When we are spoken to we shall hear for the first time what is really being said, instead of jumping to automatic conclusions. The function of man is to transfer the planet's energy to one another and to allow it free passage between us and the sky and the ground. But this can only be achieved by keeping ourselves open. We have to connect in a clearer way than we do at this moment. Not just clearer as in making the connection, but clearer as in emptying our own emotional bins first. The rubbish we have trudged around since infancy is blocking our senses to the real world itself. The illusions that we keep fuelled by wrong thinking are merely keeping us away from the place we should be. Totally present in the now!

Only we can bring ourselves back to reality with our feet planted firmly on the ground. Only we can take each new

243

day as it comes and make it worth its weight in gold. Only we can live everyday we are given as though it is our last one. We need to clear the backlog of tasks that we take forward with us with every dawn that breaks. I, too, have a mountain that follows me – one step at a time, but I can say that it is slowly diminishing. It cannot be rushed, nor can this task be forgotten because it is all of this that drains our energy steadily away. I, too, am working through my own trail of rubbish.

(I am I). Rubbish can take many forms and it can come in many disguises. It can range from a stack of half finished projects, to unfulfilled promises, to cluttered cupboards and drawers. It can cover decades of time and as you begin to wade through it you will see how deep the pile is. Don't let this worry or dishearten you. It is natural. The bonus is that you are now waking up to yourself and 'your stuff'. You have made a choice to move forward and to clean up. You know now why you must and why it's actually worth it. These things have taken life times to build up, and they can take your own lifetime to clear. But the point is that as long as you attack it earnestly, then you are. You are clearing it – one step at a time. A mountain in its totality can never be moved, but one boulder, one stone at a time, it is possible to move the whole thing.

And another point to remember is that you are not (not ever – anymore) alone. All that you will do will constitute a fraction of what is occurring on your behalf by spirit. (I am I).

Man can do much to help himself if he would but know it. All the help and guidance he could ever need is right under his nose, but he is as an infant watching T.V. He operates within his own mind limitations, so that all other things fly over his head and his range of knowledge. A child might watch an adult programme but it can only understand a small part. The rest goes over his head as well, and we are little different. We, too, need to wake up in order to move up to the next level of survival. Man operates too fully on a material/physical level. He lives in a physical world but he is not completely of this world. He is made of solid matter but he is also so much more besides.

I, too, am matter but of a slightly different calibre. The energy we are made of becomes finer as we tune into ourselves on a new level of understanding. I, too, have a long way to go before I can reach my goal post, or even my God post. I, too, am still only a fraction of what my eternal capabilities can eventually be. No one here on earth can plug into their soul and see how far it has already travelled along the course of evolution, so it is only fitting that we yet cannot know how far we have left to go. All souls here on earth were born at the same time - at the beginning. There can now be no new editions. We are born into a physical life and we shall leave it behind when we cross the bridge back home. We have all done this many times before and we shall continue long into the future, as long as the need occurs. It is the destiny of man to grow and evolve. Since the time of living in caves we have come a long way. Even in our own short lives we can look back with hindsight and realise the distance we have travelled, despite any obstacles we have encountered along the way. Life is a gift. Each life is individual. It is no more special than another. We are all travelling to meet the same end. That is all there is to it. We don't really have any choice in the matter, yet we have every choice under the sun. Life is ours for the taking. It is here to be lived, to be loved and to be cherished.

(I am I). I once spoke directly to every man himself and I will do so again. Each man everywhere will hear me as plainly as he can hear his own thoughts. This book is a living example of that truth. I will talk to you, as you, too, will learn to talk with me. I am not a legend, neither am I a ghost of the past or the future. I

live in the here and now. You should also live in the here and now, because that is the only time there is. The past is time that has gone and been spent. The future is yet but an illusion; an idea. The moment you are now in – and every moment you shall ever be in at the time of its birth, is the miracle of God. It is here and only here that you will find me. It is here that all things are possible. All of life stems from this point and this point alone. Remove your automatic button and be fully aware and alive once more in the 'now'. (I am I).

Man has the world at his feet. All possibilities he could ever imagine are here in the now for his taking.

(I am I). I will help him just as soon as he asks me. Not by lip service. Not by merely mouthing the words, but when he pulls those words form deep within his heart. I will not judge him by his past actions, words or deeds. I will not do that ever. I am only here to love him as a parent unconditionally loves his child. How could I turn my back on myself? He is a part of myself. You all are. Could you disconnect your own arm and not feel it? The answer is No. So neither could I. Each man, each person, each being and living thing is a part of me that I can never replace. How could I dismantle myself and to what purpose would I do it? I am not imagination. I am real. I am not a man, not a figure looming high in the sky that threatens to tower over you through eternity. I am with you, quietly, now and have always been so. I could never be anywhere else because you live upon my own body. You breathe in my life force – into your lungs, in through your skin, through every pore in your being. I am all you are and you in return are a fraction of me. Go out into space and look down. All that you see is me. And you are a part of that. Each man is as important as the next because combined as one we make the whole. (I am I).

246

Man is important. He is the conscience of a planet that can live, breathe and comprehend all that he will ever come across. He is a living part of God. He is part of the all that is and the part he plays is irreplaceable. There is good and bad in us all, but man was equipped with self-intelligence. He can realise right from wrong, hot from cold, love from hate. The choices and rules he then lives by are his own affair. It is up to him to choose the best, and to become the best example of a person that he ever could be. It is up to him to live his life in a way that he himself would be proud to own up to. The past is past. It is up to him to move on.

Only man can wake himself up from the waking sleep that has been his life. Only he can choose to do this for himself, by himself. Yet when he does he will see that he is not by himself and never has been.

(I am I). I am here, holding his hand. I will carry him through the next few months and years if he so wishes, but first he must learn to recognise my presence. How can he know I am helping him until he does? Life can never be plain sailing. The very nature of this planet is a cycle of life and death, life and death. He, too, is part of this cycle. Pain plays as much a part as joy, but out of pain comes growth and understanding. I will not cause him pain. He does that alone by his choices - he and others around him, but I can help him through these periods of pain, a lot more easily than if he were alone, wading through it. Man is not lost; he is found. He is right back where he should be. There is no more deviation in his way. He is home if he can but realise. He is home.

Only you can take yourself into your future. You are not bound by ties of the past. You are free to travel in the direction of your choice. Not physically, but mentally. The thoughts you think do matter. They matter very much. In fact if you but realise – they 'make' matter. (I am I).

247

Only man can wake himself up to the divine presence that surrounds him in all things. I, too, have had to do this. I, too, walked for almost forty years as though blinkered, through my life. I, too, have had to wake up to the divine presence that walks with me and talks with me. I, too, have had to let go of my past mistakes, both of my own making and through the intervention of others. Only we can love ourselves, and this life enough, to have the guts to begin again on a clean slate; to take up the chance of a new beginning that has been offered to us. Life is a precious thing. Only we can choose to live it. Only we can make the difference it will take to make it work. Only we can now put back as much as we have taken out.

The Native American Red Indians knew much about life and about living in harmony with God and with the planet. They recognised the importance of balance and of prayer. They bound herbs and tobacco to give back to the planet by way of thanks for all they received. They took nothing from 'mother earth' that was not absolutely necessary for their survival. They looked upon 'father sky' as the bringer of that life to both mother earth and to themselves. They recognised the importance of a circle as a cycle. They learnt to honour all things for their own value and importance. They lived in harmony (most of the time) with life.

They believed in living life to the full and all things played their part. They recognised the many cycles that past through life each year – each season. They believed in honouring those who walked before them and they kept their life alive through tradition and through stories. They understood both the powers of word and of thought. They knew a lot that the white man is only now beginning to understand.

Life for all civilisations, both past and present, is the same. We are born of the same source and are made of the same stuff.

(I am I). I made a promise to man that I would live with him, if he would live with me. Through all of time I have kept my promise. The civilisations of the past have not all gone. They are very much alive. They have left your physical world and you but know their remains, but they are all a part of life itself as it is today. Many souls have taken the choice to be born again through other lives, whilst others have taken the choice to remain here, as they were, and experience life from this side. All life is life whether it is of the physical or the spiritual. In essence all life is spirit. It is energy in form, in motion. Only man can wake himself up to learn to understand this. I miss him. I want him back. I would like to walk by his side once more, to laugh and to cry and to love with him. Man could not live for long by himself and neither can I. We need each other, to continue. (I am I).

Only man has got lost over the space of time. Only he can find his way back home, but not alone. He is not alone. Every living day of his life he will be helped, but the cry must first come from his heart. Not just his mind or his mouth. It must come from his very being when he realises his mistake. And it is just that. He was mistaken.

Only we can live the life we are in. Only we can take it forward into the future. Neither God nor spirit can do it for us. Only we can take this Earth and turn it around once more. I, too, must play my part and this book will play its part too. Alone we feel small and insignificant. We buckle with wonder as we see the task ahead. But life will lead us along, one little step at a time and all we must do is keep up. We must not falter and we must not fall. We will walk with the aid and love of God. With the strength and support of spirit and with the help and the knowledge that they bring. Together we make a world. Together we can repair what is broken and together we can walk to the future.

Chapter Twenty-One

The Winds of Re-birth

Learning to live again

Only we can get our lives back on track. Only we can bring the spring back to our step and the laughter back into our hearts. **(I am I). I must help you. (I am I).** Now is time for reflection and for thought.

Only man can sit down to look at and understand where he is now. There is help wherever he looks. This journey has not just begun, it has always been. For years those that have re-awoken have tried to reach those that are still asleep. They have written books and songs and plays. They have tried any way they can think of to record their findings in the hope that some day it will help mankind. Alone their works seem small. But they are not alone. They are binding together more and more to make a blanket of awareness that is reaching out to man. Together they tell the truth of a life that really does exist.

A child can only understand through his capacity of awareness. All other things pass over his head. And we are the same. All these truths have always been right in front of our noses. But we have missed them because we could not see. We did not understand. We did not know.

(I am I). I must help each individual in his own area of understanding, to wake up. I must reach out and touch every one of you until you realise I am real. I am here - in the now. I am with you and I am helping you. Do not be fearful, or live in guilt. None of these can help. They will only distance you more from the reality that now you face. You are as a newborn child that is looking for guidance, for instruction. Only you can

learn to reconnect to the all that is; to myself and the richness of the past combined with present. The future does not matter. All possible outcomes are always available to man at any one time, like an interactive computer game. The only thing that really matters is the now, and it is here that you will find me. (I am I).

Only we can make the connection – by ourselves and for ourselves. Everyday is a new day – a new beginning. Take each day as it comes and do all that you must do. But before you do ask God that he shall lead you. Ask that you may walk behind him in his guidance instead of in front as you always do. This is your life to live, but to live it well man sometimes needs help.

(I am I). I will help you to get back on track, with your feet on the ground and your head in the air. I will help you sort through the rubble and the ashes of your life and I will help seeds take root. Together we will go forward with one foot in front of another. (I am I).

This book has probably rocked you to your core. It will have touched places that until now you did not realise did exist.

(I am I). I will help you through the next few years, but first you must let me in. I cannot reach you, cannot hear and feel you when you are racked with pain and guilt and stress. I am love and so are you. It is only in the love mode that we can connect once again. Not the passionate, man woman love, but the joy and happiness in your heart kind of love - the love that is born from peace and contentment - the love that first made you. (I am I).

Every person, everywhere, began in the same way. They began with a spark of love and of light - even those who were born traumatically. They too are of the same source. I must help man to understand both himself and his life better than he does right now. I, too, must make some changes in my approach to life. I, too, have some catching

251

up to do. It is easy to get hung up on the past - even the recent past such as yesterday and the day before. I, too, must keep in the now more than in the past or the future. All of life is happening here - in the 'now'. All of life stems from this moment in time. This is all there is. This is all there can be. All of the future begins from this point and the past has led us to this point as well. All you will ever be, stems from here and now.

(I am I). I, too, live in the moment. This is the only place that I am. All of my life is the sum total of all of yours and when you look at the state of the human world you can see what a mess you are leaving me in. There is very much left for us to do to rectify the mistakes of the past. These cannot be done in one go — or we would create an unbalance of a different kind - a different order. Instead all things must be addressed one single step at a time — at the exact moment that it occurs. That is the law of cause and effect. To effect a change to stop an event is to change its course entirely. This has its benefits, but it also has its downfalls. The only way to ensure correct precision is to instigate all things in the now - the time that they arise. (I am I).

There is an upward side to this. It means that in the here and now we have hit rock bottom — and from now, providing we can pull ourselves together, the only way left is up

(I am I). I also second this statement. Providing you are willing to help yourselves, slowly — starting with your own life, then I will stay with you - every step along the way. I will show you the best way forward until you are able once more to go it alone. I will show you, but you must learn to listen, to see and to hear. (I am I).

Listed at the rear of this book are a few of the countless books that can help you in your studies. I will help you find the ones that are best for you at this time. The journey you are about to begin is a solitary one. You are journeying within to find the workings and the essence of your truest self and in doing so you will also learn to understand others in a different light. With understanding also comes forgiveness. You will learn to recognise how those before you were stuck. Once upon a time they were as free and as hopeful as you are with your thoughts. The world was their oyster too – but then real life took over. It dulled the light of their inspiration. All people are just that – people. They each had their own hopes and dreams and aspirations. Don't let your own light flicker and fade into nothingness. Nurture it back to health, back to life. Find your own sense of vitality and wonder once more. Rekindle the zest you used to have for life and learn to enjoy it. Stress is a word of the moment. Stress overrides all other emotions when we let it, but most of us have no idea how to stop it. Once it takes its hold it is self-perpetuating.

(I am I). Stress is one of the main things that will draw you away from me; it is one of the things that keeps you locked into exactly where you are. When you are stressed you are closed to all else - you have switched to unbalance and overload. Take a deep breath and think of me. Ask to be given truth and light and balance once more. Ask that all illusion be removed from the situation and ask me to oversee the problem. Ask it for yourself – twenty times a day if necessary, but ask. I am powerless to help you unless you do. Don't despair if it does not work right away – it may be that there is a further reason behind it, or there might be something else you are missing. I will always do all I can to sort things out in any way I can. It is in my interest too – to keep you free of illusion. How can you know which way to go when you only see half the deck of cards? To choose correctly you need to see the whole picture. The truth of the moment you are

experiencing. By asking for my help you help to avoid further miscommunication and misconception. (I am I).

This life is for you to live. Spirit and God cannot do it for you. Only you have brought yourself to where you are now and only you can lead yourself back. Over the course of time man has given too much of his own power away and by following the trend, he has become a product of the times. He has almost left too much to others and to automatic pilot. The time is now right for him to take this back, but before he can he must again remember how.

At no time in your life will you be left flapping around, wondering what to do next for the best. When you don't know which way to turn, simply do nothing until you do. Never make a choice out of desperation or impulse. Some of our best choices were made this way, but so were some of our worst. Before we leap into the unknown it is better to see where we might land, to know what is on the other side of the hole. Life will always allow you to see both sides of the coin, but sometimes you must wait for it to do so. Time must also play its part in the game of life, but we sometimes forget that in our haste.

(I am I). I will always allow you to see the whole picture if you allow me to. I will always allow you to understand all your options before you make a choice. Life is about taking chances but it is also important to keep your feet firmly on the ground. To change too much too soon can sometimes leave you without your roots. Only you can look at your life and only you can decide how best to pull it together once more. Bridges can be rebuilt between arguing relations, once step at a time, but it is helpful to remember me. Ask me beforehand to help you where help is needed. Ask that old blockages and fences be recycled. Ask that all illusion be removed and ask that the words both you or all will need, be given to you at the time they are needed. Walk with love and hope in your heart instead

of doubt or blame or fear. One small step at a time and a miracle can be achieved.

When you are faced with a mountain again remember me. I will hand it to you one stone at a time, so you will be able to deal with it. Ask and you will be given - even if you won't always realise it at the time. (I am I).

Only we can learn to recognise the help and the support that is constantly around us. Those we have loved and lost are never far away. They are rooting for us, helping us to see the truth that is ours to see. They pop in and out to visit us much more than they sometimes could when they were here on Earth. They don't remain with us the whole time, because this is our life to live, and they have theirs too, but they do keep a watchful, loving eye on us.

(I am I). When a leaflet falls onto your mat at exactly the time you need it, it is I. When you hear a conversation by chance, that contains exactly what you need, it is I. When you watch a film or read a magazine and some vital/helpful piece of information jumps out to your attention, it is I. I will give you whatever you need, whenever you need it, but you must stay aware. You must allow time for these things to fall into place. Sometimes it is necessary for you to follow a wrong path to get to the end, to move over and make another connection. All things will lead to something, somewhere. (I am I).

Only we can walk with our eyes and our ears open as we expect the unexpected. Once you start to recognise the all too often coincidences, you will attract even more to yourself. Learn to say a mental thank you in acknowledgement that you have understood or received. Learn to remain focused in the moment as often as you can for these things to occur. Miracles can only occur in the now. If your attention wanders too far you can miss the subtleties that are there. Life is not a chore for you to carry like a milestone around your neck. It is a voyage of discovery and of fun. Not all the time, but for most of it. Let go of your rigid timetable sometimes to allow chance to step in and surprise you. You are guided and helped nearly every step of the way, but most especially when you falter and appear to fall. Never fear. Keep your mind's arena as clear and as clutter free as possible. When your mind wants to race, bring it quietly back. Ask that your thoughts be at peace and your mind be still. Ask again and again if necessary, but ask.

There may be times that things just won't leave you alone. The same thoughts may come back or you may find yourself in a place you thought you had dealt with already. At times such as these you may be missing something that needs your attention. There may be a change that needs to be made, or that perhaps you have been avoiding. Again don't worry. Ask for help to understand the problem and then to sort it out. Ask for illusion to be removed and ask that you see only the truth. Again ask and you may be pleasantly surprised how quickly and easily you can remove it. An argument that you had been dreading can fluff away into nothing. Always speak the truth, but with love and consideration - never with anger. The anger that you produce will always bounce right back to you. It will fuel a tense situation even further. Try to remain calm and say nothing if it will cause discomfort or pain. Wait for a better time to come, and be sure that it will.

All of your life stems from you. You are its centre pillar. You can make it work or you can mow it down. Only you can take it forward to work in a better fashion for you. The things that you need, will not always come to you in the form that you were waiting for, or in the way that you thought you wanted them to. Life has a way of showing its colours in an unexpected manner, so try to remain open and flexible through each day. Life will unfold before your eyes but first you must send up your thoughts and allow it to sort itself out. Only thoughts sent with an open loving mind can be heard. The pain and pleas and fears remain with us. They block our way and our actions, and that is why we must recycle them. They will only hinder and fester otherwise. They add negative energy to an already negative situation. Fearful thoughts only send fear into your future. You feed your future with them. Let it go. Send it back to where it can be transformed into something useful. Don't keep it to yourself, nor pile those thoughts onto others. Recycle them instead and allow the truth to shine through. Life is tricky. Once you begin to be aware of the things that you do that keep you where you are, you will be surprised at how often you did them. You will realise how you added unconsciously to the situations you found yourself in.

Only you can help you, and after you do you will start to help those you love. Not in monetary or material form but in a giving of your own essence, your own truths. You will stop feeding your friends illusions and you will help them also to step out of their chains. Love and light will always win through. Light is infinitely more powerful than dark, but the dark will keep you there until you learn to let it go. Until you learn to hand it up to your God, your creator. If this is too difficult at first, pass it up to someone you know in spirit; someone you are more comfortable with. They will know what to do to pass it on, on your behalf, but the point is that you must learn to pass it on, upwards, not outwards to your friends or your relations.

Only you can do these things to help yourself onto a surer, happier path. The books you will read following or even before this one will show you other ways to help yourself. They will click other things back into a more usable order. They will show you other truths that will help you along your way, perhaps on a more physical level.

No change can be instant. It often takes time, patience and practice. Be patient with yourself. Don't be so quick to judge. Wait for the truth to come to light as often as you are able. Every person is in the same boat you are. They are looking for their own life to fit as it should. They, too, are searching for their missing link. They too are looking to find peace and love and contentment on a permanent level. They, too, are searching for their guiding star, so be gentle with them too. If a truth needs to be spoken, say it with love and with kindness. Ask beforehand that the words be given to you to give to them and ask that they be received on board in the manner that they should. Ask again that illusion be recycled and ask after the event, regardless of its outcome, for it to now be handled by our father. Ask and let it go. Get on with your day in hand. Only we can do this for ourselves and for each other.

(I am I). Ask and it will be given. Ask in love and it will be done, always. I am your father, your provider, your living God. I am not vengeful, but always loving. I am tolerant and patient. I will wait for you until you are ready to accept me back into your life. Until you are ready to believe that I exist. I will always stand quietly by your side, whether you believe it or not, but if you are willing to give me a try, the proof you will see for yourself. It will not take faith anymore, because you will know beyond doubt. It will be fact. (I am I).

Only we can push past the bouts of depression that can overwhelm us when we least expect it to. I, too, have been in this place and it can still catch me out even now. It can be hard to remain uplifted and positive when all that's stretched ahead of you is doom and gloom. At these times you must accept the inevitable and hope that its storm will pass as quickly and quietly as possible. Keep your head down and keep yourself small in all that you do, until it is safe to venture out once more. Life will ebb and flow, like the tides of the sea. Sometimes it will be rough and sometimes rougher still, but at other times not a ripple will remain to be seen. Life must be this way for a reason. Life has a beat all of its own, but most of the time it is hard to notice. All things must vibrate within their own frequencies. All of life's events have their time and their place within the life that we live. Sometimes in our darkest times an unexpected glimmer of hope will emerge to surprise you. That, too, is the nature of life.

Because we don't really like change we unconsciously try to keep things exactly as they are, even when we can see that change is necessary. I, too, am guilty of this. I, too, must become more flexible and open to the mysteries of life. I, too, must learn to dance with the beat of the time I am in.

Man expects what he expects when he expects it. He is altogether too impatient. He wants everything yesterday; even when that's not possible and he will go out of his way to obtain it. Life cannot always be like that. Again, nothing can happen before it is destined to be. There is no use pushing harder to get there first. Man is too impatient for his own good. He sails through the good times without even noticing and he runs riot in the bad. I, too, must remain more consistent within myself. I should take more in my stride than I do. I find it too easy to panic when things get a little wobbly for a time. I jump to the conclusion that I must be doing something wrong, even when it is clear that I am not. I, too, find it too easy to take the blame onto myself. But then again – we should not blame others either. They, too, are on the opposite side of the same coin. At times like these all we can do is recycle once more and sit tight until the storm has sailed past.

Only we can do these things for ourselves, but we must first recognise that we need to. Over the next few days you will begin to notice when you start to beat yourself down, or perhaps others instead. The point is that this will help no one. Negativity will only attract more negativity and it will make you feel worse. Hand it up to those that know what to do with it on your behalf. Hand it up and take a breather.

Then carry on with your day and let it sort itself out. Providing you do nothing you should not, then things should settle down once more to an acceptable level.

Only man can sort his daily life into a better working order. Only he can weed each day until it runs smoothly like clockwork.

(I am I). The day you are in is the offering you will leave in your wake. Learn to use it wisely. Treasure all things that you do as though they will be your last. Learn to tie up your loose ends and never leave for tomorrow what you can do in this day. When tomorrow comes it will dance to a whole new beat of its own. And who knows, you might even smile and be happy. (I am I).

Only you can colour your life in the way you would like it to be. The place you are now is born of the sum of your past. The responsibilities you have you probably chose along the way. Stand by your obligations whenever you can, but don't stoop to carry more than your load too often. If you are a doer, make sure that others are not merely letting you do their share as well. I, too, used to do more than I was supposed to, mostly because at first I wanted to. It pleased me to be this way. Then the balance can shift and others will expect it of you automatically. Suddenly what you did to help has become the normal expected level of your task. If you are doing too much then you can be robbing others of the experience of doing enough. The balance of life should be fair and just at all times. Too much in either direction will cause an imbalance somewhere. I, too, had to learn this and it was no easy task.

(I am I). Life will come to you in the way you most expect. Expect nothing and let it take its course. Do what you have to do at the time you are supposed to do it, and leave the rest to us. (I am I).

Only you can make the necessary adjustments that will leave you free to be who you want to be. Only you can move beyond the normal constraints that you would operate within. No one else can take your hand. The journey into the self can be a solitary one, but if you remain in the truth and the light then you will never regret another day you will live. Life itself will appear too short, too fleeting for you to achieve all that you will wish to achieve. A whole lifetime just won't be long enough.

The world can be saved and we are the ones who can do it - one step by one small step at a time. We can move mountains if we would wish to, but first we must start from within. Only within will clear our rubbish and clutter, and only then can we begin to move slowly forward as we would like.

Only man can save himself because man is in the driving seat. He must learn to walk once more in the sun. He must move away from the stress that engulfs him and he must find his own inner peace.

(I am I). I will help him if he so wishes. I will lead him on in the way that is best for him. Each journey is an individual affair. Children of the same family are all on their own individual journeys. They are all striving to find their own life and their own way back home once more. (I am I).

Only we can make our own way back home, back to the peace that resides in our mind and in our heart. Only we can take the turmoil and stress and turn it around. It is up to us alone to pull ourselves together once more. To control the thoughts we think and to step out of the mundane that we have accepted as our lot. Life is too precious to allow it to dwindle recklessly away as we play the waiting game. Don't let your days drift into nothingness. Take hold of each one as a gift, as a gem, and treasure it for all its worth. You will never get it back once it's gone; and once it's gone, it's gone forever.

Life is not always easy for anyone. Neither should it always be hard. If yours is difficult most of the time then you are probably missing the triggers that would help lift you out from where you are. Begin to notice what you do to unconsciously help keep yourself there. Begin to notice how others keep you there as well. *'Families and How to survive them'* is an excellent book that could help you gain a better perspective of your self. Written by John Cleese & Robin Skinner, it will highlight many things that until now we often take for granted. This book is written in an easy to read conversation format. It will help many things slot into place.

We are lucky today in that when we realise a problem exists, all available tools are there to help us. We can talk to counsellors and professional people for advice if we want to, but otherwise a mountain of information and help is available in book form. If you are not a book reader then you could perhaps get them on tape from a company called 'Talking Books'. Your local library should have the details, otherwise failing that, you will just have to keep your wits about you and your ears open. You will stumble across all sorts of things at precisely the time that you need them, but you must remain open and in the moment in order to notice. All things will be available to us in the form that we need them, at the time that we need them. I, too, have been on this route. I read a dozen books in as many months once I began. I read what I was directed to read, and this came from intuition within. You, too, will be led if you can allow yourself to be. Notice what grabs your attention. Begin to be aware of the coincidences that occur quite naturally and follow them through when you can. A whole New World is waiting for you to notice that it's there. Nothing happens without a reason, so that means also that all that happens does so for a purpose. Relax a little and enjoy the experience of the ride. Notice what it's trying to tell you and if you have no use for it now, place it in your memory banks for later, when you can put it together with something else.

(I am I). I will help you go forward from this moment on if you ask me to. I will try to lead you in a way that's loud and clear, but you must help me. I can only use the tools that are available to me at the time, so once more you must remain vigilant, open and aware. If you are not sure then wait until you are. Ask me to recycle the rubbish until you are left with the truth. If a thought is persistent then examine it. Find out what it's trying to tell you. If it leads you on, then follow it. If it appears negative then examine it too and find out why it's bothering you. Look to understand what it relates to. It might even be your Ego that is panicking unnecessarily. There is a part of you that does not like change very much. That part served its purpose in your early youth, because it stopped you from going too far too fast. It stopped you from hurting yourself by keeping you within certain boundaries and limitations. This part of you might start to panic and it may try to throw you off course. It wants to stay in the familiar. It tries to bring you back to where you were, because then it knows or thinks that you will be safe; but wrong - it is that that has held you back. It is ego that is responsible for your unhappiness. Learn to make your own judgements. Don't just slip into automatic once more. Your ego will scream and shout at you like a spoiled little child, but learn to see beyond it. Ask that its illusions be recycled and ask for the light to shine through. (I am I).

Keep your head up and remain balanced. Learn as much as you can about yourself and go beyond the constraints that would normally hold you back. Not your personal responsibilities, they are another matter, but your own internal doubts and fears. Don't jump recklessly into the unknown, but go forward slowly and surely into your future.

263

(I am I). All time stems from this time, from the time that you are in now. Look after this time and the rest will fall surely into place. It may be bumpy for a while or it may be incredibly smooth, but it will be all that it needs to be as it takes you on with your life. (I am I).

You are at the beginning of your life. The place you are now is of the fruits of the past. You are at the start of your next phase. Look at it and protect it as you would a newborn child. You will be that child for a while. You might feel vulnerable and unsure as the armour plating you have surrounded yourself with slips away. But don't begin to worry and don't be bored with the task in hand. Look at the strengths that you have and learn to use them.

(I am I). All you are, all you have done and all you have been, will have left you with lessons and strengths that are unique to you. Learn to recognise your good points and allow the rest to fall away. It will not happen overnight, but it will happen if you let it. Notice the love that sits quietly by and accept it, as you should. You may become tearful and emotional for a while. This, too, must play its part. It is a symptom of the new that's coming of the old. Don't worry. It will pass. It may take a while, but it is just a stage. It is a little of what needs to come out from your past. It is a little of what you have kept locked away. It is a part of you that simply needs to 'be' for a while. Nurture that part and understand it as necessary. Learn to let yourself be all that you need to be; but learn to let yourself live. (I am I).

Only we can open the doors that we have kept locked against the world, and even against ourselves too. Some were banged shut so early in childhood that we don't even know they exist. Learn to be patient with the world and with yourself. No one means to harm you. They, too, are probably in the same boat you are. They, too, are just trying to live in the best way that they know how. They, too, are searching for their own happy ever after ending, but they are probably as unaware of their actions as you were. They will wake up when the time is right for them to do so, but until then, just let it go and concentrate on your own actions, on your own responses.

(I am I). Ask me and I will transform the situation into the truth. I will allow the truth to shine through when it should. I will be your strength and your armour. I will be your guide. (I am I).

Man is at the birth of a new dawn. That is why Nostradamous could not see beyond this point. That is why he signalled the end of the world. It is the end of the old and the birth of the new.

(I am I). Once again I must second this statement. Man is very much on the threshold of a new understanding - of a new wave of life. (I am I).

The world as we know it had to get to this point. It has to exhaust its limitations in order to go past them. Just like a boil must achieve its full head before it can be lanced, the trials and tribulations of man had to reach the same. It was a necessary brick of life.

Only we can take it forward now, to the next stage - the next phase. We made our pledge to do just this before we came back. All we have been through, and all that we know, has been a vital part in making the connection we should. The place you have reached in your life is exactly where you should be in order that you may go forward. You cannot be who you are until you are certain of who you are not. The path of individuality is not always as clear-cut as we would like it to be. There are times when we can sail smoothly and freely with the wind and then there are other times when all seems to go incredibly wrong. These are the seasonal challenges of life. These are the things we have to work through.

Only we can live through these moments, but when we understand the reasons behind them it is unlikely that they

265

will trouble us further. Once we have learnt a lesson we learn not to let it happen again.

Only we can go forward as we were always intended to do. Take this time as a breath of fresh air. Do all that you are required to do but use your free time as a starting point that will guide you forward on a surer path. Take this time as a gift - a chance to take stock, like the earth does in the winter months. Make yourself small and allow the dust to settle. Only you can do this for you. Allow this time to do some healing of its own. Begin to take notice of the things that surround you, the patterns that are most prominent in your life and your family. Use your free time to read and to digest what you are learning. Take it slowly and be kind to yourself in the meantime. Life will always throw its challenges at you, especially when you least expect it to. What matters most is the way you then handle both yourself and the situation. There is an old Chinese Lesson called the 'I Ching'. Books are available to help you understand the changes that are occurring both within and without yourself right now. Many have written about it, but the one that helped me was called '*The I Ching or Book of Changes*', by Brian Browne Walker (ISBN No. 0-7499-1265-0). Treat this book with respect and you will be linked with a helping guide that will tune himself in to you. This, too, is not a game. The book and the procedure you will follow each day is a tool that will link you to spirit. You will achieve the advice that you need. Learn to use what it is telling you, but remember, it is only a tool. A guide. You must do the hard work for yourself. You must fill in the missing pieces, but with a guiding hand it will be easier than fumbling around in the dark.

The way you choose to go forward is your own affair. I, too, have been here and have thankfully come out of the other side, but who knows for how long. Knowledge and understanding does not make you immune to life. It merely helps you walk through those troubled times easier than you did before. It helps you to recognise the light at the end of the tunnel.

Only we can work through the issues that need to be addressed, and each time we do we will grow a little stronger, a little surer of the path we should follow.

(I am I). I am by your side to experience with you all that you do. Learn to recognise this. Learn to trust me as you used to trust yourself. Until now you have done all that you thought you wanted. All that you thought would bring you happiness and love; but has it? Is where you would like to be where you are? (I am I). Follow each day one step at a time and gradually you will win through.

Only you can learn what the missing pieces are in your life. Books and other information will help but only you can fit the pieces of the puzzle together. And that is exactly what this is all about. It is a coming together of all the pieces of your life that are useful to you. It is a throwing away of old worn out habits and behaviour patterns that no longer serve you in the way that they should. I, too, have been here. During infancy, depending on our surroundings and the quality of interaction that was available to us, we built up an unconscious picture of life. For the most part it has served us well and has been pretty accurate in its projection, but the rest was laid aside as building foundations for a later date. In adulthood it is necessary to draw upon those foundations, as they were the original plans that we would be guided by unconsciously. Problems arise when we have mislaid those stones by wrong information or by wrong interpretation of our early life. A computer needs all its programming just so, that it may call upon what it needs at the appropriate time. It must have all things labelled correctly and in a specific order. And we are not different. We, too, must unconsciously call upon past experiences as a basis of how to go forward. These early instructions are often the guidelines we live by. If by the wrongful doing of those about us we misinterpreted or misjudged those early years then the information we have to draw upon will be flawed. It will not serve us as it should in the way that it should. We of course have no idea. We don't even know that a problem exists. Our life is just our life to us, and that is all there is to it. But wrong. Just as a computer can be upgraded from time to time, so can we. We are the most brilliant invention that nature ever put breath into. How can we be so cocky as to believe that we are perfect? That we know it all? Not physically, but mentally in our emotional memory banks. We simply accept our lot as our lot and wade through life in the best way we know how. We check our motorised engines on a regular basis. We don't expect them to run forever without any thought and update their mechanics with new technology on a regular basis too. Just look at how far formula one has come. We are magnificent in our inventions. Yet when do we ever pay even a fraction of that attention to ourselves? Our bodies and our looks yes. Some are besotted by their appearance, yet the driving force behind us is our inner workings. The thoughts we have put together over a lifetime. We have done very well to a point, but how do we get passed that? How can we ever help ourselves over the last few hurdles when we don't know how?

Man has reached a state in his life that needs learning about. He has reached as far as he can by himself, and it is now time to pull all things back into order.

(I am I). I have stood by man through all of his life. I have been witness to all of his ups and especially his downs. Until he turns to me, even now, I cannot help him. Because of free will I am bound to watch on and wait. From the first word he will utter to my direction I will help him. I will pick him up from his pain and his sadness and I will right him gently once more. I will be

as a parent that looks out for his infant. I will be that parent and man will be my child. (I am I).

Only you can help this to occur. Only you can open even the tinniest window in your mind to allow God to step in. Massive belief is not an issue. The first tiny spark from you will bring the light forward. And all the proof that you need will come flooding to your door. To notice you must simply be aware. Notice the difference in those times that you actually ask for help. Be sensible about it, but notice the difference all the same. The armour you began to place about yourself during infancy has grown as thick as the thickest steel. It is impregnable by any force, even by God. You have learned to lock things up well. This helped to guard you when it was necessary, but it also stopped much of the love you wanted from filtering in. Now it is time to begin to open up those dusty old chambers - years of dust has settled. In the safety of God and your adult discrimination abilities it is safe to finally come into bloom. This is what your life has always been about. This is the time of your fruition.

Trust in yourself. You have learned your lessons well. Right from wrong is your forte. Pick up the pieces of your life and move yourself forward to a happier place. All the help you need is right beside you. You must simply recognise it.

Chapter Twenty-Two

The Winds of Light and Love

(I am I). I am the light. I am the love. I am the lantern that will guide you. (I am I).

Only man knows all there is to know about his self and the path he has trod. He can recall at will practically all of his life as though it were only yesterday. The mind and its memories are not bound by time, nor by lock or any key.

(I am I). I am the keeper of these records. All that you have ever achieved is kept in order by me. I am the conscious mind that holds the blue print of the whole of this planet. I know all there is to know about all that has been, but the future is yet but a dream. (I am I).

All that is yet to be is contained each day in the thoughts of man. All that ever was, was first a thought, an idea, that was born into materialisation by the actions of mankind. Even the thoughts that we discarded have played their part, and because of this the possibilities of the future are endless. The thoughts we generate hold more power than we could ever imagine. It is not by chance that the things we need turn up. It is not chance that put them there but the conscious and unconscious thoughts we generate ten to the dozen. The thoughts we have are more like radar signals that send out words of instruction to the realms of the spirit. Just as there are hundreds of workers here, performing all their daily tasks, so it is more so in spirit. When we send out a thought of something we need, it is received by someone somewhere, who then tries to put it into being. Now you can see the problem of always changing your mind. Because we are usually ahead of ourselves in the daily thoughts we think, that which we need is placed in our path usually when we have changed our mind. We have already moved onto the next project by the time the cavalry has arrived. It is our fault, not the fault of God or of spirit. It is us who live in the future more than we live in the now, the present. We have left the now on automatic. We automatically drift through the day as we do most of the things that we do. Only we can bring our time back to the present, not only in our actions but in the thoughts that we think as well. I, too, attempt to catch myself out as my attention wanders from place to place. I, too, must remain more focused than I do. The time that is most important to our life is always the time we are experiencing at this moment. Yet our attention is hardly ever fully there. I, too, have a dozen things that I must think about at any one time, so it is not always easy to remain fully in tune with the task in hand. It is not easy but we should try our best. For a start it will help us finish our tasks faster and better than we would otherwise do, but it also has an added benefit. Energy flows where thought goes. When we can remain fully focused we stop wasting our precious energy. Only we can curb our thoughts. Only we can come back to the now.

Only man can slow his life back down to a walking pace. The world we are a part of is getting faster and faster in every way. This can have its benefits but it more often has none. We are creating an instant race of children who will come to expect life to always be this way. They, too, will join that bandwagon when it is time for them to take this world forward. They will come to believe that speed is of the essence - the faster the better, but wrong. All we do we should do properly and enjoy it. I, too, have played my part in an illusion of this kind. I, too, was on the treadmill, the same conveyor belt, but I, too, had to recognise that it was time to get off - to come back properly to earth and to reality. The problem is that we are living too much on the expectation of tomorrow. We are living too far into a projected future.

271

Even our wages are spent before they come. We don't buy just what we need; we buy things that we might use if... Our homes are cluttered to the brim with knick-knacks and goodies that caught our eyes. Our cupboards and draws are bursting. The shops are full from wall to wall with things that they hope we will want and in the meantime production lines can hardly keep up as they make more and more for a projected market trend. The whole of our economy is about making, buying and using products that in reality we don't really need. We are stuck in a loop that is not only drowning our resources, but our energy as well. We work, we spend, we worry and we buy. We work some more, worry some more and buy and spend even more. Man is being asked to wake up, not only to himself, but also to the part he plays in the state of the world. We are creating children who really believe that life is the way they can see it. The people of the East work hard. They use their bare hands every waking day, to produce enough products to earn a few pence. They live on bare necessities. This is not right – nor is it wrong. It is simply the way their world is. In the Middle East children have been taught they must fight. They fight for the very survival of their life. It is as natural to them as the taking of air into their lungs. When the West goes to liberate them, others believe they must fight harder still. It is the way they have grown accustomed to be. In the West we believe that we want to make something more out of our lives. We try to achieve a personal success story. We want to aim high and sure, and work hard to get up the social ladder. We have become driven by material success. Only we can now place this balance into better order. The world has become too segregated - too black and white. The changes that will most make a difference must start within, not without ourselves.

Only we can look at our life, our surroundings and our thinking. Yes it is necessary to live, and it is nice to live well if we can. But once we reach that point enough should be enough. It is very hard for us to recognise this. We have grown as far as we should materially. Man can have his hearts desire granted by a fairy and still he would want some more. He has forgotten to check when his desires will have been met.

This is not all doom and gloom. This is more about waking up to the realities of life. Is it necessary to spend hundreds and thousands of pounds on all the things that we do? **(I am I). I must second that. (I am I).** We should curb our spending in order to work less and enjoy life more. The simple things that matter go unnoticed in life each day. Man is locked tight into his own world of existence. He wants bigger, better and faster than ever before. He is trapped by his own automatic behaviour.

Just for a while try to step off the merry-go-round. Try to think twice about the things that you would usually do automatically. Try to work out if you really need what you are going to buy, or if it is a 'feel good' item. Try to see behind the actions of the self. Why you do what you do. Even I am here, but with me it is the other way around. I, just like many, have a heart that far exceeds the limitations of my purse. Most of us spend far too much trying to make others feel happier. We give away far more than we are able to realistically afford, so once more we must work harder in the meantime to catch up. Working harder means producing more products and producing more products means that there will be more to sell, therefore more to buy. More to buy means more to spend and more to spend means more hard work. Once more we can see how easily we can be caught in this loop. The only way to stop is to get off the bandwagon. Curb your own actions.

(I am I). I, too, second this once more. The only way forward is to slow all things down. Take life back to a slower, healthier pace that will have a knock on effect for us all. (I am I).

273

But even this will have its problems. We will still have a surplus of product that is floating around. We still will have to look at environmental and social issues. We have structured the world in the way that we have so now we rely too heavily on the projections of future forecasts. The East will feel the pinch if we slow down in the West. The Middle East will still be as it was. The process we must follow must be slow and sure. Panic in any way is disruptive. It once more takes things to extreme. Your life is your own affair. The way you live it and what you choose to do with it, is equally your own affair. The thing we must now do, is retrace our steps. We must pull ourselves together into a better working order. Not outwardly, but inwardly.

Only we can live in love and in light. Only we can take the life we live and make it worth its weight in gold. Only we can learn to live in a better frame of mind for the remainder of the life we have left. In times gone passed man believed that the world was flat. Then he learnt it was round. He thought he was alone and would stand before God or the Devil, depending on where he would end up. But he will not. He is always with his maker as his maker is with him. There has never been a separation. Indeed there never could be. God is us – all combined. He is all that we can see and equally all we cannot. He is as alive and living as we are. He is here in the now – everywhere, everyday. Only man thought he was not. Only man has been mistaken through the teachings and writings of other men. God is lonely and he wants us back. He feels our separation as a parent that loses a child, as a brother that loses his brother. He feels our sadness and our fear but until we reach out to touch him he is powerless to help. It is man who must remake his connection. God's has always been there.

Only we can love ourselves enough to come back on track with all that we are. We are like children that have forgotten their heritage. All our life we have been searching to find out where we belong; who and where and what we are; but we have only had half a picture to do it with. How could we ever believe when we only knew half the facts and a lot of coloration besides? Our God, our father, our creator is here. He is only and always was in the here and now.

(I am I). These words are true. If you never believe another word then believe in this. I am here. I am with you and I always will be. (I am I).

Only man can rediscover his connection to the divine source; this is not fairy tale, it is fact. All through the ages of time man has known in some part of himself that he was actually more than was obvious.

(I am I). I am made manifest in all things, in all of life, but most especially in man. I live life with him, and through him; all that he experiences he does with me, and through me. We are bound together as the sky must meet the sea. There is no split. No dividing line. All things are a part of the whole, and the whole is a part of all things. All that we are, we are together, forever. (I am I).

Man can no more distance himself from God than he can from the earth upon which he is a part.

(I am I). Neither can he distance himself from any part of himself - the good or the bad - the past or the present. He cannot dismiss a single part of his life, but he can understand the mistakes he has made. He can allow them to be recycled so that he does not carry them so heavily about with him. Each new day is just that - a new day to live and experience in a better way. (I am I).

All of the past in whatever form it has appeared has led us to this moment in time. Without one single thing we would not be where we are now. Not all has been for the best; in fact many things could have been avoided if we had understood our connection to life a little sooner, but one

275

thing is sure; we cannot turn back the clock. We can only go forward, one tick at a time.

Only we can decide more correctly the decisions we have to make. The choices we have to take. Life is an individual journey but we are not as alone in it as we think. Only we can open up to the truth of the reality in which we live.

When we are born we are given free choice. We obtain the experiences that we do, in manner and form that we can. Next we go out into the world and we live. We draw upon our past and hope it will take us forward as it should. We make a life for ourselves by our own choices and decisions. We experience all that we do because we want to. We do the things we would love to do at the time we would love to do them. We live life by our own standards, our own beliefs and our own choices. Yes we interact with others along the way and they, too, have an influence upon us. We grow and we change, we change and we grow. We reach the point that we have by our own laws of cause and effect. This is the very nature of free will. We are the masters of our universe, of our little corner of the world. We choose how we will use it and what we shall do with it. We choose all that we do out of free will.

Now it is time to take stock - to reassess - to change direction if necessary, but to audit our life just the same. We are the sum total of all we have ever been. Of all we have said, done and thought. It is time to honestly look at the person you are and the life that you live. Ask yourself some questions. Only you can update your own programme. Only you can re align the parts that you no longer want or need. Only you take your life forward from here.

By going within you can learn to see what makes you function and what is your driving force. Only you can decide or can know what it is that you are searching for. Only you can know what matters to you. When you do you can begin to see a different picture unfolding. You will see deeper reasons behind many of the things that you did. None of us are angels. We were not meant to be at this stage. We are all here in different levels of unfoldment. We are here to learn and to grow in a personal, spiritual way. Not a 'praise the lord' spiritual way, although that may come as natural progression of your self-discoveries, but by spiritual we mean the well-being and happiness of the soul, of the self. Of that part of you that is you.

You are not your arm, nor your leg or both legs. These are limbs. Without them you would be incapacitated, but you would still be you. There would be adjustments to be made on every level, but the essence of you would still be you. That is your spiritual self. That is the part that is energy. It is the blue print of who and what you are. It is this part that merely lives within your physical body as you would use a car to drive you about. Your physical body gives you your physical experience in a physical world, a world made of matter. It helps you experience all that you do in a physical way. Your body is just the vehicle that will carry you through this life. Through this existence and this experience. Your body is no more to you than that. It never was and it never can be more. It is biodegradable. It is supposed to function for the whole of your life, then return in the form of dust or smoke back to the earth once more. That part of you that is you will always be. It can never die. It is a part of life that is eternal. It is that part of you that can laugh and cry and think and know and be. It is all and everything that is you. You are spirit. You are energy in motion. You have love as your essence, as your core. You are you.

Only you can wake up to yourself and once you do, you will have a clearer understanding of where you are going; of where you have been and of what you have learned.

(I am I). **I must say that all these things are true.** **They always have been.** **The problem was that words and understanding got in the way.** **(I am I).**

Throughout the ages there have always been some, before others, that have awoken. They in their way have tried to portray the truths that they found, that they discovered and were a part of, but words are too limiting. They do not always correctly express what we are trying to say. First we are limited by our own choice of them and even when a picture is correctly portrayed it depends once more on the understanding of the receiver. We can only understand within our own personal sphere of discrimination. We can only take in the information that we can relate to, the rest falls to the ground like waste. Through the years of the past many have tried to tell us these truths, but we were not ready. We did not hear and we did not understand. We took the words that we heard and shaped them in the way that we did, or that we could. We made up our own picture by the limitations of our understandings and beliefs. We have led ourselves a merry dance.

The truth will always be the truth whether we believe in it or not. Nothing can change it. It cannot alter. The truth stands sure in the safety of itself and of time. The truth is simply the truth. Nothing that man can challenge it with will change its structure. It is just what it is and it always will be.

(I am I). **I am the truth and the light.** **Before the world (however science may explain it) there was only darkness.** **There was only space, as you know space to be.** **There became a change, an alteration to the conditions that were and over time; over hundreds of millions of years the earth was born.** **Again over hundreds of millions more years, the Earth became as it is today.** **I am that earth.** **I am the essence of this living, breathing, rotating planet, just as you are too.** **All of life**

278

must move, must rotate, and must grow. Nothing is ever stagnant or it would be dead. All of life has a pulse of its own and combined we make this planet. It is not necessary for man to know the whole picture. It is not necessary for man to understand all things as I do, but it is necessary that he understands enough to explain to him the nature of his connection to the world. He must see a clearer picture than perhaps he does now. When a child feels wanted he feels loved and connected. Man needs to feel wanted, needed and necessary to this life. He has searched for his whole life to belong on a deeper level, somewhere, to someone for something.

The nature of this earth is that all things seem to live and die, live and die. Man himself thought he was the same. He has lost his zest for life because of these thoughts. He sees himself as disposable, as insignificant. But it is the very nature of himself that is not any of these things. His existence could not be more vital than it is. He is the caretaker of this planet - this earth upon which he lives. He is a living breathing part of this Earth and all he does will leave its mark somewhere, for someone, on something, for the future and for all eternity. The planet upon which he lives will be his home again. He will most definitely come back and he will choose to do so. That is why it is important for him now to pull himself together. It is time for him to clean up his act and to live in a way that he can be proud to say 'that was my life'. 'This was the part that I played in shaping this world'. Man holds more power in his thoughts than he does in the whole of his physical body. He is like me. He is a chip off the old block. He can perform his own miracles if he would but realise it. He can be happy and content for all eternity, but first he must learn to live his own life in the best way that he can. He must first master his own inner world - the world that makes him tick.

Only man can do this for the love of this life, for his own self, for his family and for his planet that he is a part of.

Man is the instigator of all that he sees around him. He alone has shaped his past and he too will shape his future. Life for him can be all that he wants it to be. He can bow his head and let life lead him, or he can stand tall and grow under his own hand. He can make the rest of his life a happy one or he can stumble along in the dark. Life for us all can be anything we choose it to be, but the point is that we can choose. From now until the end of our days we can choose. We can walk alone as we believe we always have, or we can walk with our creator. I am only a thought away from you. (I am I).

Only you can choose where you will go from here. The books listed at the back are only a few of the tools available to help you start your journey. (I am I). I will help you in all you undertake. I will help you. (I am I).

Take some time out of the rat race. Stand by your commitments and responsibilities but use your free time to collect your thoughts together.

(I am I). I will help you again, but you must allow yourself to ask. It does not matter if you feel silly or strange. Confidence will come with time and practice. I can hear the smallest whisper of sincerity and love. I will come wherever I am invited. There are no restrictions, no limitations to my love. I have waited your whole life long for you to need me; to recognise my presence intertwined with yours. There is nothing you have done that I will not see through. That I will not help you overcome. (I am I).

Only you stand in your own way - you and your thoughts of doubt and of fear - your thoughts of guilt and of failure. How can you be blamed for the things you have done when you did them under false guidance and belief? The time is right for us to awaken. Here and now is the only thing that matters. Do not allow yourself to be bound by the past any longer. It is over. Take this day you are in and live it for all you are worth; use it in a way you can be proud of; do this for yourself; do it for those that you love. Only you can live it – so live it!

Only you can put the spring back into your step. You will not be alone in your efforts – even when you think you are. Never again will you be caught up in the chains that held you before.

(I am I). Give all your fears and doubts and pain over to me. I will recycle them. I will give you back only what you will need to work with. I will lift your burdens and your spirit. (I am I).

The rest of your life can be a joy to you, but first you must learn to walk once again. You must unlearn some of your old thought patterns and relearn some truer ones.

(I am I). The life you have lived until now was by your choice of free will alone. I will be your crutch - your support and your strength. When you have any doubt or fear at all, just call me. Make yourself small and let the moment come back into truth. Allow all illusion to fall away. (I am I). Only do what you need to do in the moment you are in.

(I am I). I will lead you one step at a time, but I will only ever be in the present – one step away from you. Ask that I should be there and I will. (I am I).

Only we can pull ourselves together once more. We can wake up to the world that really matters.

(I am I). There will always be those around you that think you are crazy. Don't listen. Ask for us to shield you. There will always be pain and violence and sadness. Ask that we may help the situation. Send us where you think we are needed. There will always be problems and obstacles to overcome – of varying degrees. Ask us to help you through them. Don't skirt them anymore. Face them as full on as you should and

281

ask that you be helped – every step of the way. Your life will turn around, in some ways instantly, overnight, and in others more slowly. (I am I).

Wherever you are right now is exactly the place you should be at this time. However bad your troubles, it has taken you your lifetime to get to that point. Therefore it is only natural that it will take a little time and effort to pull you out - to sort you out. Miracles can happen and regularly do, but they can only operate within the laws of the moment.

(I am I). I will help you through anything, but don't be too closed in your thinking. Help comes in many shapes and guises - sometimes the way is clear, sometimes it is not. Sometimes we have to travel the distance within a problem before it can be put to rest. Don't think you have not been heard and never think you are on your own. At all times I will be there. (I am I).

Life cannot stop because you want it to, but a chain of events can be softened with help. The negativity and illusion can be removed and the truth can be your shield at those times. When you ask for help things will not always be as bad as you thought they would, but it is important that you help yourself as well. It is important that you make yourself small inside. Mentally curl yourself up and still your thoughts. Think of spirit and ask them to recycle all that should not be there. Don't allow yourself to fear or to wander. Remain completely focused on the task you are doing and do not allow your mind to wander into the past or the future of this event. You may feel a little strange, as though you were watching this event happening through a window. Know that it is spirit, that they are shielding you. You may feel disconnected. Again don't worry. Remain small and in the truth of the moment you are in. From this time on spirit shall be with you and you will know.

Man is his own worst enemy. He thinks he can get away with this and a little bit of that. He thinks that as long as no one is watching he can do whatever he wants; but wrong. There is no force towering over his actions, but there is the energy of the self, and it is this that all things cling to. It is this that mirrors the true actions of his thoughts and his words and his deeds. The soul is his blue print. It vibrates on a level that man has yet to understand. Every little deed that he does is amplified. It produces either a negative or a positive reaction and this in turn will add to his feelings of self-power or negativity. As you clear more and more of the rubbish that has accumulated on your path you will find you can get away with less and less. It will not be that others will look at you and notice, but more that you will become more and more uneasy with yourself when you do things that you know you ought not. This is your spirit self that is prodding you. It is your conscience and it will become stronger as you progress on your journey. You will not become good always for goodness sake but more because you will feel uncomfortable when you don't. The little things you do will play on your mind like neon signals until you put them right once more. No one will know, but you definitely will. Peace can only stem from peace and when you set to disturb it, you will know.

There are no eternal rules of right or of wrong doing. There is only what is. Each person is equipped with the facility to judge for himself. Moral and social rules are a good starting point. They give us limitations that we can operate between, but we are also programmed with a finer judgement. When we do things that we really know we should not, we feel it on some other level within ourselves. Yes, we can and often are hardened to these feelings. We choose to ignore our better judgement and hope that all will be well inspite of our actions, and often they are. Often we can get away with all sorts of things, but do we really? The answer is that we do not. All of life must be in balance.

The laws of cause and effect always come into play somewhere. Without hate we cannot know love. Without war we cannot know peace. Without pain and stress we cannot appreciate the peace and contentment of a quiet mind. All things have their opposites to highlight them. All that we do, is given back to us in one way or another. The form it takes might be completely unrecognisable, but we will always reap what we sow eventually, if not in this life then the next. We can get away with nothing so the sooner we realise this fact the better it will be for us all.

Only man thinks that he must be the judge and jury of another, yet he forgets to monitor closely his own actions - his own thoughts and words. Very often he throws out nothing but negativity, even to his friends. How often do we back talk and re-enact scenes in our own head? How often do we replay events that have occurred and wish we had said this or done that? Little do we realise that we simply make the whole matter worse. We heap negativity onto an already negative situation when in reality we should just recycle the whole thing.

We are as much to blame for the downs in our life as are the people that put us there. We are as much responsible for the state of the world as those whose actions appal us. We are adding to the state of world affairs without even realising and this is not a good situation to be in. Yet how can we stop before we are aware of it? How can we break a habit that we do not even know exists? The answer is one step at a time. And it all begins inside with us.

Life is ours for the taking, but the way we each conduct that life has a major effect in your corner of the world.

(I am I). I will help you understand what you do. I will help you see how you add to your own pain and heartache. Then I will help you stop. I will help lift you up and out of your rut until you can run again once more. I will hold your hand until you can go it alone. (I am I).

Only you can ever take the next step forward in your life, but first you must learn how you should do it. Once again the 'I Ching' would be a good tool.

(I am I). I will help you recognise when to move forward and when to be still - when to be small and when to stand tall. Only you can learn these things for yourself with my help. (I am I).

Life will help you and work with you when you let it, but again first you must learn how.

Only you can learn to read the signals and signposts that surround you, but you must keep your feet firmly on the ground as you do. Only you can do this again for yourself by remaining utterly and completely in the moment you are in. Whenever you feel your insides beginning to flutter, or when you get over excited, pull yourself back to your centre. Imagine roots under your feet that go deep into the ground, to ground, balance and nourish you. Imagine you can let yourself go. Imagine you are a flower in reverse. Bring in the petals of your head. Allow the flower to go backwards into bud. Bring in your leaves and fold them back into bud formation too. Imagine the stem can grow backwards into the seed until you are once more as small as the seed, then open your eyes and continue as you should.

Any sign of over emotion, either sadness or excitement – is an imbalance. All emotions have their place, but all things should be equally balanced within their time and place. As you reconnect to life, to yourself and the divine presence that surrounds you, you will naturally feel a quickening, an excitement, a buzz. Acknowledge these things as they occur, but keep yourself firmly focused on the things that you should. You will feel as though you are being recharged, and indeed you are, but it is important that you do not let yourself float away in the process. Keep within the bounds of reality and at all times ask that your illusions be recycled and that only truth and light prevail.

At this point you will be vulnerable. You will be like the blind leading the blind.

(I am I). Keep yourself grounded and focused on your day and I will be with you to help you. (I am I).

Only you can help yourself by remaining aware of your feelings. Only you know where your mind is so only you can keep it in check.

(I am I). This life is to be lived. This world is to be treasured, so it is up to man to look after it properly. (I am I).

This planet Earth, is the body of God that we live upon. It feeds us and provides for all our needs. It, combined with the energies of the sky, is our life force. Take care of it for all your own life's worth. Respect it as you would respect your own home.

Only we combined, can turn this planet around, literally. Only we can pull ourselves together and bring it back on track. Only we can take this chance we have been given to rectify the mistakes of the past; not by reliving them and feeding them to keep them alive, but by putting them out to rest and by moving on. This is a time for re-growth and for pastures new.

(I am I). I will lead you every step of the way if you will only give me a spark of recognition, of faith and of love. This is our chance, combined, to place the 'now' on the map of time. It is here that I am and it is here that all things are possible. Life is asking for our help so it is up to us to hear that call. It is up to us to conduct our life in a way that we can be proud of now. Don't wait until you get back home before you wish you had sorted things out. Re-establish all the things you should do and tidy your loose ends. Place order back into your bank balance and also into your affairs. Don't follow the pack and do what others do. Take your life back into your own control and walk beside me. I will lead you if you wish. (I am I).

It is probable that right now you are feeling a little sad; a little scared; but don't. You are where you are because that is where you are. The past is over, even yesterday. None of it can be used again. Instead allow yourself to believe in the fresh start that awaits you. There may be repercussions that you must face up to, but do that with your chin held high and your shoulders back. Face up to your mistakes and move on. This life is far more precious than any amount of silver or gold.

(I am I). No amount of precious metal or stone can ever replace it. Treasure what you really are - your essence, and treasure all that you have achieved, despite the trials of your past. Lay down your defences and walk forward. Walk tall. Know that your life is now just beginning. This is your time to shine. (I am I).

Chapter Twenty-Three

The Winds that will Help You Recover

(I am I). I am not a figment of your imagination. I am real. I am as real as the air that you breathe or the light that you see. I am the words that attract your attention and the books that you read. I am in the thoughts that you think and the words that you say. I am you and you are me. I am neither your jailer nor your judge. You are. You do all this and more to yourself. I do not hold the key to your heart and your chains. You do. You have it all. You are responsible for controlling your life. You first think the thoughts that put into play all that occurs around you. You programme your own destiny with your thoughts and your words, your beliefs and your actions. You have total control of the being that is you. Recognise this and learn to accept your own power. Nobody anywhere can alter this truth. You are more, much more than you can ever dream, more than you can know in many lifetimes. You are a vital part in this living, breathing, thinking machine called Earth. The choices you make and the role you play is vital in the life of this planet. Together you are strong. Alone you believe you are small. But individually you play your part and it is a part that cannot be replaced. Without you there would be a gap - a hole - and holes have always been a nuisance. (I am I).

Only you can pick up the pieces of yourself and put them together once more. The years have taken their toll. No man is able to travel through this material existence unscathed. Pain and turmoil is a necessary part of our life, of even our birth; without it we would live as zombies. How could we ever know and appreciate the joys that surround us and that await us if we did not have an opposite to measure against. Life is like a ball of living energy. It contains all possibilities that could ever be - like a computer programme. We push the buttons with our thoughts and release the things that we need. We are in charge of the next step. We choose the category we shall work within and respond to.

If man lived the same time as the Earth has once again he could never reproduce a machine so complex. Man is himself the greatest invention that was ever grown, ever manufactured - he out does even God.

It is man himself who now shapes the world. He must wake up to the facts that are true.

(I am I). I can only guide and help when my help is needed, but it is man who directs the future of his Earth. (I am I).

God in the ways that science has explained, made the world, but it is man that will now take it forward. He can make it into a technological, mechanical world or he can take what he has learned and use it wisely. He can use his inventions to help him return back to life, to freedom and to happiness.

Only you can put your life back in order. This is not a quest for further outwardly advancement, but about reconnecting to the life that is. It is about using the machines we have made to make our lives a little more comfortable, but then about loving and enjoying the time we have left. It is about connecting properly with each other in a heart-felt way. It is about understanding our parents, our children and our friends. It is about recognising that we are all people. We are all on the same path of progressions through life. It is about recognising that we all have the same feelings, hopes, fears and dreams. It is about realising that we are all connected on a spiritual level and it is about learning to see past the faults that mess us up.

Only we can live the life that we have, just as others are trying to do the same. Don't just spot the faults of others, as you too have made your own. Help others to communicate. Help them to move forward too. Not with money or with a do-good attitude, but by your own example. Go within yourself first and foremost and understand exactly what has been holding you back and keeping you sad. Take this new day, this blank page and use it a little differently than you usually would. Take your automatic pilot off line and make your own choices as you used to when you were young, when you believed that the world really was your oyster, when you believed in yourself and in your life and when you believed in your ability to go with that life, wherever it may take you.

Today is the first day of the rest of the life you have. Take it and live it. Yes you have commitments and yes you have to work. Yes the same old bills still drop onto your doormat, but you don't have to let them get you down. Instead work out how to get rid of them - how to get them back down to a minimum. Look at the whole of your life from another perspective. Look at what you need to do to turn things around - to get out of debt, to remove the clutter and to enjoy your life. Are you doing a job you enjoy or are you simply working for your pay cheque? We all have to work in order to survive, but we should at least do it in a way that we enjoy. Life is too precious to let it dwindle away, to let it slip through your fingers day and night. Change a few of the things that drain you. Learn where others are pulling your strings. Help yourself climb out of your rut by recognising that you are probably in one. A book called *Emotional Clearing* by John Ruskan (ISBN No: 0 7126 7167 - 6) is a good starting point. It will help you recognise some of the behavioural habits that you stick with naturally. It will help you understand where you are, how you got there and more importantly how to get out. I, too, have read this book and it helped me understand some truths that I perhaps would not have liked to hear. I could not argue though with a book and you cannot ignore the truth as it is. We all have our little quirky ways but when we learn how these things do matter and hold us back then we should take the adult approach and work them through.

We have lived only a half-life up until now. We believed that we were alone and that all we ever had to do had to be done alone, under our own steam. Now we can learn a new truth - the actual truth. We can learn it for ourselves, by ourselves, one little bit at a time. We can relearn the truths about ourselves instead of just ducking and dragging along other people's opinions of how they think we are. We are not bad through and through. Neither are we headed for hell. We live in a world that was made from love. We ourselves came from an act of love. We have love in our hearts and we want others to love us, but before they can, before we can let their love in, we must first learn to love ourselves. To forgive ourselves our past mistakes. To recognise that we are worth more than we realised, not in a pretentious way but in a truthful, bottom line sort of way. We must take a look at the essence of the person we really are and we must forgive the child within ourselves for all our wrong doings. We can put to rest our discretion of the past as we take each new day and live it in a better way - a non-impressive, truthful way. We have no one to impress - no one to prove a thing to. We have simply to recognise the love and the joy that is possible for us to have.

(I am I). I, too, could not have put this better. I second these things with all that I am. (I am I).

The lump you feel inside now is your soul acknowledging the truth. This book has highlighted things that you can only admit deep within. It has accessed forgotten issues - things that you usually push away and cloud over. It has reached the essence of who you are.

This is not the end; it is the beginning. It is the start of a new life, of self-recognition and of a deeper understanding of those who are around you. All people, everywhere, are just that - people. They don't always mean to hurt each other. They are just looking to be loved and understood as you are. They want the best for themselves as you do. They are the same as you are. When you find yourself in conflict or turmoil with another, at the point where you would normally lock horns, go inside instead, and quietly ask for help. Ask for illusion to be gone and ask that truth and light and love prevail. Ask that both of you may communicate on a correct level of understanding. Ask that you may hear each other's words. Just recycle all that stands in your way – always.

(I am I). Man is at the brink of a new age. What he thought would happen at the birth of the new millennium is upon him now. I am with him to help him live in the way he would like to, to take himself back into love and happiness. (I am I).

This is not a whim any more; it will be fact. He is at a crossroads both physically and spiritually. He can stay as he is but he will always struggle as he always has, or he can choose to change direction, to explore the deeper realms of himself, and to understand his mind and emotions on a deeper level. He can make educated choices instead of haphazard, impulsive ones and instead he can set himself free. He can dance to the beat of his own tune, his own choices instead of trudging through rubbish and conditions of his past.

Only man can look at the complete picture of his life so far. He must work out for himself if it is a good and happy one, or if there are things that could be better. The picture you will see has been built up over the years gone by. Little by little you have slotted those pieces into place, some under your own steam and some by the intervention of others. There is no judge, other than you. Only you can decide if you like all you see, or not, or if there are things that could have been done better, or not. Only you can decide if you are happy as you are, or if you want to go within now to understand what always goes wrong, despite your efforts on the surface. Only you can help yourself, but first you must understand how. You are being shown an opportunity to find the tools that will do it. Until this moment in time, you could only operate within the thoughts and beliefs that you already had, within the boundaries that have existed for you since your childhood. All you will do by going within is refine and redraw a few of the automatic things you do unconsciously. You will throw away the weeds, the things that do not serve you as they should and you will allow new growth to come - to take root. You are replanting the garden of your mind and tidying up years of neglect and mistakes. You are going to learn a better way to help yourself and in so doing you will cut the unconscious cords that others until now have played upon. They will no longer be able to pull your strings. No longer will you feel bad for nothing. They will understand the words you speak and the things you do in the way you mean them to. Your life will slowly sort itself out into a better working order and in the process you will clear the arena of your mind. You will learn the power of your thoughts and perhaps you will allow them to help you in a positive way instead of a negative one. Life will take on a new and exciting look instead of the automatic existence that has become the norm.

This book will open doors that until now have been tightly locked.

(I am I). I will help you from this moment on – if you let me. I have never left your side yet, but you did not know. I had to watch and wait for you to recognise that I was there. I was powerless to interrupt. Now it can be different. Don't cry and don't be sad any more. Yes, life will still be life. It will always have its peaks and troughs, but then it is supposed to. Only now, you will turn to me. You have a few tools that will help you

along your way and you will pick up many more besides as you begin your studies. I will help you if you also learn how to help yourself. I will be there at all times. (I am I).

Life is good. It can be all that you want it to be – despite the problems that are yet to be overcome. All that is occurring in your life is only a symptom of things that are happening to everyone. A problem is a problem. Trouble and sadness are trouble and sadness. The shapes and guise of these things may vary, but they are still the same for us all. No one is out of the woods yet; we are all on our way. **(I am I). I must second this statement. (I am I).**

As we look back over time we can see the struggles that our ancestors lived through, like scars across the path of time. But we can also see how far man has come. He is not out of the woods yet but he is well on his way. Life on the whole has never been so good and once we learn to get our own acts together it will be even better. The picture we shall weave will be better and cleaner than before. We can see the traps of the past and we shall recognise the ones we are in. We all have a chance to clean ourselves up before we then go back home. We are lucky. We are luckier than we can ever realise.

Those we have loved and lost will be with us, helping us as we continue on our way. They will be cheering us on. Just as the crowd is important in a sporting event, so will they play their part as we run the event of our life. All will play their part until you return home once more - until you cross your own finish line. **(I am I). I must second this. (I am I).** Only you can go forward now.

(I am I). I will be with you every step of the way you will tread. Don't fear or worry anymore. Look at the moment in front of you with truth and allow the illusions to fall away. Always look for the bottom line. If you are in doubt then make yourself small and wait a short while until the picture is clear. I cannot do

anything for you. You must do it yourself, but I can show you the way. I can smooth the edges and I can give you strength and support. This is your life to live, so only you can live it, but you will be helped till the end of your days. I will help you flow through your obstacles, especially when you feel that the world is against you. At these times you will be at your lowest ebb, but trust in me and I will hold you up. Believe in me. (I am I).

Man is always doing his best, but sometimes it seems that that best is just not enough. When the chips are down – don't ever give up.

(I am I). I will always lift your heavy mood so that you can carry on. I will always direct you to a glimmer of light and of hope. When you think you have tried all the avenues available to you, I will show you some more. (I am I).

Sometimes it is necessary to complete a cycle of events before the new can begin, so once more don't hold on to any illusion past its 'sell by date'. Always look for the truths that are lurking on the bottom line. Don't fool yourself or others anymore and life will turn around again. Pain and sadness might be there from time to time, but it is sometimes a necessary conclusion to events that are. You cannot let go of the old until you are ready to, so once more ask for help from Our Father. Ask that he help you. Ask that the old be recycled and that love and light remain. Never forget to recycle your pain and sadness. (I am I). I will replace it with love. (I am I).

Life is a gift to be treasured. It is also not as fragile as the thoughts you think. Life is fun and you can have as much of it as you wish. (I am I). Providing all things are in balance. (I am I). I must also remember this as I go through my own life. Balance is the word that holds all things in their true and proper place. Balance is more important that we realise. Too much attention in any one direction will always throw another out of sync. All of nature must be always in balance and so must we. That is a fact of this life.

Only you can return the balance back into your life, and in turn it will have a knock on effect. As you pull yourself together once more the little things around you will also readjust. **(I am I). I will help the whole process. (I am I).** Take your life back to the basics and release yourself from that which you no longer need. You will lighten your load in the process. I, too, have had to do this and in some ways I still must. Life should never stagnate, so allow it to go forward at its own pace. All you need do is keep up. If you think it is going too fast – ask that it be slowed down. Nothing can occur before the time it is destined to do so. Learn to be patient with yourself and with others around. Take each day as it comes and learn to flex with it.

Only you can do these things for yourself now. We all can do the same. No one person is ever more important or in need than another. All men are equal in the eyes of God Our Father, and as soon as we allow ourselves to recognise our own worth, the sooner we can reconnect to the whole. Nothing you could ever do, will alienate you from your birthright, and that right is to live in love, in peace and in contentment. Reach out your hand for the help that you need and never turn your back on another. Help them not with money, but with the help you have received from the words of this book. Pass it on where necessary and pass on your love as well. **(I am I). I will always be with you – no matter what. (I am I).**

Only you can give yourself another chance - another lease of life. Each new day that you live can be a good day. A day that is full of new experiences. Learn to embrace them. Don't tar them with the brushes of the past. Ask for your old fears, your old hang-ups to be removed whenever you recognise them and try a few things that you usually would not. I, too, must remember this. I, too, must let my hair down a little more than I do.

Only man can turn this world around once more. He can put the spring back into life or he can continue to wear it out. He does not even have to go overboard with his efforts. He just has to start from within. He must learn to live and to trust himself. He must give himself a reason to trust himself. He must realise that he has a new chance in every single day that he lives and he must learn to use it. Man does not stand alone. He is an important part of the all that is - of the planet itself. The thoughts in his head have more effect than he can ever imagine, so he must realise that what he has in his mind is his offering to God - to the all that is. His thoughts direct his life and all that he finds himself doing. His thoughts are responsible for the way others treat him as well. Man must learn to respect and understand himself, and when he does then other things will fall back into place.

All we ever need is with us and it always has been. We are not alone and have never been. We never could be. We are an important working part of the Earth and a spark of the divine energy that exists in all things. We are a part of a living, breathing, loving God. We are man.

(I am I). I am here. I am with you. I am in you. All that you will ever be you will be with me. It can never be any other way. I am the spark of life, the consciousness that is in all living things and after your time is over and spent, you simply return home to me. The life you are living is a gift - a joy to be experienced with love. You are love – even though you may have forgotten. You are a living part of me. (I am I).

The place that you are right now is the place that you are. Learn to be happy. If you are not, then look at your life and figure out why. Not in an outward manner, because others have done this or they have not done that, and not because you are sour with your lot. Look to understand how you always get to this point. Look for the reasons that are springing from inside you.

(I am I). Man is never too old to step out of behaviour patterns that no longer serve him. I am with him and I will help him to stay out of the fear. I will surround him with all that he needs if he asks me. (I am I).

Your life will turn around but be patient. Look for the little miracles that happen in your day. Ask for your troubles to be recycled – one at a time. In your thoughts stay only in the day you are experiencing right now. Operate fully from within this point. Now is the only time that really exists for tomorrow is an illusion – until you get there. Until it becomes the day you are in. Be careful of the energy and thoughts that you place ahead of you in your own pathway. Recycle things a hundred times if you need to, but learn to be positive and happy. This day is your day. Events may come and go; good as well as bad, but at the end of each day look at what you have achieved. Make each one count in one small way and slowly things will turn around for the better. You hold the key to your own life - to your heart, to your happiness and to your future. Learn to recognise the person you really are and let him/her out to live.

Only you can live the life that you have. You are unique. The mistakes of the past are just that. They were mistakes – and they are now behind you. They are not to be compounded with more. **(I am I). I second this. (I am I).** Take each day and live it in a way you will be proud to own up to.

(I am I). I will be with you at all times. I am only one thought away. This is the place I have always been and it is here you will always find me. (I am I).

298

Chapter Twenty-Four

The Winds that Sum Up

(I am I). When we die we return to original energy form. When we are born we come to Earth, to physical matter. We also form our part in the Earth's physical body. The energy that is sky consists of the life force the planet needs.

Earth and Sky are designed to integrate their energy through the catalyst that is man, through his spirit, but this is not occurring successfully at this time. Man is causing a blockage. He has forgotten that he is part of a thread. He has forgotten that he is part of a past – of a living heritage. He has forgotten that he comes from a long line of hundreds of descendants. He has forgotten he is merely the latest link in a long chain that existed before he was born and will continue long after his own life span. In his turn he, too, will become a link of the past. He, too, will have others attached in front of him, namely his children and their children in decent.

The Earth needs us to remember this. It needs us to re-establish links that have been forgotten. Blockages that have occurred during his lifetime need to be opened once more.

The state of the planet's surface depicts this picture. Its barren slopes and countries represent a mirror image of the blockages that man is the cause of. Barren lands represent the amount of connections that need reconnecting in men. As we progress into the light of the future, so will we return life and greenery, balance, peace and harmony to the Earth. Until we wake up to who and what we are in terms of being energy channels, we shall simply add to the barren and dead lands that already exist.

Man was made as one of many energy conductors for the physical Earth to exist and survive, and as such he will feed the Earth for the whole of his life. He is capable of omitting both positive and negative vibrations. He alone has control of which, by his choices, his emotions and the life he leads. All through his life and as a consequence of his life he transmits the forces that then return back into the earth.

When energy is positive it is able to assist the Earth in sustaining life. It is put to good use. Negative forces have the opposite effect. They can feed nothing. They have their effect on the planet in other ways, as they attract like for like in their own magnetic way.

All moving things on the surface of the earth influence life as we know it. Man is the only variable that causes a disturbance to the planet's equilibrium and it is this that must be drawn back into balance once more.

There will always be dark areas, but over the course of the earth's existence man has created and witnessed enough negative energy to last him through all eternity. From now until the end of time there is no further necessity to create more. What the Earth must have now is light and a drawing together of positive energy. Only this can bring into focus the forces to repair its damage. It needs man to pull himself together in his 'now'.

The Earth is slowly dying. It needs the help of man to assist it now, before it is too late. Man is its only hope of survival, because it is man who is the cause of the damage. Nothing is impossible at this point. I will help. I will help man overcome himself – every step of the way, but first he must let me in. He must wake up to the reality of himself and the part that he plays in the order of life. Both in his own and in the planet that sustains his life. (I am I).

Chapter Twenty-Five

The Wind that Is

(I am I). The world of Spirit is the past. It is the all that has been before this moment you are in, but it is also the future's potential.

Man is born into a physical 'now'. His 'now' is the only time frame that is able to instigate anything at all. It is the only place that can turn possibility into material form and matter.

The future is yet to be but it is created by the actions of the 'now'.

Inside man exists the double potential of both good and bad, light and dark. These two possibilities exist side by side within him everyday of his life. It is up to man alone to choose the path he will take. It is up to each individual in turn to make his own destiny.

The past can have little effect on the now, because those who live there have no influence in this time frame, unless we allow their help to filter through.

Man holds in his hand the future outcome of Earth itself.

The present needs to reconnect with the past so that the future will be as it should.

The present is not able to carry the world forward under its own steam alone. It does not have the necessary tools to do so.

The past has had the necessary tools, but has missed its opportunity to be effective in the now. Both past and present must combine to bring the now back into balance and peace.

The now is incapable of operating alone, because it is too deeply based in fear. It needs the love of the past to filter through to dilute energies that presently overrule man.

Man needs the past to reconnect in his present to help him go forward truthfully and with confidence. Man is his own creator.

The world needs a balance of past and present to take it successfully into the future.

I need man to reconnect with me, because I am all things. I am the past that was, the present that is, and the future that will be.

I am all that there is and I need man to understand this. (I am I).

Further Reading

The following list, is merely a sample of literature available in the Mind, Body & Spirit / Self-Help section of your local bookshop.

To connect with your inner self and your own personal guides or angels, simply still your mind for a few minutes and then browse through the following list, seeing which titles you connect with and trusting in your own inner guidance.

You will be guided, one step at a time, along a path that is right for you. When you browse through your bookshop or library, notice the titles that jump out and grab your attention. These are the books most likely to take you forward at this point in your journey.

Never read a book from back to front, but always from front to back. Many can be read from beginning to end fairly quickly, but others will be better chapter by chapter, to give the information time to sink in. Because you are on a journey, you will likely experience the things you have read, in your life. This is good. It is part of the experience and the same path of learning.

Some books will feel flat in the middle, but don't worry and don't be tempted to skip over these sections. They are flat because at this particular time the information might not relate to your needs. Your mind will simply place it in store until it does.

Other books will be hard going because they are not right for you in your 'now'. Put them down and go back to them at a later date if you wish.

This mode of reading information will help you outgrow outdated boundaries and beliefs that may have lingered with you since your childhood. It is a process that will take you forward from the place you are stuck, to where you can operate more efficiently. It will open you up to the flow of life that is waiting to help. It will connect you once more to your guides.

Good Luck!

Just For Today
By Stephanie J. King
ISBN 0-9542421-9-X

'Just for Today', was written to go hand in hand with 'The Winds of Change' and is designed to be opened at random, where you will find your thought for the day. Nothing is ever by chance and you will be guided to the lesson most appropriate for your own now. It will cultivate balance and inner peace, as well as strong personal growth.

The Celestine Prophecy – An Experiential Guide
By James Redfield & Carol Adrienne
ISBN 0-552-50370-7

The Celestine Prophecy – An Adventure
By James Redfield
ISBN 0-553-40902-6

The Tenth Insight
By James Redfield
ISBN 0-553-50418-5

The Tenth Insight – An Experiential Guide (for advanced students)
By James Redfield & Carol Adrienne
ISBN 0-553-50555-6

The Bible Code
By Michael Drosnin
ISBN 0-297-82994-7

Toxic Parents
By Susan Forward
ISBN 0-553-81482-6

The Relate Guide to Starting Again
By Sarah Litvinoff
ISBN 0-09-185667-1

The Relate Guide to Second Families
By Suzi Hayman
ISBN 0-091-81358-1

Families and How to Survive Them
By Robin Skynner & John Cleese
ISBN 0-7493-1410-9

Emotional Clearing
By John Ruskin
ISBN 0-712-67167-6

Living in the Light
By Shakti Gawain
ISBN 1-870845-32-3

In The Meantime
By Iyanla Vanzant
ISBN 0-671-03399-9

Yesterday I Cried
By Iyanla Vanzant
ISBN 0-671-02968-1

One
By Richard Bach
ISBN 0-330-31173-5

Jonathan Livingston Seagull
By Richard Bach
ISBN 0-006-49034-4

Bridge Across Forever
By Richard Bach
ISBN 0-330-29081-9

Conversations with God
By Neale Donald Walsch
Book 1 – ISBN 0-340-69325-8
Book 2 – ISBN 0-340-76544-5
Book 3 – ISBN 0-340-76545-3

The Road Less Travelled
By M. Scott Peck
ISBN 0-7126-1819-8

The Road Less Travelled and Beyond
By M. Scott Peck
ISBN 0-7126-7076-9

A Course in Miracles
By The Foundation for Inner Peace
ISBN 0-670-86975-9

The I Ching – Book of Changes
By Brian Brown
ISBN 0-7499-1265-0

Finding The Spirit Within
By Linda Williamson
ISBN 0-7126-0487-1

Men are from Mars and Women are from Venus
By John Gray
ISBN 0-00-715259-0

Men are from Mars and Women are from Venus – Children
are from Heaven
By John Gray
ISBN 0-09-182616-0

Seven Steps to Eternity
By Stephen Turoff
ISBN 1-902636-17-1

Spirit Guides and Angel Guardians
By Richard Webster
ISBN 1-56718-795-1

One Day My Soul Just Opened Up
By Iyanla Vanzant
ISBN 0-684-84134-7

Ambika's Guide to Healing and Wholeness
By Ambika Wauters
ISBN 0-7499-1290-1

Signposts
By Denise Linn
ISBN 0-7126-7449-7

Awakening the Buddha Within
By Lama Surya Das
ISBN 0-553-50537-8

Dictionary of Dreams
By Gustavus Hindman Miller
ISBN 0-75253-545-5
The Complete Book of Dreams
By Edwin Raphael
ISBN 0-572-01714-6

Learning to Meditate
By Patricia Carrington PhD
ISBN 1-86204-191-1

The Path to Love
By Deepak Chopra
ISBN 0-7126-7224-9

Illusions
By Richard Bach
ISBN 0-099-42786-9

Messages from the Masters
By Dr. Brian Weiss
ISBN 0-7499-2167-6

The Soul's Code
By James Hillman
ISBN 0-553-50634-X

The Awakened Mind
By C. Maxwell Cade & Nana Coxhead
ISBN 1-85230-004-3

Chicken Soup for the Soul
By Jack Confield & Mark Victor Hansen
ISBN 0-09185-428-8

A Guide for the Advanced Soul
By Susan Hayward
ISBN 0-959-0439-3-4

The Rock of Truth
By Arthur Findlay
ISBN 0-947823-04-2

A Mind of your Own
By Betty Shine
ISBN 0-00-255894-7

Animals as Teachers and Healers
By Susan Chernak Mcelroy
ISBN 0-7126-7264-8

To Begin Again
By Naomi Levy
ISBN 0-7225-3819-7

Inner Beauty
By The Brahma Kumaris World Spiritual University
ISBN 0-9637396-3-8

Confessions of a Pilgrim
By Paulo Coelho
ISBN 0-00-711437-0

The Alchemist
By Paulo Coelho
ISBN 0-7225-3293-8

The Valkyries
By Paulo Coelho
ISBN 0-0076-3955-4

The Fifth Mountain
By Paulo Coelho
ISBN 0-0076-3956-2

The Pilgrimage
By Paulo Coelho
ISBN 0-7225-3487-6

Wings of Soul
By The Brahma Kumaris World Spiritual University
ISBN 1-886872-12-0

Black Elk
By Wallace Black Elk & William S Lyon
ISBN 0-06-250074-0

Black Elk Speaks
By Nicholas Black Elk
ISBN 0-8032-6170-5

Black Elk Lives
By The Black Elk Family
ISBN 0-8032-3340-X

Meetings with Angels
By Dr H.C. Moolenburgh
ISBN 0-85207-260-0

Angel Inspiration
By Diana Cooper
ISBN 0-340-73323-3

A Little Light on Angels
By Diana Cooper
ISBN 1-899171-51-7

The Field
By Lynne McTaggart
ISBN 0-00-714510-1

Footprints

One night a man had a dream. He dreamed he was walking along the beach with the Lord. Across the sky flashed scenes from his life. For each scene, he noticed two sets of footprints in the sand: one belonging to him and the other to the Lord.

When the last scene of his life flashed before him, he looked back at the footprints in the sand. He noticed that many times along the path of his life there was only one set of footprints. He also noticed that it happened at the very lowest and saddest times in his life.

This really bothered him and he questioned the LORD about it. "LORD, you said that once I decided to follow you, you'd walk with me all the way, but I have noticed that during the most troublesome times in my life, there is only one set of footprints. I don't understand why when I needed you most you would leave me."

The LORD replied, "My precious, precious child, I love you and I would never leave you. During your times of trial and suffering, when you see only one set of footprints, it was then that I carried you."

The Last Wind

Man must pull in one direction – together. This is the only way that we can survive. This is the only way that we can go forward. We create our reality with our own thoughts and wishes. To believe in the power of thought is to re-establish our link with the universal consciousness - the all that is.

A closing note from the author...

The Winds of Change is unique and we hope that you have enjoyed it. The experience you have gained from it was also individual and unique for you. If you have benefited by it in any way, we ask that you pass its details on towards a friend.